Affective Disorders

Postcolonialism across the Disciplines 21

Postcolonialism across the Disciplines

Series Editors
Graham Huggan, University of Leeds
Andrew Thompson, University of Exeter

Postcolonialism across the Disciplines showcases alternative directions for postcolonial studies. It is in part an attempt to counteract the dominance in colonial and postcolonial studies of one particular discipline – English literary/cultural studies – and to make the case for a combination of disciplinary knowledges as the basis for contemporary postcolonial critique. Edited by leading scholars, the series aims to be a seminal contribution to the field, spanning the traditional range of disciplines represented in postcolonial studies but also those less acknowledged. It will also embrace new critical paradigms and examine the relationship between the transnational/cultural, the global and the postcolonial.

Affective Disorders

Emotion in Colonial
and Postcolonial Literature

Bede Scott

Liverpool University Press

First published 2019 by
Liverpool University Press
4 Cambridge Street
Liverpool L69 7ZU

Copyright © 2019 Bede Scott

The right of Bede Scott to be identified as the author of this book has been asserted by him in accordance with the Copyright, Design and Patents Act 1988. All rights reserved. No part of this book may be reproduced, stored in a retrieval system, or transmitted, in any form or by any means, electronic, mechanical, photocopying, recording, or otherwise, without the prior written permission of the publisher.

British Library Cataloguing-in-Publication data
A British Library CIP record is available

ISBN 978-1-78694-170-1 cased

Typeset in Amerigo by Carnegie Book Production, Lancaster
Printed and bound in Poland by BooksFactory.co.uk

For Ingrid and Sappho

Contents

Acknowledgements	ix
Introduction	1
1 Anger: Naguib Mahfouz's *Midaq Alley*	31
2 Reticence: Vikram Seth's *A Suitable Boy*	55
3 Jealousy: Joaquim Maria Machado de Assis' *Dom Casmurro*	79
4 Boredom: Upamanyu Chatterjee's *English, August: An Indian Story*	105
5 Fear: Michael Ondaatje's *Anil's Ghost*	127
6 Stuplimity: Vikram Chandra's *Sacred Games*	147
Works Cited	169
Index	183

Acknowledgements

I owe a large debt of gratitude to many people, but I would like to mention, in particular, Graham Huggan, Sharanya Jayawickrama, Chloe Johnson, John McLeod, Michael Neill, Francesca Orsini, Ato Quayson, and Janet Wilson. For their congeniality over the last decade, I would also like to thank my colleagues, both past and present, in the Division of English at Nanyang Technological University, Singapore. And on a more personal note, I am especially grateful to my mother, Naomi Estall, and my father, Dick Scott, for all the support they have provided over the years (despite the intervening time zones).

Earlier versions of some of the chapters have appeared in the *Journal of Arabic Literature* (42.1 [2011]), *Contemporary Literature* (53.3 [2012]), the *Cambridge Journal of Postcolonial Literary Inquiry* (3.2 [2016]), and *Modern Fiction Studies* (65.2 [2019]). I am grateful to the editors and publishers of these journals for their permission to use this material in the following pages.

Finally, I would like to thank my wife, Liz, and our two boys, Conrad and Arlo. Together, they have made this project (and everything else) possible. The book itself I have dedicated to our daughters, Ingrid and Sappho, who arrived in the spring of 2016 and have inspired nothing but good feelings ever since.

Introduction

[T]he affective quality of the world matters more than its geography.

                          Mikel Dufrenne, *The Phenomenology of Aesthetic Experience*, 1953

[Feeling] is nothing without form.

        Gustave Flaubert, Letter to Louise Colet, 12 August 1846

I

I would like to begin, if I may, in a rather unpredictable place: provincial France in the summer of 1789. At this time, the country was undergoing a political and economic crisis that has been well-documented. The harvest had failed, food prices were rising, and unemployment was rife. In Paris, the Revolution was gathering momentum, and as news of the fall of the Bastille filtered through to the provinces, a number of rumours began to circulate. It was said that the aristocracy were planning to subdue the uprising by force, and that they had recruited foreign soldiers and 'brigands' in order to do so. It was also said that this army of mercenaries would be marching through the provinces to quell the various disturbances that had taken place there too. These rumours travelled with astonishing speed, and as they moved from village to village, they produced a particular kind of affective response that has come to be known as the Great Fear of 1789. People everywhere experienced an overwhelming sense of panic and anxiety, but this was not a vague and intangible national mood; it was a circulation of feeling whose speed and specific coordinates, at any given point in time, can be traced with remarkable accuracy (see Figure 1). According to Georges Lefebvre, the fear travelled from Clermont-en-Beauvaisis to the Seine, a distance of about fifty kilometres, in twelve hours. As it moved more slowly at night, it covered the five hundred kilometres from Ruffec to Lourdes in nine days, while elsewhere it travelled 'from Livron to Arles – a hundred and fifty kilometres – in forty hours, which makes [an average of] four kilometres an hour, night and day' (Lefebvre, *Great* 155).[1] In his classic study of the Revolution, Lefebvre was able to follow the progress of this emotion as it was transmitted throughout the provinces:

> A 'disturbance' at Nantes alarmed Poitou. At Estrées-Saint-Denis, in the Beauvais, another spread fright in all directions. A third in southern Champagne sowed terror through the Gâtinais, Bourbonnais, and Burgundy. A fourth, originating near the Montmirail forest, close to La Ferté-Bernard, alerted Maine, Normandy, Anjou, and the Touraine. From the edge of the Chizé forest fear struck Angoulême, spread into Berry and the central mountains, alarmed Aquitaine as far as the Pyrenees. In the east, agrarian revolts in Franche-Comté and the Mâconnais drove fear to the shores of the Mediterranean. (*French* 123–24)

By exploring this phenomenon in such detail, Lefebvre was attempting to rectify a tendency, among other historians of the period, to ignore the affective dimensions of the Revolution – or to ascribe the events of that year, in passing, to the irrational and pathological nature of 'crowd psychology.' For Lefebvre, by contrast, the Great Fear played a central role in the Revolution of 1789. It emerged as a response to quite specific political and economic circumstances, and it directly influenced the subsequent course of the Revolution – by mobilizing various rural militias, by bringing disparate communities together, and, above all, by disseminating revolutionary fervour throughout the provinces, so that many of those who experienced the Great Fear would later participate in the uprising against the 'seigneurial regime' (Lefebvre, *Great* 211).

---

1 If Balzac is to be believed, however, this was a good deal slower than the speed at which rumour moved through the residential areas of nineteenth-century Paris – i.e., nine miles (or roughly fourteen kilometres) an hour (Robb 52).

Introduction

Figure 1. The Great Fear of 1789

Affective Disorders

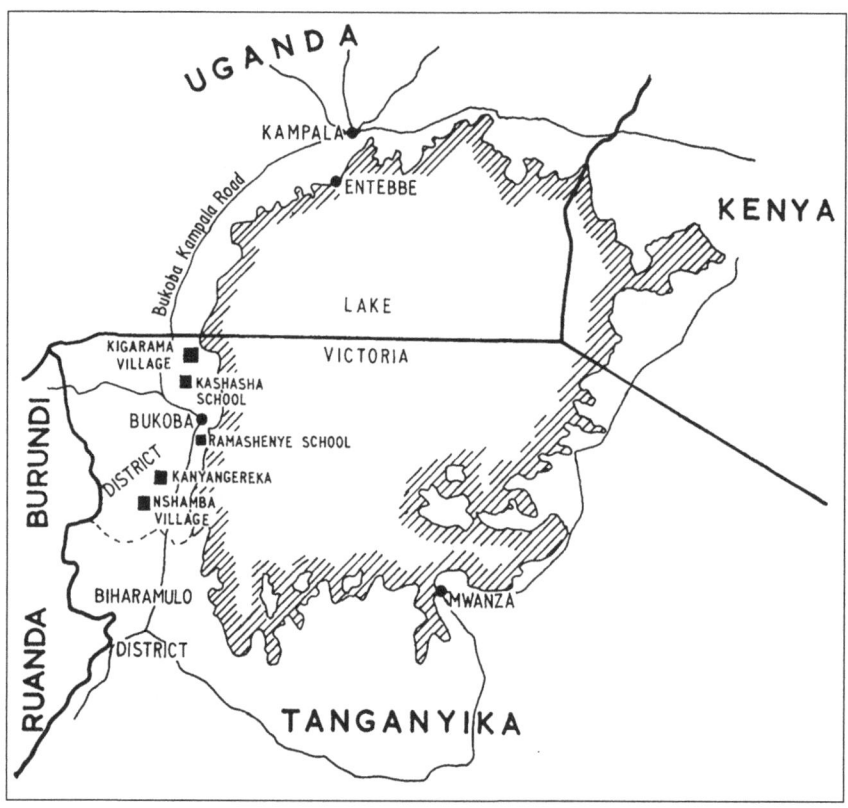

Figure 2. The Tanganyika Laughter Epidemic of 1962

As we shall see, the Great Fear demonstrates many of the features that will be essential to my discussion of emotion in *Affective Disorders*. But I could easily have begun elsewhere too – in Tanganyika (Tanzania), say, in the early sixties. On 30 January 1962, three girls in a mission school in the village of Kashasha (see Figure 2) started to laugh uncontrollably. This laughter spread rapidly throughout the student body and showed no sign of diminishing as the weeks passed. By the time the school was forced to close, on 18 March, ninety-five out of 159 students had been infected. During this period, the 'disease' was also transmitted to the neighbouring villages of Nshamba (where 217 people were infected), Ramashenye (where forty-eight were infected), and Kanyangereka (where the rate of infection was not recorded). In every case, the symptoms were the same: the afflicted person would succumb to hysterical laughter that might last anywhere between a few minutes and a few hours, followed by a respite and then a recurrence. This pattern would be repeated for several hours or up to sixteen days, depending on the severity of the episode, during which time the individual would be unable to perform his or her normal duties and would be difficult to control. An epidemic of this kind was unprecedented, and so there was no traditional name for it in the local languages. The Bahaya people, who constitute the majority in north-western Tanzania, referred to it either as *enwara yokusheka* ('the laughing disease') or as *akajanja*, which simply means 'madness.' Although some people believed that the disorder was a consequence of poisoned maize flour, this possibility was quickly eliminated – as was the theory that the laughter may have had a viral aetiology. In a contemporary article on the subject, A.M. Rankin and P.J. Philip conclude that as none of the infected people demonstrated any physical abnormalities, and the possibility of poison had been eliminated, the condition was almost certainly 'culturally determined' – that is to say, it was a type of 'mental disorder' that had been influenced by the precise social and cultural circumstances in which the afflicted found themselves (170). 'As the commoner epidemics are caused by the spread of viruses, bacteria, or parasites,' Rankin and Philip write, 'there is a tendency to forget that abnormal emotional behaviour may spread from person to person and so take on an epidemic form' (167). In this instance, the emotion that was being transmitted was not as congenial as it may have appeared to be at first glance. Such episodes were often accompanied by feelings of restlessness and anxiety, as if the person was 'frightened of something' (168) or being pursued; and in some cases, they would become so agitated that they would have to be physically restrained. As François Sirois observes, hysteria of this kind frequently coincides with a 'state of ideological or cultural transition' and may also occur during 'periods of uncertainty and social stress,' such as those occasioned by war, famine, or even rapid technological change (106). In the case I have just outlined, it may be worth noting that Tanganyika had gained full independence on 9 December 1961, less than two months before the outbreak of the 'laughter epidemic' – and some of the uncertainties generated by this moment of profound social and political transformation may well have contributed to the 'abnormal emotional behaviour' that subsequently occurred.[2]

2 Along with the political and economic difficulties it was facing during this period, Tanganyika had also been suffering from a famine since 1960 (the worst for seventy years); and as the country declared its independence, nearly half a million people were still receiving famine relief (Iliffe 576). According to Robert R. Provine, the 'laughter epidemic' only came to an

Affective Disorders

In this study, I will be exploring the process by which certain sociopolitical forces give rise to dominant 'structures of feeling' within colonial and postcolonial societies. I shall be arguing, furthermore, that these affective qualities also make their presence felt within literary discourse, where they penetrate even the deeper reaches of form, genre, and style.[3] In order to make such an argument, I will be placing particular emphasis on three characteristic features of emotion (as demonstrated by the Great Fear and the 'laughter epidemic') – namely, (1) the fact that emotion is both psychogenic and sociogenic (i.e., socially transmitted); (2) the fact that emotion may be determined by quite specific historical processes; and (3) the fact that emotion is inherently mobile, a quality of feeling that moves easily from one body to another, from one structure to another, and from one place to another (see Figures 1 and 2).[4] Of course, all three of these features are interrelated and mutually enabling. In other words, it is precisely because it is sociogenic (and subject to various historical contingencies) that emotion acquires such mobility; and this is also why it is able to penetrate the deeper reaches of literary discourse, for good or for ill. Once emotion becomes detached from the individual consciousness, circulating freely within the larger community, it becomes, to quote Mikel Dufrenne, 'a supervening or impersonal principle in accordance with which we [might] say that there is an electric atmosphere or, as Trenet sang, that there is joy in the air' (168). And once an emotion becomes depersonalized in this way, once it merges with the general 'atmosphere' of a particular place or time, it very quickly achieves a kind of ubiquity, percolating into almost every

---

end two and a half years later, in June 1964, having infected an estimated one thousand people (131). For more on this subject, see Hempelmann.

3 It goes without saying that the study of emotion has a long transdisciplinary genealogy – encompassing philosophy, evolutionary biology, anthropology, aesthetics, history, sociology, rhetoric, psychology, cognitive science, psychoanalysis, neurobiology, and literary and cultural studies. For a useful overview of these intertwined genealogies, see Plamper; and for an intellectual history of the 'emotion sciences' that traces their development since the 1960s, see Leys.

4 If we turn to the *Oxford English Dictionary*, we find that the etymology of the word itself alludes to each of these characteristics. Originally derived from the Latin *emovere* ('to remove,' 'to shift [or] displace'), 'emotion' would go on to accrue a social significance ('a public commotion or uprising' [1562]), an historical connotation ('any strong mental or instinctive feeling [deriving] from one's circumstances' [1602]), and a sense of mobility ('[a] movement from one place to another; a migration' [1596]).

area of social and cultural life.⁵ Indeed, I would go so far as to argue that emotion (thus understood) is what ultimately unites the categories of the literary-aesthetic and the sociopolitical – not only in a straightforward mimetic sense, but also at a deeper, discursive level, as the literary artefact itself internalizes the dominant structures of feeling circulating within society at large.

Rather than understanding emotion as necessarily subjective or individualized, then, I shall regard it here as a relational practice that may be socially or even politically determined. Or to put it another way, I will argue that literary representations of emotion need not be interpreted solely at the level of character, individual psychology, or the contingencies of plotting, but could also be related to wider historical processes. This shift in emphasis acknowledges the intersubjective quality of such emotional responses and, in so doing, challenges some of the boundaries that have traditionally insulated the individual from the collective, the psychological from the social. In *The Transmission of Affect*, Teresa Brennan makes a similar point, arguing that the feelings of 'one person, and the enhancing or depressing energies these affects entail, can enter into another' (3). According to Brennan, this process of affective transmission 'alters the biochemistry and neurology of the subject. The "atmosphere" or the environment literally gets into the individual. Physically and biologically, something is present that was not there before, but it ... was not generated solely or sometimes even in part by the individual organism or its genes' (1). Although such a claim may blur the boundaries between self and other, subject and object, the psychological and the social, I believe it is important to maintain *some* distinction between these 'opposing' categories – rather than seeing ourselves as mere repositories of disembodied affective energies, whether they be positive or negative, euphoric or dysphoric. And this is

---

5 In *Melancholy and Society*, for instance, Wolf Lepenies describes the collective sense of boredom that plagued the French aristocracy as they were increasingly marginalized by Louis XIII and Louis XIV. 'This boredom,' he writes, 'which stemmed directly from the position of an aristocracy both disempowered and relieved of its duties,' was 'socially transmitted and a phenomenon of interpersonal action' (40); it 'took hold of everyone, the members of the salon as well as the [courtiers], the former Frondeurs as well as nobles loyal to the king' (39). One may also be reminded of the 'objective neurosis' that Jean-Paul Sartre, in his multivolume biography of Flaubert, attributes to Second Empire society following the Revolution of 1848 – and the connection he draws between this social pathology and the 'subjective neurosis' of Flaubert himself (*Family* 619).

something that Brennan herself readily concedes: 'We may influence the registration of the transmitted affect in a variety of ways,' she writes, as 'affects are not received or registered in a vacuum. If I feel anxiety when I enter [a] room, then that will influence what I perceive or receive by way of an "impression" (a word that means what it says)' (6).[6] So although I will be arguing here that emotion is at least partly sociogenic, I shall also be retaining some sense of individuality (or the 'subject') in order to acknowledge our capacity to *resist* affective interpellation – our ability to defy the 'psychology' of the crowd, or the social rules that govern our emotional behaviour, or the dominant structures of feeling that may be characteristic of the historical period in which we live.

I have employed the phrase 'structure of feeling' more than once now, and I should probably define this term more precisely before proceeding. It is, of course, derived from the work of Raymond Williams, who uses it to describe the 'specifically affective elements of consciousness' (*Marxism* 132) that could be said to characterize any given historical period. For Williams, the term 'structure of feeling' designates the affective quality of our lives at a particular point in time – not the dominant ideologies or doctrines of the day, but the way in which these more 'concrete' and easily delineated forces are registered at an intuitive, emotional level. 'The most difficult thing to get hold of, in studying any past period,' Williams writes in *The Long Revolution*,

> is [a] felt sense of the quality of life at a particular place and time: a sense of the ways in which the particular activities combined into a way of thinking and living ... The term I would suggest to describe it is *structure of feeling*: it is as firm and definite as 'structure' suggests, yet it operates in the most delicate and least tangible parts of our activity. (63–64)

The structure of feeling was, for Williams, a way of collectivizing our affective lives. Although we may register the 'atmosphere' of an

---

6 Similarly, in *The Promise of Happiness*, Sara Ahmed argues that 'to be affected by another does not mean that an affect simply passes or "leaps" from one body to another. The affect becomes an object *only given the contingency of how we are affected*. We might be affected differently by what gets passed around ... If bodies do not arrive [somewhere] in neutral, if we are always in some way or another moody, then what we receive as an impression will depend on our affective situation ... [H]ow we arrive, how we enter this room or that room, will affect what impressions we receive' (39–40).

Introduction

historical period individually, the fact that we are all doing so at the same time gives these individual feelings a broader social significance:

> We are talking about characteristic elements of impulse, restraint, and tone; specifically affective elements of consciousness and relationships: not feeling against thought, but thought as felt and feeling as thought: practical consciousness of a present kind, in a living and interrelating continuity. We are then defining these elements as a 'structure': as a set, with specific internal relations, at once interlocking and in tension. Yet we are also defining a social experience which is still in process, often indeed not yet recognized as social but taken to be private, idiosyncratic, and even isolating, but which in analysis ... has its emergent, connecting, and dominant characteristics, indeed its specific hierarchies. (*Marxism* 132)[7]

Such feelings are, by definition, ephemeral and elusive. They are barely registered at the time, and as they lie at 'the very edge of semantic availability' (Williams, *Marxism* 134), they leave few traces in the historical record. According to Williams, the 'best evidence' of a structure of feeling can be found encoded within 'the actual conventions of literary or dramatic writing' (*Politics* 159) – in the affective and aesthetic qualities, the phobic and philic impulses, that achieve a certain salience within a work of literature. In *Politics and Letters*, for instance, Williams observes that 'one of the determining characteristics of so much of the English writing of the late 1840s was an anxious oscillation between sympathy for the oppressed and fear of their violence' (166). This combination of sympathy and fear, he argues, constituted one of the dominant structures of feeling in England during the 1840s, and can be identified in a number of literary narratives produced during this period. Williams' structure of feeling is particularly useful for our purposes as it delineates the same affective qualities that I will be emphasizing in the following pages. Here, too, emotion will be seen as essentially sociogenic, as a response to specific historical processes, and as a quality of feeling – an 'atmosphere,' if you like – that infiltrates literary discourse, with often profound formal and generic consequences. In other words, using the structure of feeling as a general theoretical principle, I shall be exploring

---

[7] It is important to acknowledge the fact that a particular historical period may have more than one structure of feeling – so, for example, we could speak of an aristocratic structure of feeling (as Lepenies does, without explicitly saying so, in *Melancholy and Society*), an imperial structure of feeling, or even a generational or gendered structure of feeling.

the process by which sociogenic and historically contingent feelings are 'materialized' within literary narratives, transforming the 'affective elements of consciousness,' such as 'impulse, restraint, and tone,' into a tangible structure 'with specific internal relations, at once interlocking and in tension.'[8]

As suggested earlier, the fact that emotion becomes detached from the individual consciousness and assumes the quality of an objective 'atmosphere,' circulating freely throughout the public and private spheres, makes it possible for such structures of feeling to find their way into literary narratives. Once they do percolate into literary discourse, they are most easily identified in the form of the atmospheric or tonal qualities that any given narrative generates.[9] This is what allows us to describe a particular work of literature as melancholy, say, or joyful, although it may be difficult to ascertain precisely where this affective quality resides. Typically, we register it as a vague, all-encompassing 'climate' or feeling-tone – the kind of feeling that Mikel Dufrenne calls a 'world atmosphere' (178). 'When we name the world of the aesthetic object by its creator,' Dufrenne writes, 'we emphasize the

---

8 There are, of course, other ways of theorizing the sociality of emotion. We have, for instance, Sara Ahmed's notion of *affective economies* ('emotions [that] circulate or are distributed across a social as well as psychic field, [following] the logic of capital' [*Cultural* 45]); Peter N. Stearns and Carol Z. Stearns' *emotionology* ('the attitudes or standards that a society, or a definable group within a society, maintains toward basic emotions and their appropriate expression' [813]); Barbara H. Rosenwein's *emotional communities* ('groups in which people adhere to the same norms of emotional expression and value – or devalue – the same or related emotions' [2]); Arlie Russell Hochschild's *feeling rules* (the social guidelines governing the 'type, intensity, duration, timing, and placing of [our] feelings' [85]); William M. Reddy's *emotional regimes* ('[t]he set of normative emotions and the official rituals, practices, and emotives that express and inculcate them; a necessary underpinning of any stable political regime' [129]); and Nina Eliasoph and Paul Lichterman's *group style* ('recurrent patterns of interaction [and emotional behaviour] that arise from a group's shared assumptions about what constitutes good or adequate participation in the group setting' [737]). Although these are all productive theories, I have found Williams' notion of the structure of feeling – combining as it does the social and the literary, the affective and the 'structural' – more suitable for my particular purposes.
9 For a fascinating discussion of the relationship between emotion and literary tone, one that has influenced my own understanding of the subject, see Ngai, *Ugly* 38–88.

presence of a certain style, a unique way of treating a subject' (167). In the case of literature, this quality saturates the discourse, creating an 'internal cohesion which is amenable only to the logic of feeling' (180). For Dufrenne, the unity of such an atmosphere emerges out of 'the vital metaphysical element in all men, [their] way of being in the world which reveals itself in a personality.' Simply put, just as someone who is feeling euphoric may be surrounded by a 'nimbus of joy' (177), so too an aesthetic object – whether it be a novel, a painting, or a piece of sculpture – will radiate a particular affective quality, a 'world atmosphere,' that gives it both substance and unity. To gain a better understanding of how this 'world atmosphere' actually operates, it may be useful to refer to Erich Auerbach's masterly reading of Balzac's *Old Goriot* (1835). In his analysis of the novel, Auerbach focuses on its opening pages, where we are offered a lengthy description of Madame Vauquer and her rather squalid boarding-house on the rue Neuve-Sainte-Geneviève. ('The atmosphere has the stuffiness of rooms which are never ventilated, and a mouldy odour of decay. Its dampness chills you as you breathe it, and permeates your clothing. Smells of all the meals that have been eaten in the boarding-house linger in the air' [31], etc.) As Auerbach notes, this opening passage produces 'an intense impression of cheerless poverty, shabbiness, and dilapidation'; and 'with the physical description the moral atmosphere is [also] suggested' (468). Like Stendhal, he goes on to argue, Balzac not only

> places the human beings, whose destiny he is seriously relating, in their precisely defined historical and social setting, but also conceives this connection as a necessary one: to him every milieu becomes a moral and physical atmosphere which impregnates the landscape, the dwelling, furniture, implements, clothing, physique, character, surroundings, ideas, activities, and fates of men, and at the same time the general historical situation reappears as a total atmosphere which envelops all [of] its several milieux. (473)

For Auerbach, as for Dufrenne, the affective or tonal quality of a narrative permeates every level of the discourse, settling nowhere in particular yet influencing everything it touches. And this may be why it is so difficult to identify exactly where this feeling resides – because of its discursive ubiquity, because of the fact that it can be found in every piece of furniture and every article of clothing, but also because it resides within the reader, too, who is obliged to register the atmosphere of a work of literature, even if they find themselves resisting it (as may sometimes be the case).

Although Dufrenne's notion of the 'world atmosphere' is a productive way of theorizing this tonal quality, this governing structure of feeling, it may also be useful to invoke the Indian aesthetic concept of *rasa* (which literally means 'essence,' 'juice,' or 'flavour'). In classical Indian aesthetics, the term *rasa* refers to the artistic transformation of certain core feelings (*sthāyī bhāva*) into an objective, impersonal mood that is communicated to – and shared by – the audience or reader. According to Bharata's *Nāṭyashāstra* (c. second or third century AD), there are eight core *sthāyī bhāvas*, all of which are relatively stable emotional states. These feelings are as follows:

1. *rati* – sexual love, desire
2. *hāsa* – laughter, merriment
3. *shoka* – sorrow, grief
4. *krodha* – anger, rage
5. *utsāha* – enthusiasm, courage
6. *bhaya* – fear, terror
7. *jugupsā* – disgust, horror, hatred
8. *vismaya* – astonishment, wonder[10]

Needless to say, in a theatrical performance or a work of literature, it is impossible to render such states in their ontological totality, so instead they are subject to a process of artistic distillation (*rasa*) by which the audience or reader is offered a 'taste' of the *sthāyī bhāva* that is being evoked. In order to create this 'flavour,' a performer or writer is obliged to transform the core feelings listed above into eight corresponding *rasas* (Dharwadker 1384–87).[11] It is only at this level, once the *sthāyī bhāva* has been transformed into an objective or impersonal *rasa*, that an emotional state can be experienced (or 'savoured') collectively. And here, too, it becomes difficult to identify the precise location of such affective qualities – whether they reside in the aesthetic object

---

10 In the *Nāṭyashāstra*, Bharata delineates a further thirty-three transitory feelings (*vyabhichārī bhāva*), each of which can be ascribed to one of these core emotional states (*sthāyī bhāva*).

11 These *rasas* are: (1) *shṛṅgāra* – eros; (2) *hāsya* – mirth; (3) *karuṇa* – compassion; (4) *raudra* – fury; (5) *vīra* – heroism; (6) *bhayānaka* – terror; (7) *bībhatsa* – revulsion; and (8) *adbhuta* – wonder (Dharwadker 1387).

Introduction

or performance itself, or whether they only 'come to life' through the hermeneutical act of reading, viewing, or listening. In fact, as Sheldon Pollock observes, this is ultimately a false dichotomy. With specific reference to literature, he argues that *rasa* can be 'regarded as a property of a text-object, a capacity of a reader-subject, and also a transaction between the two. The whole process ... exists as a totality even while its several moments can be analytically disaggregated.' In this respect, *rasa* 'precisely resembles the "taste" it metaphorically references, which may be regarded as existing at once in the food, the taster, and the act of tasting' (26).[12] Despite their cultural and historical differences, then, both Dufrenne and Bharata theorize the relationship between emotion and aesthetics in a remarkably similar way – emphasizing the 'impersonality' of aestheticized emotion, its collective quality, and also its capacity to defy the boundaries that traditionally insulate the (perceiving) subject from the (aesthetic) object, the phenomenal world of the reader from the purely referential world of discourse.[13]

It is important to note that the structures of feeling that find their way into literary discourse may in some cases acquire a pathological dimension; and this is particularly so within colonial or postcolonial societies, where one frequently encounters accelerated processes of social transformation, sudden historical ruptures, civil instability, authoritarian governance, and profound socioeconomic disparities. In *The Wretched of the Earth*, Frantz Fanon describes a range of pathologies that came about as a direct consequence of the colonial war in Algeria (1954–62). As a psychiatrist, Fanon was especially attuned to these pathologies, and in a

---

12 For more on the subject of *rasa*, see Appadurai 92–112, Rowell 327–34, and Schwartz.
13 In his article on the *Nāṭyashāstra*, Vinay Dharwadker expresses surprise at the extent to which the treatise anticipates modern theories of emotion such as those found in Charles Darwin's *The Expression of the Emotions in Man and Animals* (1872), William James' *The Principles of Psychology* (1890), and even Silvan Tomkins' *Affect Imagery Consciousness* (1962–92). 'These intersections across time and space,' he writes, 'are not the result of accidental or idiosyncratic textual juxtaposition. For reasons that we still cannot formulate after nearly three centuries of intellectual excavation, the fabric of thought in several modern European languages, as in Latin and Greek previously, is thickly interwoven with the thought that started to emerge in Sanskrit early in the first millennium BCE. Far from being foreign, Bharata's concepts and categories have been domesticated in European culture for a long time, in the intertextures of word and idea beneath the visible tissues of textuality' (1381–82).

chapter entitled 'Colonial War and Mental Disorders,' he provides us with a fascinating series of case studies. In Case No. 2 (Series A), for example, we are told of an Algerian *fellah* who had survived a massacre perpetrated by the French forces, and who subsequently developed a pathological 'aggressivity' (260) that manifested itself in the form of indiscriminate homicidal impulses. Similarly, in Case No. 1 (Series B), Fanon discusses the murder by two young Algerian boys of their European schoolmate, and he concludes that this crime was a consequence of the 'atmosphere of total war which reign[ed] in Algeria' (270) at the time. As we read these case studies, it becomes clear that the colonial presence in Algeria not only gave rise to a number of quite specific 'psycho-affective injuries' (218), but also produced a more general 'pathology of atmosphere' (289) that influenced every aspect of Algerian society. Under such circumstances, as I have suggested, these pathologies also infiltrate literary narratives, creating significant disturbances both at the level of character psychology – be it individual or collective – and at the level of form and structure, where the narrative itself may experience a series of discursive or generic crises. In an essay on the Arabic novel, for instance, Edward Said explores some of the underlying differences between Naguib Mahfouz (whom we shall be discussing in Chapter 1) and writers of a later generation from Lebanon and Palestine. According to Said, Mahfouz's work has always been able to depend on the stability, continuity, and 'vital integrity' of Egyptian civil society. '[T]hroughout all the turbulence of the country's wars, revolutions, and social upheavals,' he writes, 'civil society was never eclipsed, its identity was never in doubt, was never completely absorbed into the state' ('After' 319). In Lebanon and Palestine, however, such discursive stability is simply impossible to achieve – given the 'fractured, decentered, and openly insurrectionary' (320) nature of these societies. Instead, we find narratives such as Ghassan Kanafani's *Men in the Sun* (1962) or Elias Khoury's *Little Mountain* (1977), whose 'underlying aesthetic form,' Said notes, is characterized by 'rejection, drift, errance, [and] uncertainty' (325).[14] For these writers, who are obliged to contend with the 'fragmented realities' (323) of civil war and social disintegration, form is 'an adventure, narrative both uncertain and meandering, [and] character less a stable collection of traits than a linguistic device, as self-conscious as it is provisional and ironic' (321).

I believe that Said is quite right when he draws this connection between the sociopolitical circumstances in which a work of

---

14 An earlier version of Said's essay, with only minor stylistic differences, was published in 1989 as a foreword to Khoury's novel.

literature is produced and the formal or stylistic qualities of the narrative in question.[15] But how, precisely, does this process of transmission occur? What is it that ultimately unites the domains of the sociopolitical and the literary-aesthetic? In what follows, I will be suggesting that emotion, as I understand it here, serves as an intermediary between these two categories. Once the literary artefact has internalized the affective energies that are circulating within a particular society at a given point in time, it processes or 'materializes' these energies at the subliminal level of form, structure, and style – before integrating them into the affective economy of the narrative itself in the guise of a 'world atmosphere' or governing structure of feeling. As the Brazilian critic Roberto Schwarz argues, the original historical circumstances in which a novel is produced (or situated) reappear 'as a sociological form ... on the fictional plane and as a literary structure.' In this sense, he writes, 'forms are the abstracts of specific social relationships, and that is how ... the difficult process of [transforming] social questions into properly literary or compositional ones ... is realized' ('Importing' 53). Consider, for example, Ato Quayson's notion of the systemic uncanny (which we will be exploring in more detail in Chapter 1). According to Quayson, when an individual is confronted by a situation of 'acute political chaos or the general collapse of the social order,' he or she will often convert this 'perception of ... systemic disorder into a negative affect' (a feeling of guilt, say, or anxiety) that may not be traceable to its original source (*Calibrations* 80). Within literary narratives, this 'repressed negative energy' generates a strong sense of the uncanny and ultimately gives rise to a particular kind of discursive pathology – one that Quayson refers to as 'symbolization compulsion.' He employs this term, more specifically, to describe a narrative's drive toward an 'insistent metaphorical register even when this register does not help to develop the action, define character or spectacle, or create atmosphere.' In fact, Quayson says, such an excessive use of figurative language serves as a defence mechanism for the discourse itself, a way of avoiding or denying a traumatic experience that 'cannot be named except through symbolized digressiveness' (82).[16]

---

15 Of course, the 'sociology of form' has a long history too. See, for instance, Adorno, *Aesthetic* 225–61, Jameson, *Political* 89–136, and Moretti, *Signs* 1–41.
16 For more on the systemic uncanny and symbolization compulsion, see Quayson, 'Symbolization' and *Aesthetic* 141–46.

Quayson's discussion of this subject is located within a precise set of sub-Saharan coordinates; yet in the following pages, I shall argue that the social, psychological, and literary-aesthetic dynamic he describes here can be identified elsewhere too – whether it be Rio de Janeiro during the nineteenth century, Cairo in the early forties, or Sri Lanka at the height of the civil war.

II

Affective Disorders is situated at the juncture of three different critical perspectives. In addition to its obviously postcolonial qualities, it also engages with the areas of affect studies and narratology. Over the last few decades, there has been a tendency in postcolonial literary studies to focus on the purely traumatic consequences of colonialism – to the exclusion of all the other feelings that achieve a certain prominence, for one reason or another, in colonial and postcolonial societies.[17] In an essay published in 2012, the South African critic Gerald Gaylard discusses this omission in some detail, asking 'why it is that [postcolonial] literature is still associated with social issues and politics rather than feeling.' After all, he writes, 'it is hardly the case that [such] literature is lacking emotion'; and yet for some reason, '[w]hen emotion in postcolonial literature has been explored, this has usually been in the guise of trauma studies' (99). In *Affective Disorders*, then, I have decided to focus on a wider range of feelings than is typical for a work of postcolonial criticism – discussing states such as anger, jealousy, and boredom – while also engaging more substantially with the field

---

17 See, for example, Craps, Ifowodo, and Ward. This entirely legitimate emphasis on the traumatic consequences of the colonial project has also led to a number of studies that focus on the psychic/affective states of mourning and melancholia (see Gilroy, Durrant, and Khanna). More recently, however, some postcolonial critics have begun to explore feelings that are not necessarily 'traumatic' in origin (see Kim, Majumdar, and Bewes). In *Prose of the World: Modernism and the Banality of Empire*, for instance, Saikat Majumdar argues that '[b]anality and its often-attendant emotion boredom need to be understood as key motifs for colonial and postcolonial literary criticism as they help to aestheticize the relation between the imperial metropolis and the colonial periphery' (4). According to Majumdar, the 'material, economic, and infrastructural inadequacies felt across the margins of the historical expanse of the British Empire' move their 'victims not only toward the intense theatre of trauma but also toward the pervasiveness of banality and the iterative cycle of boredom' (23).

of affect studies (as a broadly construed, interdisciplinary enterprise). The third major critical perspective I employ here is that of narratology. Once again, there has been a tendency in postcolonial studies to neglect or deprioritize the formal and stylistic qualities of a narrative in favour of thematic readings or ideological critique. As the editors of the *Cambridge Journal of Postcolonial Literary Inquiry* put it, 'literature and the aesthetic at large have suffered a regrettable abeyance as prime sites for generating theoretical perspectives on the conditions of the postcolonial' (Quayson et al. 6). In this case, however, I will be emphasizing the formal and structural consequences of the aforementioned emotional disturbances – exploring the way in which feelings such as anger or boredom can often destabilize narratives, provoking crises of representation, generic ambivalence, and discursive rupture. By bringing all three critical perspectives together in this manner, I hope to provide a deeper understanding of the relationship between various sociopolitical forces (colonial modernity, bureaucracy, communal violence, etc.) and the affective and aesthetic 'disorders' to which they give rise.

As the reader may have noticed, I have chosen to focus on an historically and geographically diverse range of narratives, some of which originate in quite different corners of the colonial and postcolonial world. Proceeding chronologically, we begin with Joaquim Maria Machado de Assis' *Dom Casmurro* (1899), which is set in Rio during the reign of Dom Pedro II (1831–89). Although Brazil achieved independence from Portugal in 1825, many colonial practices, such as slavery and patronage, continued well into the postcolonial period – creating, as we shall discover, a peculiar dissonance within nineteenth-century Brazilian society. Naguib Mahfouz's *Midaq Alley* (1947) is set in Cairo during the Second World War, a time when the city was occupied by over 140,000 Allied soldiers. Under the terms of the Anglo-Egyptian Treaty of 1936, Egypt was obliged to accommodate an unlimited number of these foreign forces for the duration of the war, although the country itself would remain officially neutral until the spring of 1945. Vikram Seth's *A Suitable Boy* (1993) surveys the early years of Indian independence, focusing in particular on a period spanning from 1950 to 1952, when the fundamental features of the postcolonial nation-state, as envisaged by Jawaharlal Nehru, were being established.[18] In Upamanyu Chatterjee's

---

18 The so-called Nehruvian Consensus involved the general acceptance of four basic principles: socialism, secularism, democracy, and a foreign policy of non-alignment with any major power bloc. For more on this 'consensus' (and its eventual collapse), see Vanaik 301–3.

English, August: An Indian Story (1988), we return to India several decades later to find that the optimism of the 1950s has long since dissipated and the Nehruvian nation-state, which held so much promise in those early, formative years, has become notorious for its bureaucratic inefficiency, petty corruption, and 'rule-bound incompetence' (Nandy, 'Culture' 68). The action in Michael Ondaatje's *Anil's Ghost* (2000) takes place during the Sri Lankan Civil War (1983–2009), a brutal conflict that claimed an estimated 100,000 lives. Although the war itself lasted for twenty-six years, the novel focuses on a particularly violent period in the late eighties and early nineties that came to be known as the *beeshana kalaya* – or the 'time of great fear.' And finally, in Vikram Chandra's *Sacred Games* (2006), we make our way to Mumbai at the turn of the twenty-first century, where we discover a city that has been deeply traumatized by the communal violence and terrorism that occurred in 1992–93 (following the destruction of the Babri Masjid in Ayodhya), and whose inhabitants continue to suffer the malign influence of majoritarian politics, corruption, and organized crime.

Although a chronological overview is always beneficial, I have decided, for the purposes of analysis, to trace the various stages of the colonial/postcolonial life cycle as it unfolded in these different locales. We therefore begin our journey in colonial Cairo during the Second World War (*Midaq Alley*), before exploring India's transition from colony to postcolony during the late forties and early fifties (*A Suitable Boy*). In the following chapters, we advance even further into the postcolonial period, albeit in different places and at different times. After visiting nineteenth-century Rio (*Dom Casmurro*), which for many years served as the capital of a postcolonial monarchy, we return once more to India, roughly four decades after independence (*English, August*). We then travel to Sri Lanka during the 'time of great fear' (*Anil's Ghost*), before bringing our journey to an end in a Mumbai that is recognizably contemporary (*Sacred Games*). By structuring *Affective Disorders* in this way, I am not suggesting that every colonial or postcolonial experience is perfectly analogous. Quite the opposite. In the case of *Dom Casmurro*, for instance, I will be focusing on the colonial legacy of slavery and the fact that Brazil would remain a slave-owning economy until 1888 (by which time it would be the only such economy in the Western world). When I come to discuss *English, August*, on the other hand, I will be addressing the bureaucratic legacy of the British Empire, which survives to this day in the form of the Indian Administrative Service (IAS). Although both of these practices could be considered a colonial 'inheritance,' they are, of course, more notable for their differences than for their similarities. But this is precisely what makes it so interesting to consider one alongside the other – and to explore the different emotions that these quite distinct historical experiences generate. In Brazil, as I shall argue, we have a destructive and pathological jealousy that emerges out of the conflict between the social reality of slavery and the liberal ideologies to which the élite ostensibly subscribe. Turning to *English, August*, however, we find an altogether different type of feeling – an overwhelming sense of boredom that is a direct consequence of the bureaucratic procedures of the IAS. This is the kind of 'minor' emotion that is characterized, in Sianne Ngai's words, by its 'flatness or ongoingness,' by its 'remarkable capacity for duration' (*Ugly* 7); and given the nature of Indian bureaucracy, it is entirely appropriate that this should be the case.

The similarities between such disparate narratives can also be instructive. Despite their obvious differences – despite the intensity of the jealousy we encounter in *Dom Casmurro*, for example, and the languid, apathetic quality of the boredom we find in *English, August* – there are a number of fundamental correspondences that all six narratives share. To put it briefly, these similarities can be summarized as follows:

1. All six narratives trace the process by which certain social, political, or economic forces penetrate the private sphere, where they induce corresponding (although frequently displaced or sublimated) affective states.

2. All six narratives demonstrate the way in which such affective states assume an intersubjective quality, becoming depersonalized 'structures of feeling' (although this collective quality may not always be recognized by the characters themselves, who in some instances continue to regard their feelings as 'private, idiosyncratic, and even isolating' [Williams, *Marxism* 132]).

3. All six narratives reveal the narratological consequences of these affective disturbances, as in each case the dominant emotion (whether it be anger, jealousy, or boredom) infiltrates the structure of the narrative itself, which thereby comes to serve as a discursive correlative for the social, political, or economic forces mentioned above, and for the various affective disorders to which they give rise.

In addition to these general correspondences, it may also be useful to provide a more detailed summary of what can be found in the following pages – beginning with Chapter 1, which seeks to explain the ubiquity of anger in Naguib Mahfouz's *Midaq Alley*. I argue here that this dominant emotion could be read as a collective response to the contradictory social forces, the radical disjunctures and discontinuities, initiated by colonial modernity. I then move on to discuss the role of rumour in the novel and the significance of its pronounced melodramatic qualities, both of which represent an attempt to contain or 'quarantine' such dysphoric feelings. As we shall see, though, this strategy ultimately fails, and the melodramatic conclusion that we are expecting never arrives. Instead, the novel itself suffers something of a generic crisis, shifting without warning from the melodramatic mode into the tragic. Rather than focusing on a particular emotion, Chapter 2 explores the way in which strong feelings of any kind are actively discouraged in Vikram Seth's *A Suitable Boy*. In the days following the Partition of India in 1947, Jawaharlal Nehru delivered numerous speeches in which he asserted that social and political unity could only be achieved by renouncing 'hatred, violence, [and] anger' (*Speeches* 23). This rhetoric, I suggest, profoundly influences the novel's affective disposition, its 'world atmosphere,' causing it to internalize the Aristotelian virtue of *metriopatheia* (or 'equanimity') and obliging the reader to adopt a similar stance if he or she is to survive 1,349 pages of carefully modulated prose. Chapter 3, as indicated above, focuses on the significance of jealousy in Joaquim Maria Machado de Assis' *Dom Casmurro*. On the face of it, this fictional memoir relates a straightforward story of marital infidelity from the perspective of the 'betrayed' husband, Bento Santiago. As the narrative progresses, however, the story we are told becomes increasingly implausible, and we begin to suspect that Bento's wife may have been unjustly maligned. Although our narrator locates the source of his jealousy in the private sphere, I propose that it actually arises out of the conflict between the archaic socioeconomic practices of nineteenth-century Brazil (i.e., slavery and patronage) and the liberal principles that were so closely affiliated with European modernity. In Chapter 4, I turn my attention to the subject of boredom in Upamanyu Chatterjee's *English, August*. Here, I explore the connection between bureaucracy, boredom, and realist discourse. More specifically, I argue that the narrative internalizes many of the features that we tend to associate with the Indian Administrative Service and, in so doing, becomes ever more lethargic, repetitive, and 'boring.' Although these qualities undermine the novel's governing aesthetic principles, the fact that it survives such a grave challenge suggests that realism may be a good deal more agile and accommodating, as a mode of representation, than is often allowed. Chapter 5 discusses the climate of fear that dominates Michael Ondaatje's *Anil's Ghost*. We can find ample evidence of such fear at the representational level of the narrative – where all the violence and torture and enforced disappearances take place – but it also penetrates the novel's underlying structure, activating a phobic response on the part of the discourse itself. After analysing this response in some detail, I explore the way in which it defies the generic imperatives that would typically govern a narrative of this kind, making it impossible to achieve the linearity, the hermeneutic closure, and the 'localization of culpability' that we associate with classic crime fiction. Finally, Chapter 6 addresses the affective (and aesthetic) consequences of violence and criminality in Vikram Chandra's *Sacred Games*. I begin by discussing the minor crimes to be found within its pages (the petty burglaries, the routine corruption, the domestic disputes, etc.), before moving on to address various instances of 'exceptional' criminality, such as the communal violence that took place in Mumbai in 1992–93, killing an estimated 900 people, and the retaliatory bombings that occurred on 12 March 1993, claiming another 257 lives. The affective state that emerges out of this combination of the mundane and the extraordinary, I argue, could best be described by invoking Sianne Ngai's notion of 'stuplimity' – a somewhat contradictory aesthetic response in which 'the initial experience of being aesthetically overwhelmed involves not terror or pain ... but *something much closer to an ordinary fatigue*' (*Ugly* 270).

So what is to be gained, then, by approaching these works of colonial and postcolonial literature from the perspective of affect studies? In the first place, I would contend, it provides us with a deeper understanding of the way in which the social, political, and economic forces that are produced under such circumstances influence the affective lives of ordinary people – whether these forces are encountered in the form of colonial modernity (Chapter 1), communal violence (Chapter 2), slavery and patronage (Chapter 3), bureaucracy (Chapter 4), civil war (Chapter 5), or crime and terrorism (Chapter 6). By analysing the affective consequences of these historical processes, we are able to gain a 'felt sense of the quality of life at a particular place and time' (Williams, *Long* 63). And as such experiences typically lie at the 'very edge of semantic availability' (Williams, *Marxism* 134), the evidence they leave behind can be identified most clearly, I would argue, at the level of literary form, structure, and style. Hence the emphasis on narratology in what follows; and hence my decision to combine narratology with affect studies (broadly construed). Only thus are we able to trace the process by which a sociogenic feeling penetrates the private sphere, and then infiltrates the structure of the literary narrative itself, where it makes its presence felt in the form of proairetic sequences, plot nuclei, temporal anachronies, and so on. In the opening pages of *The Bourgeois*, Franco Moretti discusses the relationship between the study of literature and that of history. 'What kind of history,' he asks, 'what kind of [historical] *evidence*' do we find in literature?

> Clearly, never a direct one: the mill-owner Thornton in *North and South* (1855), or the entrepreneur Wokulski in *The Doll* (1890), proves exactly nothing about the Manchester or Warsaw bourgeoisie. They belong to a parallel historical series ... where the spasms of capitalist modernization are matched and reshaped by literary form-giving ... [I]f we accept the idea of literary form as the fossil remains of what had once been a living and problematic present; and if we work our way backwards ... then formal analysis may unlock ... a dimension of the past that would otherwise remain hidden. Here lies its possible contribution to historical knowledge: by understanding the opacity of Ibsen's hints to the past, or the oblique semantics of Victorian adjectives, or even ... the role of the gerund in *Robinson Crusoe*, we enter a realm of shadows, where the past recovers its voice, and still speaks to us ... But speaks to us *only* through the medium of form. (14–15)

While it may be difficult to prove, incontrovertibly, the connection between the diminution of the proairetic code in *English, August* and the bureaucratic procedures of the IAS, or between the abundance of 'catalyzers' that can be found in *A Suitable Boy* and the placatory content of Nehru's speeches during the late forties and early fifties, the formal *correspondences* between these narratives and their actual or imagined historical circumstances, the structural *analogies* that serve to conjoin the literary-aesthetic and the sociopolitical in such cases, will, I hope, prove to be reasonably persuasive. As Roberto Schwarz writes, an argument of this nature 'requires a moment of extraliterary reflection, whose relevance, impossible to prove on the model of $2 + 2 = 4$, can be substantiated in the increased understanding [of the narrative that] it ... allows' (*Master* 20). And that will certainly be my objective in *Affective Disorders*, too, where the reader will be asked to pursue these often elusive feelings as they take on a decentred, intersubjective quality, as they colonize the private sphere, and as they saturate the very tissue of the narratives we will be discussing. Such a process may not yield incontrovertible 'proof' in the manner of $2 + 2 = 4$, but it does provide enough circumstantial evidence, I believe, to make a plausible (even compelling) case.[19]

Something else the reader will be asked to do in *Affective Disorders*, as we have noted, is to follow a rather meandering historical and geographical itinerary, one that includes destinations as diverse as Rio during the reign of Dom Pedro II, wartime Cairo, and contemporary Mumbai. So what logic has informed the selection of these particular texts, and what do we learn by bringing them together in such a way? By choosing to focus on four different countries and two different empires, I am attempting to emphasize the international (or, as Robert Young might say, the 'tricontinental') nature of the processes outlined above, while also revealing the various correspondences and specificities that only become clear once we bring these narratives into direct contact with each other.[20] Generally speaking, then, I have selected these six narratives precisely *because* of their historical and geographical range

19 By arguing that literary discourse internalizes the dominant structures of feeling within a particular society, and by identifying the traces of such feelings in the formal, generic, and stylistic qualities of these individual narratives, I have clearly consigned the figure of the author to the periphery of my analysis – and I have done so quite deliberately. As a matter of critical principle, I believe that literary narratives assume a certain autonomy from their author and are ultimately responsible for generating their own (polysemic) meaning. I also believe that literature is capable of internalizing various social, political, and economic forces, and that we may learn more about this process by analysing the formal qualities of a narrative than by discussing the biography of its author (although in some cases this may be a productive enterprise too). More specifically, however, given the nature of this particular project and my attempt to move away from individualistic or subject-centred theories of emotion, it seemed important that the affective qualities I explore here should not be seen to originate from an authorial figure (even if such a figure were merely serving as an 'intermediary'), but instead should be allowed to circulate freely between the public and private spheres, between the domains of the sociopolitical and the literary-aesthetic, as a disembodied and depersonalized structure of feeling.
20 In *Postcolonialism: An Historical Introduction*, Young uses the term 'tricontinental' instead of 'postcolonial' or 'Third-World' in order to emphasize the international dimension of anti-colonial and postcolonial resistance. 'Above all,' he writes, 'the tricontinental marks an identification with the great Havana Tricontinental [Conference] of 1966, which initiated the first global alliance of the peoples of the three continents [i.e., Africa, Asia, and Latin America] against imperialism, and the founding moment of postcolonial theory in its journal, the *Tricontinental*' (5).

Affective Disorders

– because of their differences, but also because each one demonstrates, in a nuanced and multilayered way, the process by which a collective structure of feeling can infiltrate literary discourse, whether the narrative in question is produced (or situated) in Rio in 1899 or Cairo in 1947. Moreover, all six narratives emphasize the tendency, in colonial and postcolonial societies, for such feelings to acquire a pathological quality; and it is in this regard that the aforementioned similarities and differences become especially instructive.

In Chapter 1, on *Midaq Alley*, we are confronted by an anger that emerges out of the various inequalities, disparities, and instabilities generated by colonial modernity. Yet given the political circumstances in which the characters find themselves (living in a city under military occupation), this anger must be severely repressed; and as a consequence, it undergoes a process of displacement, being directed instead at more easily mastered substitutes such as wives, employees, and acquaintances. This is what makes the anger in the novel so disproportionate and 'ill-fitting': the fact that it is a product of obstructed agency, the fact that it is an emotion *looking for a cause*, and the fact that it denies the characters the possibility of genuine cathartic release.[21] Chapter 2, which offers a close reading of *A Suitable Boy*, is slightly different to the other five chapters in that it does not explore a particular emotional state, but focuses instead on the *attenuation* of feeling, on the discipline and self-control that Nehru promoted in response to the communal violence that accompanied Partition in 1947. Even so, the fact that this reticence acquires such prestige within the narrative, and within the society it delineates, draws our attention to the volatility (the underlying 'passion and prejudice' [Nehru, *Speeches* 33]) that made the imposition of such a rigid 'emotional regime' necessary in the first place. Moving on to *Dom Casmurro*, in Chapter 3, we also encounter a disproportionate and displaced feeling. In this case, however, the pathological jealousy that our narrator experiences emerges out of the conflict between his professed liberal values and the archaic system of slavery on which his socioeconomic privilege relies; and it could thus be seen as an affective correlative for the more general tendency among the Brazilian élite to misrecognize

---

21 I have borrowed the phrase 'obstructed agency' from Sianne Ngai, whose 2005 book *Ugly Feelings* explores some of the 'negative affects' (envy, anxiety, paranoia, etc.) that such an obstruction produces, 'regardless of whether [it] is actual or fantasized, or whether the agency obstructed is individual or collective' (3).

the true nature of their social reality. Such jealousy also became a dominant structure of feeling during this period as a consequence of the patronage that continued to serve as Brazil's primary form of social mediation, encouraging a fierce competition for favour at every level of society. Chapter 4 focuses on *English, August* and the debilitating boredom that arises out of the bureaucratic procedures of the Indian Administrative Service (which, prior to independence, was known as the Indian Civil Service [ICS]). In some ways, we could relate this boredom to the renunciation of strong feeling advocated by Nehru in Chapter 2 – for boredom also de-intensifies our lives, leaving us, as Heidegger observes, 'equally distant from despair and joy' (*Introduction* 2) – but again there are some fundamental differences that ought to be acknowledged. The 'reticence' in *A Suitable Boy*, for example, is designed to protect the narrative from dangerous upsurges of intradiegetic feeling, while the boredom in *English, August* brings it to the verge of a complete discursive collapse. And whereas the emotional regime in *A Suitable Boy* still endorses *moderate* affective states, in *English, August* the attenuation of feeling assumes a pathological quality that leaves our lethargic hero utterly drained of energy and desire. In Chapter 5, which explores *Anil's Ghost*, we discover a feeling of fear that has also acquired a pathological quality. During the Sri Lankan Civil War, the use of violence and intimidation as a deliberate political strategy gave rise to a general 'culture of terror' within the country. By the late eighties, as one Amnesty International report indicates, violence had become 'so widespread that it [was] often difficult to establish with certainty who the agents of specific killings were – or even to identify the victims,' whose bodies may have been 'grossly mutilated' or 'burned to ashes' (qtd. in Senaratne 146). Under these circumstances, as we shall see, the kind of fear that is created cannot be easily localized in the form of an unidentified corpse or a representative of the state, but instead moves from body to body, and from place to place, creating a dysphoric atmosphere that permeates every level of the discourse. Finally, in Chapter 6, we address the significance of stuplimity – the conjunction of the stupefying and the sublime, the boring and the astonishing – in *Sacred Games*. As mentioned earlier, this term was first employed by Sianne Ngai to 'highlight certain limitations in classic theories of the sublime,' which fail to account for the boredom that has become 'increasingly intertwined with contemporary experiences of aesthetic awe' (*Ugly* 8). In Chandra's novel, however, the feeling of stuplimity assumes a broader social significance. Instead of being inspired by an encounter with an aesthetic object, it is generated by the intermingling of two different types of crime: the 'ordinary' criminality that has become a feature of everyday life in Mumbai, and the episodes of 'spectacular' criminality, such as communal violence and terrorism, that have also come to be associated with the city.

Before proceeding any further, I would like to clarify precisely what I mean when I use the word 'emotion.' In some recent theoretical writing within the field of affect studies, a crucial distinction has been drawn between affect and emotion – the former term being employed to describe pre-subjective, asignifying bodily 'intensities,' while the latter refers to feelings that have been recognized as 'subjective' and granted both social and linguistic significance. According to Brian Massumi, for instance, affect and emotion follow 'different logics and pertain to different orders.' Whereas affect is 'embodied in purely autonomic reactions most directly manifested in the skin – at the surface of the body, at its interface with things' (25), emotion involves the 'sociolinguistic fixing of the quality of an experience which is from that point onward defined as personal' (28).[22] Although I have found this formulation useful at times, by and large I agree with Sara Ahmed that the distinction between affect and emotion can 'under-describe the work of emotions which involve forms of intensity, bodily orientation, and direction that are not simply about "subjective content" or [the] qualification of intensity' (*Promise* 230). In other words, drawing such an emphatic distinction between affect (as an asignifying bodily 'intensity') and emotion (as a clearly defined, subjective feeling) can conceal the extent to which these categories merge into one another. It is possible, as Ahmed notes, to 'separate an affective response from an emotion' at a theoretical level – to separate the bodily sensation of fear, say, from the *feeling* of being afraid – but this 'does not mean that in practice, or in everyday life, they are separate' (*Promise* 231).[23] In the present study, therefore, I shall not be observing this particular theoretical distinction. For one thing, my interest lies not in dividing the bodily from the cognitive, but in exploring the interaction between these two categories. Or to put it another way, I shall be focusing on the point at which feelings such as anger or boredom achieve a certain discursive

---

22 For more examples of this theoretical distinction, see Grossberg, *We Gotta* 79–87, Terada 4, and Jameson, *Antinomies* 28–44.
23 Other critics who have chosen not to make use of such a distinction include Brennan 3–6, Ngai, *Ugly* 25–28, and Flatley 12. For an especially forceful critique of the affect/emotion dichotomy, see Greco and Stenner 10–12.

legibility, coming into view by way of the 'impression' they leave on the literary narratives they infiltrate. These are the structures of feeling we discussed earlier – the feelings that lie at 'the very edge of semantic availability' (Williams, *Marxism* 134) yet nonetheless reveal themselves in 'the actual conventions of literary or dramatic writing' (Williams, *Politics* 159). Although such structures of feeling have assumed a certain significatory presence, this does not mean that they have lost their physiological qualities. On the contrary, what literature provides is a site where the subjective and the objective, the semiotic and the asignifying, the cognitive and the somatic, can come together; and it is the conjunction of these different categories, as revealed, enacted, or produced within the domain of the literary-aesthetic, that we will be exploring in the following pages. As we do so, I shall be using the term 'emotion' to describe *a state of feeling that combines, to varying degrees, the categories of the physiological, the psychological, and the sociocultural*. And I will also be emphasizing the three characteristic features of emotion that I mentioned at the beginning of this introduction – (1) the fact that it is both psychogenic and sociogenic, (2) the fact that it is historically constituted, and (3) the fact that it is inherently mobile, an affective quality that slides all over the place, defying all boundaries, even those that would distinguish between a feeling you register on your skin, as a bodily 'intensity,' and your cognitive understanding of what that sensation signifies.

As we have seen, the texts I have chosen to analyse in this study are notable for their diversity – encompassing four different countries, two different empires, and three different centuries. By discussing such a wide range of narratives, I am not suggesting, of course, that emotion can be easily universalized. Again, quite the opposite: I view emotion not as the product of some ahistorical psychic essence, but as a 'felt response' to specific social, political, and economic forces (hence my reliance on the 'structure of feeling' as a theoretical principle). At the same time, however, this does not mean that our affective lives are *entirely* determined by our circumstances, or that the anger we feel in Cairo in 1942 bears no resemblance at all to the anger that may be felt elsewhere in the colonial or postcolonial world at different historical junctures.[24] Rather than opting for a biological *or* a cultural understanding of emotion, then, I shall be attempting to combine these

---

24 For more on the universality of certain narrative structures and affective states, analysed from a cognitive perspective, see Hogan, *Affective* and *Mind*.

two categories by situating various emotional 'utterances' (or *parole*, to use Saussure's linguistic terminology) within a larger affective structure (or *langue*) that is not confined to any one culture.[25] If we are to deny the humanistic notion that different cultures share certain underlying similarities, many of which may be located in the psyche or the realm of the affective, then we create a world of unassimilable, untranslatable cultural difference, which immediately forecloses the possibility of meaningful intercultural dialogue.[26] Earlier, if you recall, we compared the affective and aesthetic theories of Bharata, the author of the *Nāṭyashāstra* (c. second or third century AD), and Mikel Dufrenne, the author of *The Phenomenology of Aesthetic Experience* (1953). This would not have been possible if these two writers did not share at least some similarities (despite their various differences); and I believe it is the responsibility of the literary critic to identify such correspondences, however unlikely they may be, while also remaining alert to the cultural and historical specificities that situate every narrative, every theory, every aesthetic object or representational gesture, within a particular place and time. It might be best to elaborate on this point, in conclusion, by discussing the example of psychoanalysis.

Traditionally, the relationship between psychoanalysis and postcolonialism has been a rather fraught one. According to its critics, psychoanalysis as a discipline is grounded in, and serves to perpetuate, certain racist ideologies and colonial binaries, such as the opposition between the civilized and the savage.[27] It has also

---

25 As the reader may know, Ferdinand de Saussure employed the term *langue* to refer to the underlying structure of a language (which is 'both a social product of the faculty of speech and a collection of necessary conventions that have been adopted by a social body to permit individuals to exercise that faculty' [9]) and the term *parole* to describe an individual utterance or act of linguistic communication.

26 Ernesto Laclau makes this argument very persuasively in *Emancipation(s)* 20–35.

27 One need only read the opening passage of Freud's *Totem and Taboo* (1913), subtitled *Some Points of Agreement between the Mental Lives of Savages and Neurotics*, to understand what motivates such a critique. 'There are men still living,' Freud writes, 'who, as we believe, stand very near to primitive man, far nearer than we do, and whom we therefore regard as his direct heirs and representatives. Such is our view of those whom we describe as savages or half-savages; and their mental life must have a peculiar interest for us if we are right in seeing in it a well-preserved picture of an early stage of our own development' (1).

been accused of universalizing a particular Western model of subjectivity that is inapplicable to other cultures (where subject-formation occurs in contrasting ways and 'subjectivity' itself may be understood differently). Such critiques are to be taken seriously, but in some cases they may underestimate the cultural pliability of psychoanalysis, the manner in which it changes shape as it moves from one place to another (again depending on the precise circumstances in which it is employed). It is this pliability that makes it possible for Frantz Fanon, in *Black Skin, White Masks*, to use the psychoanalytical categories of narcissism and neurosis to explore the pathological consequences of the colonial presence in the French Antilles. Or, elsewhere, this is what allows J.M. Coetzee to analyse the psychopathology of South African society during the apartheid era, as demonstrated by the obsessive and neurotic writings of Geoffrey Cronjé (19–22). Or to offer yet another example, it is this pliability, this shape-shifting quality, that enables the anthropologist Gananath Obeyesekere to invoke the Freudian notion of transference when describing his relationship with an informant in Sri Lanka (9, 231–36). In each of these cases, we see the way in which a body of thought that originated in a particular place and time (Western Europe at the end of the nineteenth century) can be used in other places and at other times to understand the formation of individual or collective identities, the pathologies to which they may give rise, and the complicated psychosocial dynamic they bring into being. In his discussion of *Moses and Monotheism* (1939), Edward Said freely acknowledges Freud's Eurocentric perspective, yet he also recognizes the wide-ranging applicability of psychoanalysis. Freud, he writes,

> was an explorer of the mind, of course, but also, in the philosophical sense, an overturner and a re-mapper of accepted or settled geographies and genealogies. He thus lends himself especially to rereading in different contexts, since his work is all about how life history offers itself by recollection, research and reflection to endless structuring and restructuring, in both the individual and the collective sense. That we, different readers from different periods of history, with different cultural backgrounds, should continue to do this in our readings of Freud strikes me as nothing less than a vindication of his work's power to instigate new thought, as well as to illuminate situations that he himself might never have dreamed of. (*Freud* 27)

In what follows, then, I shall be exploring different feelings as they emerge in different places and at different times. But I also believe it is important to identify some of the cultural and historical correspondences that make such a study possible in the first place. Even if we do not always experience feelings in precisely the same way, it is essential, in my view, to acknowledge the fact that such feelings *can be shared*; and if we go so far as to acknowledge the possibility of a 'structure of feeling' that may be characteristic of a particular society or a particular culture, at any given point in time, then we also need to consider the possibility that there may be qualities of feeling, shades of emotion, that we share with other people, with still larger collectives, elsewhere and at other times. Or to end this introduction where it began, I would like to suggest that there may be some connection, however slight, between the fear experienced by a French peasant in the summer of 1789, as rumours of invading armies spread throughout the provinces, and the anxiety felt by a young Tanganyikan schoolgirl in 1962, as her country negotiated the various social, political, and economic challenges that accompanied its declaration of independence.

CHAPTER ONE

Anger
Naguib Mahfouz's *Midaq Alley*

The native's muscles are always tensed.

        Frantz Fanon, *The Wretched of the Earth*, 1961

A moment arrives when one can no longer feel anything but anger, an absolute anger.

        Jean-Luc Nancy, *The Birth to Presence*, 1993

I

Set in Cairo during the Second World War, Naguib Mahfouz's *Midaq Alley* (1947) introduces the reader to a small circle of characters living in one of the old city's more dilapidated alleyways. It traces their interwoven lives and focuses, in particular, on the accelerated processes of social transformation that many of these characters are forced to undergo. As Magda Baraka has observed, the socioeconomic influence of the war made the 1940s 'a decade of sharp contradiction' in Egypt (87). For some, the presence of over 140,000 Allied soldiers in Cairo led to greater employment opportunities, and many local businesses flourished. The average earnings of the young men employed by the British Army at Qantara and Tel el-Kebir increased tenfold (Cooper 137), while for a privileged minority the war would prove even more lucrative: between 1940 and 1943, to cite one especially revealing statistic, the number of (sterling) millionaires in the country rose from fifty to

Affective Disorders

four hundred (Lacouture and Lacouture 99). But of course there was another side to this story; and in many ways, during the early forties, Cairo was becoming an increasingly divided city. While fortunes were being made in the financial district, in the poorer quarters they were storming the bakeries for bread (Vatikiotis 347). Between August 1939 and September 1941, the cost of living index rose by 45 per cent, and during the same period the price of food showed an average increase of 94 per cent (Cooper 136, 161). This sudden rise in the cost of living was aggravated by a scarcity of basic commodities such as sugar, flour, fuel, and bread (Vatikiotis 347) – leading one Member of Parliament to accuse the Allied forces of 'starving the people' (Lacouture and Lacouture 99).

As ever, these economic disparities were also reflected in the topography of the city itself. While the European quarter was being expanded and developed, Islamic Cairo was largely abandoned: 'its streets were neglected, cleaning was haphazard, [the] water supply was only partial, and the sewers were poor or insufficient.' This deterioration was exacerbated by the 'rapid increase in [a population] whose density weighed heavily on the crumbling infrastructure and inadequate public services' (Raymond 334). And as the old city went into an irreversible decline, the upper classes relocated to the European quarter – where political power, economic activity, and capital were now concentrated – leaving Islamic Cairo to the poor and uneducated majority.[1] Such developmental and demographic differences in turn served to underscore the broader social and cultural disparities that separated the two halves of Cairo. Whereas the European quarter contained all the usual signifiers of Western modernity (department stores, shopping arcades, movie theatres, etc.), the old city was, as Janet Abu-Lughod notes, 'still essentially preindustrial in technology, social structure, and way of life' (98).[2]

By the early 1940s, then, when the action in *Midaq Alley* takes place, Cairo had been divided into two quite distinct spheres of urban culture: 'traditional versus modern, native versus foreign, Egyptian

---

1 In the 1940s, half of the city's children were dying of diarrhoea and malnutrition before the age of five; and although an estimated 90 per cent of foreigners were literate, only one in seven Egyptians could read (Rodenbeck 147).
2 For more on the topographical duality of colonial Cairo (and the liminal zones that at least partially defied such binaries), see Naaman, Reynolds, and Scott, 'Colonial.'

versus European, old versus new, *baladi* ["of the country"] versus *ifrangi* (Western style)' (Reynolds 3). And it is the tension between these two spheres that generates much of the novel's proairetic substance, as continuity collides with change, and the inhabitants of the alley struggle to maintain a fragile sense of social order and stability. Perhaps not surprisingly, the conflict between tradition and modernity has also tended to dominate critical readings of *Midaq Alley*, with many commentators approaching the novel from a broadly sociological perspective.[3] In what follows, however, I would like to trace in greater detail the affective, formal, and generic consequences of this encounter. I shall begin by discussing the significance of anger within the narrative, arguing that this dominant structure of feeling could be read as a collective response to larger historical forces.[4] Or to put it another way, rather than understanding emotion as the 'subjective property' of the individual (Grossberg, 'Postmodernity' 79), I shall regard it here as a relational practice embedded within and determined by quite specific sociopolitical circumstances. Only thus can we hope to account for the curious ubiquity of such negative feelings in *Midaq Alley*, their hyperbolic nature, and the insufficient explanatory force of the localized causes we find distributed throughout the narrative. I will then proceed to discuss the role of rumour in the novel and the significance of its pronounced melodramatic qualities. In the first case, I shall argue, the circulation of rumour provides a way of containing or 'quarantining' the negative feelings produced by modernity, while also reinforcing the boundaries of a community facing the very real possibility of its own

---

3 For examples of this tendency, see El-Enany, Moosa, Deeb, Somekh, and Moussa-Mahmoud.

4 I do not claim to be entirely original here, as the broader social and political significance of (colonial or postcolonial) anger has been acknowledged elsewhere too. In her analysis of Tsitsi Dangarembga's *Nervous Conditions* and *The Book of Not*, for instance, Sue J. Kim distinguishes between the 'large anger' we find in the former ('grand, explosive, and raging at structures') and the 'minor rages ... over apparently trivial things' that occur in the latter. Yet despite these differences, Kim argues that both varieties of anger are ultimately political in origin – the characters' dysphoric feelings being produced and shaped by the various 'ideologically conditioned' spaces they occupy. 'In *Nervous Conditions* and *The Book of Not*,' she observes, 'spaces such as bathrooms, kitchens and dining halls, and other private spaces are charged battlegrounds, particularly for women, sparking anger that arises from their inhabiting of clashing ideologies and structures' (101–2).

demise. In the second case, I would like to suggest that the narrative's tendency to privilege the melodramatic mode creates a sense of social order and moral intelligibility by channelling these feelings into a stable and predictable generic structure. As we shall see, though, the latter project is ultimately frustrated when the forces of evil emerge to destroy the novel's principal representative of virtue – thus ensuring that the trajectory of the narrative itself, the melodramatic logic of its unfolding, should also be severely disrupted by the intervention of colonial modernity.

II

If we agree with Sianne Ngai that 'every literary work has an organizing quality of feeling akin to an "atmosphere"' (*Ugly* 174), then the emotion that most clearly dominates *Midaq Alley* would have to be anger – the instinctive rage that drives the narrative forward, providing it with its underlying dynamic force. Simply put, everyone in the novel is angry, and they seem to be angry all the time. Here are just a few randomly selected examples of the anger to be found on almost every page:

> Her temper had always, even in Midaq Alley itself, been something no one could ignore. (24)

> She was one of those alley women renowned for their tempers ... and she was particularly famous for the furious rows she had with her husband concerning his dirty habits. (72)

> He was filled with scorn and his small eyes flashed in anger. (73)

> Anger seethed within her and she stared hard at him, her eyes red from sleeplessness and rage. (75)

> Kirsha was now standing behind the till, his anger having locked his tongue, his face pale with fury. (100)

> He always seemed overcome with rage, exasperation, and a desire to curse. (116)

> She turned her attention to the stage in angry exasperation ... Her blood boiled. (157)

> As soon as he was left alone [Salim] Alwan's vindictive thoughts returned and, as was usually the case with him these days, his anger enveloped everyone. (176)

Anger

> She opened her mouth in horrified amazement and an awful look darkened her eyes as her face went white with rage. (196)

> The memory flowed through him like a gentle spring breeze, but, meeting the glare of his troubled heart, it was transformed into a raging sirocco. (238)

And so it goes. Over the course of the novel, this constant reiteration of anger comes to dominate the narrative, producing what we might call a surplus of dysphoric energy.[5] Indeed, at times, even the characters themselves are surprised by the overdetermined, excessive nature of their anger. When, for instance, the wealthy businessman Salim Alwan learns that Hamida has become engaged to Abbas, he flies into an uncontrollable rage. Taken aback, the girl's mother replies: 'Don't be angry with me, Mr. Alwan. You're the kind of man who only has to issue a command when you want something … Please don't be angry with me. Why are you so angry?' (139). It is a question we will hear more than once as the novel progresses, and eventually we will be obliged to ask ourselves the same thing. Yes, why *are* they so angry? Why are these people always shouting at each other? Why must every encounter in the alley take on an adversarial quality?

The very overdetermined nature of the characters' anger, however, along with its striking ubiquity within the narrative, complicates many of the interpretive procedures we would ordinarily bring to bear on such issues. In other words, a reading of this dominant structure of feeling based solely on character, individual psychology, or the contingencies of plotting would seem to be inadequate – or at least incapable of accounting for the privileged position that anger occupies within the novel's affective economy. The disparity between the intensity of the characters' negative feelings and the incidental causes scattered across the surface of the narrative is simply too great to sustain such a reading. Instead, I would like to suggest that the anger in *Midaq Alley* emerges out of much deeper social, political, and economic processes. As will become clear, the intervention of colonial modernity in the novel radically destabilizes the old social order, yet without implementing a new order that can be easily comprehended by the characters or assimilated into their lives. And because they are unable to understand fully the processes of transformation they are undergoing, because

---

5 Envy also features prominently in *Midaq Alley*, yet this minor emotion is subordinated to (and ultimately serves to generate) the anger that I would consider to be the novel's primary affective quality.

these processes are located just beyond their cognitive range, many of the characters internalize a vague sense of social crisis that eventually resurfaces in the form of displaced anger. Ato Quayson, to whom this chapter is greatly indebted, has used the term 'systemic uncanny' to describe a similar phenomenon involving 'the conversion of the perception of a systemic disorder into a negative affect' (*Calibrations* 80).[6] In the face of social disruption of one kind or another, he writes, an 'internalization of these perceived disorders takes place … The internalized translation of disorder does not, however, remain merely internalized, but gets cathected into inchoate senses of guilt, inexplicable terror, or a general sense of disquiet that may or may not be consciously traceable to a direct source' (*Aesthetic* 142). To Quayson's list of dysphoric feelings we could, of course, add anger – the blind rage that drives (and disfigures) almost every social encounter in *Midaq Alley*. And once we register the fact that these encounters have been invested with *too much* affective energy, once we acknowledge their overdetermined quality, we are compelled to look elsewhere for the ultimate source of such disproportionate rage. According to Freud, the process of displacement involves shifting the 'psychical accent' from something of key importance to the psyche to something of minimal significance, 'which thenceforward plays the psychological part of the former [idea]' ('Further' 308–9). It is the responsibility of the psychoanalyst, he argues, to recognize the affective disparity such a process creates and to identify, by following a 'chain of associations' (*Interpretation* 58), the original cause of the displaced feeling. 'If [such] displacements can be reversed,' Freud concludes, 'the way is open to the discovery of the repressed ideas, and the relation between affect and idea is found to be perfectly appropriate' ('Claims' 173). In *Midaq Alley*, as I say, this is precisely what the attentive reader is obliged to do if the novel is to achieve any kind of emotional plausibility. Rather than accepting the characters' anger at face value, we must trace it back to its source in the public sphere, for only at this deeper, social level does the rage they all share begin to make sense.[7]

---

6 It was Quayson who first drew my attention to the preponderance of anger in *Midaq Alley* and suggested that this structure of feeling could be related to the disruptive pressures of modernity.

7 Aristotle's theory of anger, as outlined in the *Nicomachean Ethics*, may also be instructive here. Rather than rejecting this 'passion' altogether, he advocates a moderate form of anger that is situated, like all his virtues, between two negative extremes. One can be too angry or not angry

Although the narrator of Mahfouz's novel describes the eponymous alley as an 'ancient relic' living in 'isolation from all surrounding activity' (1), it soon becomes obvious that this is not altogether true. In the opening scene, we witness a radio being installed in the local café, displacing the old poet who has been allowed to recite his verses there for as long as anyone can remember. 'Public reciters still have an appeal which won't disappear,' the poet announces as he is leaving. 'The radio will never replace us.' To which the café owner, Kirsha, replies: 'That is what you say, but it is not what my customers say and you are not going to ruin my business. Everything has changed!' (6). This altercation is just the first of many such disturbances; and over the course of the novel, the characters will continue to grapple with the contradictory social forces, the radical disjunctures and discontinuities, initiated by colonial modernity.[8] Indeed, in *Midaq Alley*, every effort is made to bring these contradictory tendencies to the fore, reminding us that modernity can be at once emancipatory *and* repressive, dignifying *and* degrading. When Hussain Kirsha leaves the alley to work for the British Army, for example, his wages increase from three piastres to thirty, and his lifestyle changes accordingly: 'He bought new clothes, frequented

---

enough; yet the 'man who is angry at the right things and with the right people, and, further, as he ought, when he ought, and as long as he ought, is [to be] praised' (73). It is not easy, Aristotle concedes, to 'define how, with whom, at what, and how long one should be angry, and at what point right action ceases and wrong begins.' But what is clear is that 'the middle state is praiseworthy – [the state in] which we are angry with the right people, at the right things, in the right way, and so on' (74). At one extreme, then, we have those people who suffer a deficiency of anger, and who therefore seem 'not to feel things nor to be pained by them,' while at the other, we have those 'irascible' people who 'get angry quickly and with the wrong persons and at the wrong things and more than is right' (73). As I have suggested, the inhabitants of *Midaq Alley* clearly belong to the latter category – their anger being disproportionate to the minor provocations they suffer, cathected with far greater intensity than it ought to be, *because* it has been misdirected or displaced.

8 On the one hand, as Perry Anderson writes, this form of modernity 'tears down every ancestral confinement and feudal restriction, social immobility and claustral tradition,' bringing about a 'tremendous emancipation of the possibility and sensibility of the individual self.' On the other hand, the very same system 'generates a brutally alienated and atomized society, riven by callous economic exploitation and cold social indifference, destructive of every cultural or political value it has itself brought into being' (98).

restaurants, and delighted in eating meat, which he considered a luxury reserved especially for the rich. He attended cinemas and cabarets and found pleasure in wine and the company of women' (33). We are also told that Hamida envies 'the freedom and obvious prosperity' of the young women who work in the factories, women whose very bodies come to signify the invigorating pleasures of modernity:

> They were girls from the Darasa district, who, taking advantage of wartime employment opportunities, ignored custom and tradition and now worked in public places just like the Jewish women. They had gone into factory work exhausted, emaciated, and destitute. Soon remarkable changes were noticeable: their once undernourished bodies filled out and seemed to radiate a healthy pride and vitality. They imitated the Jewish girls by paying attention to their appearance and in keeping slim. Some even used unaccustomed language and did not hesitate to walk arm in arm and stroll about the streets of illicit love. They exuded an air of boldness and secret knowledge. (40–41)

But needless to say, there are two sides to this story as well. Hussain will eventually lose his job and be forced to return, destitute and disillusioned, to Midaq Alley, while Hamida, for whom the outside world held so much promise, will only be able to fulfil her 'dreams of clothes, jewelry, money, and men' (255) by prostituting herself to the Allied forces.

It is perhaps not surprising, given these contradictory qualities, that modernity should generate a strong sense of ambivalence in many of the novel's characters. They simply do not know what to make of it, and so they respond, for the most part, with profound equivocality – torn between feelings of repulsion and attraction, between 'phobic strivings "away from" [and] philic strivings "toward"' (Ngai, *Ugly* 11). In Hamida's case, these feelings attach themselves most obviously to Faraj, the predatory pimp who offers to rescue her from the 'graveyard of decaying bones' (Mahfouz 195) in which she lives. His arrogance, we are told, 'infuriated' her, and yet his 'respectable appearance and his handsome masculinity attracted her' too. Try as she might, 'she could not sort out her feelings for him' (161). As the novel progresses, Hamida's libidinal impulses toward Faraj are repeatedly disrupted by surges of anger, animosity, and a 'bestial desire to fight' (184). Consider the following passage, for instance:

> She noticed [Faraj] had snuggled close to her, and she began to sense the effect of his touch creeping over her. This enraged her, and she

pushed him away more forcibly than she intended. He glanced at her to see what was the matter and then took her hand and gently placed it between his own. He was encouraged by her permissiveness and searched for her lips with his mouth. She seemed to resist and drew her head back slightly. However, he did not find this a sufficient restraint and pressed his lips to hers. (189)

It is worth noting the vacillations of meaning that occur here. Almost every sentence produces a collision of contraries – sliding from one antithetical category into another, weaving its way through a series of equivocations and inconsistencies, 'ceaselessly posit[ing] meaning ceaselessly to evaporate it' (Barthes, 'Death' 147). Force fades into delicacy without quite losing its coercive qualities. Resistance becomes 'permissiveness' under the guise of continued defiance. Phobic strivings 'away from' give rise to philic strivings 'toward.' And all of these minor slippages ultimately testify to the presence of much deeper instabilities and equivocalities, circulating just beneath the surface of the narrative. For many of the novel's characters, as we have seen, modernity is a source of considerable ambivalence. They are 'moved at once by a will to change – to transform both themselves and their world – and by a terror of disorientation and disintegration, of life falling apart' (Berman 13). And it is this underlying tension, I would argue, this sense of cognitive dissonance, that contributes more than anything to the novel's dominant structure of feeling, transforming a vague sense of disquiet into full-blown 'loathing and rage' (Mahfouz 99).

Although the characters themselves may not always know why they feel the way they do, it is difficult for us as readers to ignore the connection between modernity and its affective consequences. Let us focus, by way of illustration, on one case in particular. At the beginning of the novel, we learn that the eccentric Sheikh Darwish had once been 'a teacher of the English language.' When the religious foundation schools merged with the Ministry of Education, however, 'his position changed, as did that of many of his associates, who, like him, lacked higher qualifications.' As a consequence of this restructuring, Sheikh Darwish became a clerk in the Ministry of Religious Endowments, and 'went down from the sixth to the eighth [bureaucratic] grade' (12), with a corresponding reduction in his salary. It was only natural, the narrator says, that 'he was hurt by what happened to him,' and so he began 'a continuous rebellion' against those in authority:

> Occasionally he rebelled openly; at other times he felt defeated and concealed his rebellion. He had tried every method, issuing

petitions, appealing to his superiors, and complaining about his poverty and the size of his family. All without success. At last he gave way to despair, his nerves almost in shreds. His case became famous in his ministry and he became notorious as a rebel, always complaining, extremely stubborn and obstinate, and very quick tempered. Scarcely a day went by without his becoming involved in an argument or quarrel. (13)

We can see quite plainly here the way in which the forces of modernity enter into, and ultimately disrupt, the novel's affective economy. Sheikh Darwish's life has been transformed by processes of structural change that he can neither control nor fully understand. At first, he strives to master these processes by 'issuing petitions, appealing to his superiors, and complaining about his poverty and the size of his family,' but when all of this proves futile, he finally '[gives] way to despair.' The profound sense of social instability he experiences is thus internalized, only to resurface almost immediately in the form of displaced anger and irascibility: '[H]e became notorious as a rebel, always complaining, extremely stubborn and obstinate, and very quick tempered.' Once his career at the ministry comes to an end, Sheikh Darwish loses his mind altogether, 'desert[ing] his family, friends, and acquaintances, and wander[ing] off into the world of God, as it is called' (14). And by the time we are introduced to him in the novel's opening pages, he has become a kind of sacrificial figure, a *pharmakos*, whose only purpose is to bear the psychological burden of these 'innovations' and to provide a choric commentary on the other characters' lives.

One question we might ask, though, is why this anger should be displaced at all. If the processes of social transformation initiated by colonial modernity are the ultimate source of these affective disturbances, then why is the anger we witness here not directed at some of the more tangible attributes of modernity itself? For one thing, as I have noted, the characters in *Midaq Alley* are simply unable to identify the underlying cause of their rage ('Don't be angry with me, Mr. Alwan ... Why are you so angry?' [139]). They may register these social pressures at a subliminal level, but they cannot understand precisely why it is that they should feel this way; and so they focus their displeasure on anyone (and anything) within range.[9] It is also significant

---

9 In this respect, the anger they demonstrate resembles Freud's notion of 'expectant anxiety,' as described in one of his introductory lectures from 1917. If we study a condition of this kind, Freud says, 'we find a general

that these characters should be living in a colonial city, a city that has been occupied since 1882 and currently accommodates over 140,000 Allied soldiers. Under these circumstances, in the colonial Cairo of the 1940s, the inhabitants of Midaq Alley have no choice but to direct their rage at more easily mastered substitutes (wives, employees, colleagues, etc.), and this is what finally denies them the possibility of genuine cathartic release. 'When the native is confronted with the colonial order of things,' Frantz Fanon observes, 'he finds [that] he is in a state of permanent tension,' and he 'will first manifest [the] aggressiveness which has been deposited in his bones against his own people.' This is a period of time 'when the [natives] beat each other up, and the police and magistrates do not know which way to turn when faced with the astonishing waves of crime in [the colonies]' (*Wretched* 52). Having been deprived of a legitimate political voice, Fanon concludes, the colonial subject is forced to find other, more oblique ways of releasing these dysphoric energies – 'in tribal warfare, in feuds between [families], and in quarrels between individuals' (54).[10] And that is why the anger that dominates *Midaq Alley* is so clearly disproportionate: because it has been displaced, because it has been denied cathartic release, and because it has been directed at an innocuous 'third party' rather than its true source, which continues to hover just beyond the characters' field of cognition.[11]

---

    apprehensiveness, a kind of freely floating anxiety which is ready to attach itself to any idea that is in any way suitable, which influences judgement, selects what is to be expected, and lies in wait for any opportunity that will allow it to justify itself' (*Introductory* 446).

10 According to Fanon, however, the self-destructive violence that occurs during this period will eventually be redirected at the colonizers themselves. 'In spite of the metamorphoses which the colonial regime imposes upon it in the way of tribal or regional quarrels,' he writes, '[this] violence makes its way forward,' until the native finally 'identifies his enemy and recognizes all his misfortunes, throwing all the exacerbated might of his hate and anger into [the] new channel [of anti-colonial resistance]' (*Wretched* 71).

11 As I shall argue in Chapter 3, Machado's *Dom Casmurro* also explores the affective consequences of the encounter with European modernity – and it is worth considering, just briefly, some of the correspondences between these two narratives. In *Midaq Alley*, the intervention of colonial modernity (in the particular form that it assumed in Cairo during the Second World War) initiates a period of rapid social transformation that many of the characters find unsettling and disorientating. This in turn produces a collective feeling of anger, which is directed not at its true source (i.e.,

Affective Disorders

In *Aesthetic Nervousness*, Ato Quayson makes another point that is of some relevance to our discussion here. 'The systemic uncanny,' he writes, 'may be social as well as personal, public as well as private' (142); and that would certainly seem to be the case in *Midaq Alley*, where the feelings of anger and animosity we have been exploring take on an intersubjective quality, transgressing the boundaries of individual consciousness. Roland Barthes has argued, quite persuasively, that literary characters are essentially composed of semes (or units of meaning) clustered around a single proper name. According to Barthes, '[w]hen identical semes traverse the same proper name several times and appear to settle upon it, a character is created ... The proper name acts as a magnetic field for the semes; referring in fact to a body, it draws the semic configuration into an evolving (biographical) tense' (*S/Z* 67–68). Despite their superficial differences, though, the characters in *Midaq Alley* all seem to share the same fundamental attributes, or 'semic configurations,' and what we eventually come to realize is that the ubiquity of ill feeling in the alley makes it difficult to distinguish *between* individual subjectivities. (It appears to be difficult for the narrator, too, whose struggle to say the same thing differently moves the narrative on more than one occasion toward blatant redundancy: e.g., 'rage and anger, spite and malice' [271].) Indeed, we could even go so far as to argue that the novel only has one subjectivity, one 'character,' for although we are presented with a wide range of proper names, they all occupy the same magnetic

---

modernity itself) but at a number of more easily mastered substitutes; and it is the displaced nature of this rage that gives it such a strong sense of disproportionality. In *Dom Casmurro*, on the other hand, the dominant structure of feeling emerges out of a conflict between the archaic social reality of nineteenth-century Brazil and the 'modern' European values to which the élite subscribed – despite the fact that they were the principal beneficiaries of the last slave-owning economy in the Western world. Although this ideological dissonance creates a feeling of jealousy, rather than anger, it is an emotion that has also lost all sense of proportion ('I came to be jealous of everything and everyone' [196], our narrator confesses). And this is where the point of connection between the two narratives can be located. In both *Midaq Alley* and *Dom Casmurro*, the encounter with European modernity (under quite specific circumstances in each case) generates a sense of social incongruity and dissonance, which in turn gives rise to a structure of feeling (anger in one novel, jealousy in the other) that is equally disproportionate and 'ill-fitting' – thus allowing it to serve as an affective correlative for the very social forces that brought it into being.

field and produce the same configuration of affective semes – a configuration, incidentally, that resists being drawn into anything like an 'evolving' or biographical tense.

The narrative's use of variable internal focalization also contributes a great deal to this sense of communality.[12] Rather than privileging any one character or seeking to individuate emotion, it offers us what Teshome Gabriel has called a 'hetero-biography' of the collective subject. In his influential analysis of Third Cinema aesthetics, Gabriel distinguishes between two different types of autobiographical narrative: (1) 'autobiography in its usual Western sense of a narrative by and about a single subject,' and (2) 'a multi-generational and trans-individual autobiography, i.e., a symbolic autobiography where the *collective* subject is the focus' (58). *Midaq Alley* provides us with a particularly good example of this second type of 'autobiographical' narrative – deliberately blurring the distinction between the individual and the collective, between the private and public spheres, until one category appears to collapse into the other.[13] As a consequence of this shift in emphasis, emotion becomes detached from the individual consciousness, circulating freely within the larger community and within the structure of the novel itself. It becomes, to quote Mikel Dufrenne once more, 'a supervening or impersonal principle in accordance with which we [might] say that there is an electric atmosphere or, as Trenet sang, that there is joy in the air' (168).[14] Yet in *Midaq Alley*, of course, the dominant structure of feeling is one of anger rather than joy; the atmosphere is not 'electric' but full of animosity and belligerence. And this affective quality, I would like to suggest, is what motivates many of the characters to spend their

---

12 Gérard Genette has distinguished between two different types of internal focalization: *fixed*, where the point of view is restricted to one particular character, and *variable*, 'as in *Madame Bovary*, where the focal character is first Charles, then Emma, then again Charles' (189).
13 It is worth noting, however, that none of the characters are able to recognize the collective quality of their anger. Like the structures of feeling we discussed in the Introduction, the rage they feel is a 'social experience' that is 'not yet recognized as social but taken to be private, idiosyncratic, and even isolating' (Williams, *Marxism* 132).
14 In *The Particulars of Rapture*, Charles Altieri uses the term 'mood' to describe this depersonalized, freely circulating form of emotion. 'Moods,' he writes, 'are modes of feeling where the sense of subjectivity becomes diffuse and sensation merges into something close to atmosphere, something that seems to pervade an entire scene or situation' (2).

Affective Disorders

time gossiping about each other's lives. For only by narrativizing their experiences in this way, only by arranging them into what Leo Bersani calls a 'governing pattern of significance' (52), can they hope to assert some control over the dysphoric energy that has been released into the novel's atmosphere.

III

On 15 January 1934, the Indian province of Bihar was struck by a catastrophic earthquake measuring 8.4 on the Richter scale. Some thirty thousand people are believed to have died in the disaster, and the urban centres of Monghyr and Muzaffarpur were almost completely destroyed. In the days following the earthquake, according to the psychologist J. Prasad, various rumours began to circulate throughout the province. The river Ganges had disappeared, it was said, leaving bathers embedded in the sand. The grounds of the High Court in Patna had been 'rent into wide fissures' and 'big holes of immeasurable depth' (1) had appeared there. Thirteen thousand dead bodies had been discovered when clearing the debris of the main street in Monghyr. Local astrologers had predicted 'evil days for the world from the beginning of 1934 until the end of the year' (3). And that was not all. It was also foretold that there would be another severe earthquake on the night of the lunar eclipse (21 January), that Patna itself would 'cease to exist' (4) on 26 February, and that within twenty-four hours of this disaster the men and women of the province would change gender.

For Prasad, writing in 1935, these rumours represent 'attempts on the part of the popular mind to comprehend a strange phenomenon in such forms of thought as are inherited by, and prevalent in, the group, and acceptable to all its members' (7). He goes on to describe rumour more generally as a 'response of a cognitive nature' to an event that has 'set up an emotional disturbance, and contains many unknown parts' (9). This 'distracting sense of incompleteness,' he argues, 'arouses a tendency to try to understand the meaning of the changed situation by a process of completing the incomplete' (7). As Prasad observes, however, such rumours not only constitute a collective response to a 'widespread emotional disturbance' (6), but also seem to 'alter the character of the effective social bonds between the individuals belonging to the group concerned,' creating what he describes as 'an intensification of the comradeship response' (13–14):

> The moment a rumour spreads about a matter of even private and personal importance ... the matter is at once converted into a social situation which is of interest and importance to the group, and is no longer a merely private affair ... [A] well-known reaction of the individual on hearing a rumour [is] his almost uncontrollable impulse to pass it on to another person ... This impulse is of fundamental importance in group psychology, since the communication of a report to other members of the group implies an underlying bond of community among the members ... Thus rumour, both in its rise and in its communication, is properly treated as a social phenomenon. (8–12)

In this study, Prasad raises a number of issues that also have some bearing on the role of rumour in *Midaq Alley*. As things begin to fall apart in Mahfouz's novel, the characters are increasingly given to discussing each other's private lives, 'fill[ing] the air' (9) with gossip and hearsay. Like anger, I would argue, these micronarratives could be read as a collective response to the crisis provoked by colonial modernity. Narratives of one kind or another have always served as a way of structuring, ordering, and plotting reality – allowing us to ascribe form and significance to the enigmatic contingencies that govern our lives. And this, of course, is precisely what the characters in *Midaq Alley* hope to achieve by producing their own narratives: a sense of order, stability, coherence, and, above all, intelligible meaning. Confronted by a 'strange phenomenon' that defies complete understanding, they attempt to clarify the 'meaning of [their] changed situation' (Prasad 7) by translating it into narrative, by telling and retelling the various stories to which it gives rise. So when the characters gather to discuss Hamida's sudden disappearance ('[S]he didn't just run away, she ran away with a strange man. In English they call that an "elopement"' [244]) or Abbas' death ('[The police] carried his body off to Kasr el-Aini Hospital and took the whore off for first-aid treatment' [283]), they are not simply indulging in idle gossip; they are, in fact, attempting to understand and lay claim to the larger historical forces that have had such a decisive influence over their lives.

Many of the rumours in the novel could also be seen as a response to the 'widespread emotional disturbance' (Prasad 6) created by colonial modernity – for only by narrating these stories are the characters able to achieve some degree of control over the negative feelings that have come to dominate their social reality. Take Umm Hamida, for instance. Her tongue, we are told, 'was hardly ever still and she scarcely missed a single report or scandal concerning anyone or any house in the neighborhood.' So when she is visited by Mrs Afify in the novel's opening pages, it is not surprising that she should provide the latter with a comprehensive 'résumé of the news of the alley':

> Had she heard of Kirsha's new scandal? It was just like the previous ones and the news got back to his wife, who had a fight with him and tore his cloak. Husniya, the bakeress, the day before struck her husband so hard that blood had flowed from his forehead. Radwan Hussainy, that good and pious man, had rebuked his wife most strongly, and why would he treat her in this way, the good man that he was, if she were not a vile and wicked hussy! Dr. Booshy had interfered with a little girl in the shelter in the last air raid and some upright citizen had struck him for it. The wife of Mawardy, the wood merchant, had run off with her servant, and her father had informed the police. Tabuna Kafawy was secretly selling bread made of pure flour – and so on. (16–17)

By integrating these disputes and episodes of violence into a clearly demarcated narrative structure, Umm Hamida does her best to quarantine the dysphoric energy she senses within the alley – energy that might otherwise prove severely disruptive to the community at large. It is her way of giving such dissonance and strife the reassuring shape of a story; and seen in this light, the seemingly casual 'and so on' that brings her narrative to a close assumes a far greater significance. According to Barthes, if the 'classic [readerly] text has nothing more to say than what it says, at least it attempts to "let it be understood" that it does not say everything.' This allusion to meaning, he suggests, is 'coded by pensiveness, which is a sign of nothing but itself: as though having filled the text but obsessively fearing that it is not *incontestably* filled, the discourse insist[s] on supplementing it with an *et cetera* of plenitudes' (*S/Z* 216–17). In this case, similarly, the narrator's final *et cetera* expresses a deep anxiety about all the negative energy that has *not* been contained within the structure of Umm Hamida's narrative, all the anger and animosity that continues to exceed its boundaries. Prasad, you may recall, described rumour as a 'process of completing the incomplete,' and that is exactly what our narrator is attempting to achieve here. He or she is attempting to 'fill' the narrative, to compensate for the 'parsimony of its plural' (Barthes, *S/Z* 217), by gesturing vaguely (and desperately) toward everything it is incapable of accommodating.

As well as enabling the characters to assert some control over modernity and the negative feelings it generates, such rumours also serve to delineate and reinforce the contours of a community in peril. In his article on the 1934 Bihar earthquake, as we have seen, Prasad consistently emphasizes the social significance of rumour, arguing that the impulse to communicate in this way is of 'fundamental importance in group psychology.' For Prasad, rumour reinforces the 'underlying bond of community' by initiating the individual into a larger collective whose boundaries it also serves to define, and by instilling in them 'an almost uncontrollable impulse to pass [the rumour] on to another person.' This transitive quality is what makes rumour a particularly effective unifying or interpellatory device, for the movement it traces is, in Peter Brooks' words, 'one of "contamination": the passing-on of the virus of narrative, the creation of the fevered need to retell' (*Reading* 220–21). None of the characters in *Midaq Alley* can resist exchanging gossip, and every time they do so, they are unconsciously performing their own communality – marking the difference between self and other, inside and outside, those who belong here, in this 'graveyard of decaying bones' (Mahfouz 195), and those who belong somewhere else.

Near the end of the novel, moreover, we witness the process by which the narrative we have been reading is itself transformed into gossip. Hussain Kirsha has just arrived back in the alley, having failed to prevent Abbas' violent death at the hands of the Allied soldiers: 'He came slowly and heavily up the alley, went over to his father, and threw himself into a chair facing him. Without a greeting he said hoarsely, "Father, Abbas has been killed …"' (283). The story that follows leaves Hussain's father, Kirsha, possessed by a 'fevered need' to retell everything he has heard – thus ensuring its transition from mimetic novelistic discourse (280–81) into the diegetic discourse of rumour: 'The news soon spread as Kirsha told his son's tale repeatedly to people who came to ask. Their tongues in turn circulated the story, along with many additions and variations' (284). Indeed, one could go even further and suggest that the narrative itself becomes an integral part of this process, disseminating Hussain's tale far beyond the parameters of Midaq Alley.[15] And as a consequence of this transformation, the novel's literary discourse is also 'contaminated' by the rhetorical features of rumour, taking on many of the qualities that we tend to associate with the latter. In certain non-focalized passages, for example, the narrator's field of omniscience suddenly recedes:

---

15 I am naturally reminded here of Truman Capote's claim that '*all* literature is gossip, certainly all prose-narrative literature' (337).

> [During this period] Mrs. Saniya Afify decided to clear out the flat which Dr. Booshy had occupied before he went to jail and Uncle Kamil volunteered to carry Dr. Booshy's personal belongings ... into his [own] flat. In explanation *it was said* that Uncle Kamil preferred to share his dwelling with Dr. Booshy rather than continue to endure unaccustomed loneliness. No one blamed him and indeed they *may well have* considered the act a kindness on his part [as] a term in prison was not the sort of thing to bring disgrace on a man in the alley. (285; my italics)

Like a rumour, the narrative is also generated anonymously, for although the narrator may in fact be located within the community, it is never made clear to us which character (if any) he or she might be.[16] And perhaps most significantly, the story that this anonymous figure relates is notable for its hyperbolic impulses, its tendency to overdo everything, to charge every encounter and every state of being with heightened emotional force. Prasad's article identifies exaggeration as one of the defining characteristics of rumour, and this is something that the historian Gyanendra Pandey has also commented upon. 'Rumour,' Pandey writes, 'is marked characteristically not only by indeterminacy, anonymity and contagion, but also by a tendency to excess' (70). This hyperbolic register is of course typical of all narratives produced in the melodramatic mode. Yet in *Midaq Alley*, I shall argue, such tendencies take on additional significance – representing one last attempt to contain and control the dysphoric energy released by colonial modernity.

IV

As Peter Brooks has observed, the connotations of the term 'melodrama' are probably similar for us all. They include: 'the indulgence of strong emotionalism; moral polarization and schematization; extreme states

---

16 One may recall that in the closing pages of Albert Camus' *The Plague*, the hitherto anonymous narrator finally decides to reveal his true identity: 'This chronicle is drawing to an end, and this seems to be the moment for Dr Bernard Rieux to confess that he is the narrator.' He does so in order to reassure the reader that he has given 'a true account of all he saw and heard' and 'confined himself to describing only such things as he was enabled to see for himself' (246). In *Midaq Alley*, by contrast, no such disclosure takes place and no such assurances are offered – preserving to the end the novel's casual, gossipy quality.

of being, situations, actions; overt villainy, persecution of the good, and final reward of virtue; inflated and extravagant expression; dark plottings, suspense, [and] breathtaking peripety' (*Melodramatic* 11–12). Needless to say, we do not have to look very hard to find these qualities in *Midaq Alley*. The strong emotionalism and extreme states of being we have already discussed in some detail ('She clung to him, her head raised toward his face, her mouth open and trembling with passion …' [223]); there are examples of 'inflated and extravagant expression' on almost every page; many of the novel's characters, both major and minor, undergo episodes of 'breathtaking peripety'; and the narrative does everything it can to establish a sense of ethical legibility and predictability. One of the ways in which it strives to achieve this last objective is through the schematic personification of moral absolutes, ensuring that characters are either good (Abbas) or evil (Faraj), and refusing to accommodate any intermediate states of ethical being. These qualities are almost always externalized, too, so that the reader has no difficulty distinguishing between the representatives of good and those of evil. And finally, we are offered a plot trajectory that (ostensibly) promises to bring about the destruction of vice and the ultimate apotheosis of virtue, thereby restoring the natural order of things within the narrative.

In *Midaq Alley*, as I have suggested, these melodramatic tendencies could be interpreted as one more response to colonial modernity. Modernity obliges many of the novel's characters to inhabit a kind of floating world – a world in which they are surrounded by historical processes they cannot quite understand and troubled by disruptive forces they cannot quite see, a world in which everything appears to be 'pregnant with its contrary' and all that was once assumed to be solid 'melts into air' (Marx 368, 248). Under such circumstances, melodrama serves to allay the threat of ineffability, rendering these occult forces legible, bringing them to the surface of the narrative where they can be more easily identified and apprehended. As Brooks writes,

> Melodrama starts from and expresses the anxiety brought by a frightening new world in which the traditional patterns of moral order no longer provide the necessary social glue. It plays out the force of that anxiety with the apparent triumph of villainy, and it dissipates it with the eventual victory of virtue. It demonstrates over and over that the signs of ethical forces can be discovered and can be made legible … Melodrama is indeed, typically, not only a moralistic drama but the drama of morality: it strives to find, to articulate, to

demonstrate, to 'prove' the existence of a moral universe which, though put into question, masked by villainy and perversions of judgement, does exist and can be made to assert its presence and its categorical force among men. (*Melodramatic* 20)

The 'melodramatic imagination' is, then, essentially conflictual, motivated by a desire to reveal the agonistic forces operating beneath the surface of our daily lives; and this brings us back to the dominance of anger within the narrative, for it could be read not only as a displaced and pathological response to colonial modernity, but also as a strategy by which the novel's characters seek to reaffirm, through 'heightened dramatic utterance and gesture' (Brooks, *Melodramatic* 14), a sense of social order and stability. In other words, one could argue that the characters in *Midaq Alley* are themselves responsible for determining the generic characteristics of the narrative they have been made to occupy – favouring, in their encounters with each other, 'intense, excessive representations of life' that 'push *through* manners to deeper sources of [social] being' (Brooks, *Melodramatic* 3–4). Here, as Brooks writes of Balzac, the 'world is subsumed by an underlying manichaeism, and the narrative creates the excitement of its drama by putting us in touch with the conflict of good and evil played out under the surface of things.' For the inhabitants of the alley, '[n]othing is spared because nothing is left unsaid; [they] stand on stage and utter the unspeakable, give voice to their deepest feelings, dramatize through their heightened and polarized words and gestures the whole lesson of their relationship' (*Melodramatic* 4). And by doing so, they render legible (at least in symbolic form) the underlying pressures and imperatives of modernity – bringing these forces to the surface of the narrative through a 'metaphoricity of gesture that evokes meanings beyond its literal configuration' (Brooks, *Melodramatic* 10). All this anger, that is to say, all this animosity and conflict, gestures toward or makes visible deeper social polarities that can only be articulated indirectly, by way of oblique metaphorical correlatives. Bringing these polarities to light also serves to delineate and reinforce the very boundaries that modernity threatens to destroy, making clear once more the distinction between tradition and modernity, self and other, good and evil. According to Brooks, melodrama 'can offer no terminal reconciliation, for there is no longer a clear transcendent value to be reconciled to. There is, rather, a social order to be purged, a set of ethical imperatives to be [revealed]' (*Melodramatic* 17). But in the case of *Midaq Alley*, as we shall see, such ethical clarity and predictability is ultimately confounded

Anger

when the forces of evil emerge to destroy Abbas, the novel's principal representative of virtue.

Of course, the predictability of melodrama is largely dependent on its formulaic structure, on the promise (and eventual delivery) of a certain narrative outcome. This structure, as Brooks observes, usually follows a very clear trajectory:

> In the typical case … melodramatic structure moves from the presentation of virtue-as-innocence to the introduction of menace or obstacle, which places virtue in a situation of extreme peril. For the greater part of the play, evil appears to reign triumphant, controlling the structure of events, dictating the moral coordinates of reality … The third act … most often includes duels, chases, explosions, battles – a full panoply of violent action which offers a highly physical 'acting out' of virtue's liberation from the oppressive efforts of evil. This violent action of the last act is possibly melodrama's version of the tragic catharsis, the ritual by which virtue is freed from what blocked the realization of its desire, and evil is expelled from the universe … The play ends with public recognition of where virtue and evil reside, and the eradication of one as the reward of the other. (*Melodramatic* 30–32)

In *Midaq Alley*, though, despite the best efforts of the characters themselves, this standard plot trajectory is violently disrupted by the intervention of colonial modernity. Up until the novel's penultimate chapter, everything has proceeded with reassuring predictability. In the opening pages, we are introduced to Hamida, the innocent young girl whom our hero Abbas loves. They become engaged, and Abbas leaves the alley in order to earn money for their future together. While he is away, however, Faraj, the representative of evil, makes his appearance – placing 'virtue [Hamida] in a situation of extreme peril.' Eventually, he manages to lure Hamida away from the alley, ensuring the temporary ascendance of evil within the narrative, but our hero soon returns and everything looks to be heading toward a satisfactory (i.e., formulaic) conclusion. When Abbas discovers what has become of his sweetheart, he promises both her and the reader 'a highly physical "acting out" of virtue's liberation from the oppressive efforts of evil' – 'a panoply of violent action' that will restore, once and for all, the natural order of things. 'I can never forget that you abandoned me and that people saw you with him,' he says. 'It's over between us … But that monster must suffer. Where can I find him? … I'll smash the filthy pimp's head … I'll break his neck; I'll strangle him!' (266–67). And those readers who are familiar with melodramatic conventions will be expecting nothing less – but unfortunately things do not quite work out that way. Before Abbas can confront Faraj, he discovers Hamida entertaining Allied soldiers in a bar and flies into a terrible rage. Seeing him enter the bar, she too loses her temper, which only makes matters worse:

> Her anger and shouting acted like gasoline on flames, and Abbas' rage turned to sheer fury. His normal hesitancy and reserve disappeared as he felt all the sorrow, disappointment, and despair he had suffered in the past three days boil up within him to burst forth in a mad frenzy. He noticed some empty beer glasses on the bar, took one, and, not really aware of what he was doing, hurled it at her with all the force of the anger and despair within him. He acted so quickly that no one, neither the soldiers nor any of the tavern employees, could stop him, and the glass struck her in the face. Blood poured in a stream from her nose, mouth, and chin, mixing with the creams and powders on her face and running down onto her neck and dress. Her screams mingled with the enraged shouts of the drunks in the tavern, and angry men fell on Abbas from all sides like wild animals. (280–81)

This moment represents the fulfilment of all that has been threatened over the course of *Midaq Alley* and the refutation of all that has been promised. Although the Allied forces have always hovered on the periphery of the narrative, it is only at this late stage that they emerge into the light to destroy Abbas and erase the crucial distinction that has been established between the novel's foreground (the alley) and its background (everything else). At this point, too, the anger that has always threatened to spill over into violence finally does so, with a cataclysmic ferocity that leaves Abbas 'quite defenseless' (281). This episode of violence is also particularly significant as it forces the novel we are reading to shift, without warning, from the melodramatic into the tragic mode, short-circuiting its generic wiring and subverting its project of ethical predictability. Instead of vice being punished and virtue rewarded, the reverse outcome is achieved, denying the characters (and the novel they occupy) their final opportunity to tame the disruptive forces of modernity. Rather than being safely contained within a melodramatic frame, the dysphoric energy produced by modernity leaks into the structure of the novel itself, disturbing its trajectory and forcing it to move abruptly from one generic mode into another. In an essay on Ben Okri's early novels, the critic Biodun Jeyifo argues that the narrative and stylistic organization of [Okri's] material is informed by a *problematic* which assumes that the work of fiction can no longer complacently proffer a fictional 'reality' axiomatically at variance with the socio-historical reality of alienation, degradation, chaos and instability for the vast majority of its living generations. It is necessary to clarify that what is implied here ... is not merely a thematic exploration of social malaise but the insinuation of this sense of social disjuncture into the very form and structure of these novels. (qtd. in Quayson, *Strategic* 148)

I would like to suggest, in conclusion, that exactly the same process takes place in *Midaq Alley*. As we have seen, the radical disjunctures and discontinuities initiated by colonial modernity give rise to a dominant structure of negative feeling within the novel. This feeling, I have argued, could be read both as a response to modernity and as an attempt to contain it through the enactment of various melodramatic tropes. But such a strategy ultimately fails, and as a consequence, the structure of the novel itself becomes saturated by these dysphoric energies, depriving the characters of any genuine sense of social order and stability. The discursive universe they occupy has shifted its generic coordinates, just as the material world they inhabit has shifted its sociocultural coordinates, and there is simply nothing they can do to stop it happening. They can only resign themselves to the inevitability of these historical processes, and to the inevitability of further disruptive change. For as Sheikh Darwish observes in the novel's final lines, '[A]ll things have their end ... Oh yes, everything comes to its *nihaya*. And the word for this in English is "end" and it is spelled e-n-d ...' (286).

CHAPTER TWO

Reticence
Vikram Seth's *A Suitable Boy*

[V]irtue must have the quality of aiming at the intermediate.

Aristotle, *Nicomachean Ethics*, c. 340 BC

The consequences of acting in passion are always bad for an individual; but they are infinitely worse for a nation.

Jawaharlal Nehru, 'Let the People Decide,' 1952

I

According to Roland Barthes, every literary narrative is structured around a series of textual enigmas, and it is the narrative's hermeneutic code that is ultimately responsible for their formulation and resolution. Under the category of the hermeneutic, Barthes argues, we may 'list the various (formal) terms by which an enigma can be distinguished, suggested, formulated, held in suspense, and finally disclosed' (*S/Z* 19). The significance of this particular code lies in its control over the pace and duration of the narrative – something it achieves by creating a number of 'dilatory morphemes' whose purpose it is to defer, for as long as necessary, the moment of full disclosure. Or as Barthes himself writes,

[T]he hermeneutic code has a function, the one we ... attribute to the poetic code: just as rhyme (notably) structures the poem according

> to the expectation and desire for recurrence, so the hermeneutic terms structure the enigma according to the expectation and desire for its solution. The dynamics of the text ... is thus paradoxical: it is a static dynamics: the problem is to *maintain* the enigma in the initial void of its answer; whereas the sentences quicken the story's 'unfolding' and cannot help but move the story along, the hermeneutic code performs an opposite action: it must set up *delays* (obstacles, stoppages, deviations) in the flow of the discourse; its structure is essentially reactive, since it opposes the ineluctable advance of language with an organized set of stoppages: between question and answer there is a whole dilatory area whose emblem might be named 'reticence,' the rhetorical figure which interrupts the sentence, suspends it, turns it aside. (S/Z 75)

In Vikram Seth's *A Suitable Boy* (1993), the narrative's central enigma is stated, quite clearly, in the opening sentence (if not in the title itself). 'You too will marry a boy I choose' (3), Mrs Rupa Mehra says firmly to her younger daughter. The hermeneutic sequence initiated by this simple declaration will determine much of what follows – sustaining the narrative, driving it forward, until the identity of the 'suitable boy' in question is finally revealed on page 1335. Here, at long last, we learn just who Lata Mehra will marry, and it is typical of the narrative that this epic, seemingly unending hermeneutic sequence should be resolved in the most understated manner possible: 'The civil ceremony,' we are told, 'was such a brief and dry affair that almost no one attached any significance to it, although from the moment it was over, Haresh and Lata were legally man and wife' (1335). At this point, the reader could be forgiven for wondering why it was necessary to dedicate 1,332 pages to resolving such a commonplace, even banal, enigma. Why did the discourse find it necessary to produce *so many* delays ('obstacles, stoppages, [and] deviations') before bringing things to a close? Why was it necessary to make so many detours, to trace so many elaborate arabesques, before finally arriving at a conclusion that, as we shall see, offers the reader very little in the way of narrative satisfaction? The answer to these questions can be found embedded within the passage from *S/Z* given above. 'Between question and answer,' Barthes writes, 'there is a whole dilatory area whose emblem might be named "reticence"'; and it is precisely this reticence, this affective moderation, that *A Suitable Boy* seeks to emphasize by expanding its own 'dilatory area' over so many pages. Indeed, there are very few narratives in world literature that have been able to resist the 'ineluctable advance of language,' and the closure it promises, for as long as this one does.

In what follows, I will be exploring the various ways in which the novel manages to privilege this quality of affective moderation. I shall begin by addressing the broader political significance of such reticence – relating it, more specifically, to the placatory content of the speeches made by Jawaharlal Nehru during the late forties and early fifties. I will then trace the process by which Nehru's 'meandering pleas for mutual tolerance' (Seth, *Suitable* 1241) eventually find their way into the very structure of *A Suitable Boy*, directly influencing both its affective and aesthetic qualities. In other words, I would like to suggest that the narrative not only privileges this Nehruvian virtue at the representational level – by explicitly advocating the renunciation of strong feeling – but also *practises* it at the formal or structural level. And by doing so, I shall argue, it ultimately obliges the reader to adopt a similar affective stance. According to Barthes, another key function of the hermeneutic code is to instil a sense of desire in the reader, a desire for meaning, for the retrospective coherence that the resolution of any hermeneutic sequence provides; and it is only once we reach the end of a narrative, where the final predication of meaning traditionally takes place, that we can fully satisfy this craving for closure (*S/Z* 75–76). In the case of *A Suitable Boy*, however, we are required to practise the same kind of reticence and self-control that the novel itself demonstrates – deferring the final discharge of meaning for over a thousand pages, and learning to appreciate, in the meantime, the value of everything that stands between us and the object of our readerly desire.[1]

---

1 As mentioned in the Introduction, this chapter differs from the other five in that it does not focus on a specific emotion, but instead explores the repression of strong feelings such as hatred and anger. Nonetheless, there are some interesting correspondences between the reticence we find in *A Suitable Boy* and the structures of feeling that dominate the other narratives. For one thing, although reticence may not qualify as an emotion *per se*, it could be described as an *affective style*, a way of expressing (or repressing) strong feelings that is particularly susceptible to social or cultural conditioning. In India during the late forties and early fifties, emotional reticence became a highly privileged affective style, an example of what Arlie Russell Hochschild refers to as a *feeling rule* (a social guideline governing the 'type, intensity, duration, timing, and placing of [our] feelings' [85]) or what Peter N. Stearns and Carol Z. Stearns call *emotionology* ('the attitudes or standards that a society, or a definable group within a society, maintains toward basic emotions and their appropriate expression' [813]). So even though reticence is not, strictly

II

Set during the years 1950 to 1952, *A Suitable Boy* covers a period that was crucial to the consolidation of the postcolonial Indian nation-state – and to the foundation of the secularism that would become one of its guiding principles.[2] The late forties and early fifties were also a time of considerable social and political turbulence in India. The nation had only recently achieved independence, and its long-term viability was far from assured. In addition, the country was still recovering from the trauma of Partition, during which an estimated one million people had been killed and twelve million displaced. As part of the project of ethnic cleansing that accompanied Partition on both sides of the border, between 75,000 and 100,000 women were also abducted – to be raped and murdered, sold into prostitution, or forced into marriage. In 1947, according to one social worker, women were distributed 'in the same way that baskets of oranges or grapes are sold or gifted' (Kamlaben Patel qtd. in Menon and Bhasin 76). Some were sold in the marketplace for ten or twenty rupees apiece, while others were sent as gifts to friends and acquaintances (Talib 287; Basu 123). During this period, Jawaharlal Nehru delivered numerous speeches denouncing communal violence and appealing for an end to such atrocities. In June 1947, for instance, on the day that the plan to divide India was announced, he issued the following appeal by radio:

---

speaking, an emotion, it is a way of responding to affective impulses – and a way of converting these impulses into emotional behaviour that will be deemed normative or socially appropriate within those cultures where such 'feeling rules' are observed. Moreover, the reticence we shall be exploring in this chapter also follows a similar trajectory to the anger, jealousy, boredom, fear, and stuplimity discussed elsewhere. Like these other feelings, it originates in the public sphere yet gradually filters into the private sphere, where it gives rise to a corresponding affective state. Like these feelings, it assumes an intersubjective quality (i.e., more than one character demonstrates this particular affective style). And like these feelings, it eventually infiltrates the structure of the narrative itself, with profound discursive consequences.

2 In a 1961 essay on the subject, Nehru provided a useful definition of the Indian secular state: 'It is not very easy,' he wrote, 'to find a good word in Hindi for "secular." Some people think that it means something opposed to religion. That obviously is not correct. What it means is that it is a state which honours all faiths equally and gives them equal opportunities; that, as a state, it does not allow itself to be attached to one faith or religion, which then becomes the state religion' (*Anthology* 330).

> On this historic occasion each one of us must pray that he might be guided aright in the service of the motherland and of humanity at large. We stand on a watershed dividing the past from the future. Let us bury that past in so far as it is dead and forget all bitterness and recrimination. Let there be moderation in speech and writing. Let there be strength and perseverance in adhering to the cause and the ideals we have at heart. Let us face the future not with easy optimism or with any complacency or weakness, but with confidence and a firm faith in India. There has been violence – shameful, degrading and revolting violence – in various parts of the country. This must end. We are determined to end it. We must make it clear that political ends are not to be achieved by methods of violence now or in the future. On this the eve of great changes in India we have to make a fresh start with clear vision and a firm mind, with steadfastness and tolerance ... We should not wish ill to anyone, but think always of every Indian as our brother and comrade. The good of the [people] of India must be our supreme objective. (*Anthology* 73–74)

Despite such persuasive rhetoric, however, communal violence would continue to plague both India and Pakistan throughout the 1950s. Time and again, Nehru would be required to make similar speeches, reiterating the same theme of intercommunal tolerance. In 1950, for example, an outbreak of violence across the border in East Bengal led to reprisal attacks against the Muslim community in Calcutta; and in February of that year, Nehru was obliged to release the following statement:

> I would like to make an earnest appeal to the people of Calcutta to help in controlling the situation and bringing it back to normal in every way they can ... I can well understand the strong feelings that have been roused by the gruesome accounts brought from East Bengal by the refugees and others. We share those feelings. But action should not flow from emotion alone. In order to be effective and firm, it has to be calm, well thought out and based on right principles ... On no account must we fall prey to communal passion and retaliation. (*Speeches* 135–36)

Although Nehru was responding to specific episodes of communal violence throughout this period, the general point he sought to make was always the same. India's social and political stability, and the security of its minorities, could only be achieved by renouncing 'hatred, violence, [and] anger' (*Speeches* 23). And by repeating himself in this way, by tirelessly promoting the same two or three core values, he obviously hoped to influence the affective atmosphere within the country – to create a climate of tolerance and amity among the different religious communities. In *The Navigation of Feeling*, the anthropologist William M. Reddy argues that any stable political system must establish a normative emotional order that either endorses or anathematizes certain affective qualities. He describes this order as an 'emotional regime,' and offers as an example 'the impact of the Iranian revolution on the experience of grief in that country.' Although previously a symbol of resistance, Reddy writes, 'grief is now an emotion mandated by the state' (48), and as a consequence, it has become one of the dominant structures of feeling within Iranian public life.[3] Similarly, in the decade or so following Partition, Nehru was attempting to establish an emotional regime that would ensure the stability (and durability) of the postcolonial Indian nation-state. In order to counteract the divisive legacies of 1947, it was essential that he anathematize 'strong feelings' (*Speeches* 135) of any kind, and instead promote the virtues of tolerance and temperance.[4] For Nehru, such virtues were to be practised not only socially or politically, but also linguistically – at the level of language and discourse. In the first passage quoted above, it is significant that he should appeal for moderation *in speech and writing*, and we find the same emphasis

---

3   For more on the development of this particular emotional regime, see Good and Good. By contrast, the medical anthropologist Arthur Kleinman has described the way in which the Chinese Communist Party sought to anathematize affective states such as depression and anxiety after it came to power in 1949 – claiming that these feelings were bourgeois pathologies that a programme of 'socially productive labour' (128) would quickly eradicate.

4   By doing so, Nehru was really endorsing the Aristotelian ideal of *metriopatheia*, which advocates affective moderation rather than the complete absence of emotion (*apatheia*). According to Aristotle, it is possible to feel emotions such as anger or fear 'both too much and too little, and in both cases not well; but to feel them at the right times, with reference to the right objects, towards the right people, with the right motive, and in the right way, is what is both intermediate and best, and this is characteristic of virtue.' In other words, virtue is 'concerned with passions and actions in which excess [*hyperbole*] is a form of failure, and so is defect [*elleipsis*], while the intermediate is praised and is a form of success; and being praised and being successful are both characteristics of virtue. Therefore virtue is a kind of mean [*mesotes*], since, as we have seen, it aims at what is intermediate' (*Nicomachean* 30).

elsewhere too. Responding to the violence in Calcutta in 1950, he declared that people should 'remain calm and determined and not indulge in loose language ... which is improper and harmful' (*Speeches* 146). And then a short time later, during a debate in parliament, he made it clear that this injunction applied to everyone, even the prime minister himself. 'I happen to hold a responsible position,' he said,

> and my decisions are not merely expressions of opinion but may have to be translated into action. Therefore, *I must be careful that at this moment I am not led away by emotion, excitement or indignation.* Normally, I speak without having to keep a tight hold of myself. In this instance, however, I dare not allow myself to go because the responsibility and the consequences are too grave. That does not mean that I am unaware of what has happened; it is because of the very nature of the crisis, the depth of it and its far-reaching consequences, that *I hesitate to speak in unrestrained language.* (*Speeches* 147; my italics)[5]

In *A Suitable Boy*, we find several direct references to the placatory speeches – the 'meandering pleas for mutual tolerance' (1241) – that Nehru made during this period. After Partition, we are told, he had 'preached against communal enmity in every speech he had given' (955), and by doing so, he had managed to 'keep a volatile country ... safe [from] religious fanaticism,' not 'merely in those early and most dangerous years but throughout his own lifetime' (1241).[6] As we shall see in the following pages, however, the affective moderation advocated by Nehru operates at every level of the novel – giving rise to an 'emotional

---

5 Here, Nehru is clearly acknowledging the performative nature, the perlocutionary force, of such utterances – however remote they may appear to be from the lived reality of communal violence.

6 Neelam Srivastava has pointed out that *A Suitable Boy*'s endorsement of Nehruvian secularism carried a broader social and political significance at the time of its publication in the early nineties, 'when Nehru's idea of the Indian secular state was subject to severe erosion in the political sphere, with the rise of the pro-Hindu Bharatiya Janata Party [BJP].' As Srivastava observes, 'The cultural and social mores of 1950s India [were] still easily recognizable in the India of the 1990s. But the political present of 1993 had witnessed a radical shift in the hegemonic ideology of the Indian public sphere: Nehruvian secularism was out, Hindutva ideology was in ... The novel can [thus] be read as a way of addressing the "present needs" of the Indian polity by proposing a return to Nehruvianism, by recreating a national narrative set in the heart of the Nehru era, the heyday of secular nationalism in the aftermath of Partition' (11).

regime' within the narrative itself, one that makes a virtue of restraint and reticence while categorically rejecting any feelings (dysphoric or otherwise) that might compromise the stability of the discourse.

Before proceeding, it may also be worth acknowledging, just briefly, the tension between Nehru's rhetorical moderation and the underlying radicalism of his political programme following independence. In *A Suitable Boy*, the revolutionary potential of Nehru's post-1947 social policies is most obvious in those passages that deal with the introduction of the Zamindari Abolition Act (which did in fact take place during the early 1950s). This legislation was designed, in principle, to abolish feudal estates and institute a more equitable distribution of land. In the novel, it is Mahesh Kapoor, the revenue minister for the (fictional) state of Purva Pradesh, who introduces the act into the Legislative Assembly; and the debates we witness there (see chapters 5.15–16) demonstrate just how divisive this issue would prove to be.[7] By advocating moderation during these transitional years, then, Nehru was attempting not only to quell specific episodes of communal violence, but also, one could argue, to contain and control the revolutionary political energies that he himself was responsible for creating. And to some degree, the same thing could be said of *A Suitable Boy* – for it is one of the novel's central ironies that it should demonstrate such a strong aversion, at the discursive level, to the volatile and melodramatic substance of its own story. On the one hand, like Nehru, it does everything it can to discourage upsurges of strong feeling, yet on the other hand, it actively contributes to this affective disorder by creating a narrative of profound social and political change. Indeed, this tension may also partly explain the rather anticlimactic nature of the novel's conclusion, in which the values of bourgeois (Hindu) respectability are finally allowed to reassert themselves – thus containing, or at least dissipating, some of the 'revolutionary' energy that the narrative itself has brought into being.

---

7 There was, however, a significant disparity between the act's proclaimed objectives and its practical implementation. In Bihar, for instance, '[t]he state government did not have the administrative competence to implement it fully. Former *zamindars* [landlords] were well advised and knew in advance the provisions of the forthcoming abolition legislation, and they were in many cases able to circumvent the intentions of the measure and retain for themselves significant landholdings' (Brown 234).

III

A Suitable Boy is structured around the interconnected lives of four different families: the Khans, the Mehras, the Chatterjis, and the Kapoors (the first of these being an aristocratic Muslim family, while the other three, related by marriage, belong to the Hindu élite). Over the course of several years, each family generates multiple plotlines that are also, inevitably, woven together. There are, among other things, love affairs, infidelities, court cases, political alliances and rivalries, communal disturbances, medical crises, suicides, academic intrigues, and, in the words of one character, 'God knows what else' (261). But despite these diverse plotlines, *A Suitable Boy* is, in essence, a classic narrative of courtship and marriage. In the very first sentence, as we have noted, Mrs Rupa Mehra delivers the 'maternal imperative' (3) that initiates much of what follows. And it is in this narrative strand that the virtues of reticence and rationality are most clearly thematized.[8] As Lata's quest to find a 'suitable boy' progresses, she is presented with three very different suitors: Kabir, the romantic young undergraduate with whom she falls in love; Amit, the '[f]amous poet' (385) and composer of whimsical acrostics; and Haresh, the manufacturer of shoes, who is really only notable for his practicality and mercantile 'good sense.' Of the three, Kabir is certainly the most appealing, and so it comes as something of a disappointment when we learn, in Chapter 18.21, that Lata has decided to reject him in favour of Haresh. Her reasons for doing so are simple. For one thing, the fact that Kabir is Muslim makes him, from Lata's perspective, 'the most unsuitable boy of them all' (1138); and she is also deeply disturbed by the emotions that he inspires in her – the 'erratic swings of mood' (14), the feelings of love and desire. So in the end she decides to marry Haresh, whose stability and pragmatism she finds reassuring. (He is, she tells herself, 'as solid as a pair of Goodyear Welted shoes' [1291].)[9] Appalled by this decision,

---

8 Needless to say, I am not alone in having noticed this thematic emphasis in *A Suitable Boy*. In her review of the novel, for example, Anita Desai argues that it implicitly endorses 'Aristotle's golden mean – the avoidance of excess, the advisability of moderation, the wisdom of restraint, temperance, and control' (24); and David Myers makes a similar claim in an article entitled 'Vikram Seth's Epic Renunciation of the Passions: Deconstructing Moral Codes in *A Suitable Boy*.' Where my analysis differs, however, is in its focus on the formal and structural consequences of these Aristotelian (and Nehruvian) virtues.

9 Interestingly, we find the same renunciation of strong feeling in *The*

Affective Disorders

Lata's friend Malati asks her to explain herself, and the following dialogue takes place:

> 'Malati, I can't describe it – my feelings with [Kabir] are so confused. I'm not myself when I'm with him. I ask myself who is this – this jealous, obsessed woman who can't get a man out of her head – why should I make myself suffer like this? I know that it'll always be like this if I'm with him.'
> 'Oh, Lata – don't be blind –' exclaimed Malati. 'It shows how passionately you love him –'
> 'I don't want to,' cried Lata, 'I don't want to. If that's what passion means, I don't want it. Look at what passion has done to the family. Maan's broken, his mother's dead, his father's in despair. When I thought that Kabir was seeing someone else, what I remember feeling was enough to make me hate passion. Passionately and forever.' (1296)[10]

Seeing that Malati is still unconvinced, Lata invokes the poet Arthur Hugh Clough, whose *Amours de Voyage* (1849) offers a similar critique of strong romantic feeling. 'I can't remember [the passage] exactly,' she says, 'but he talks about a calmer, less frantic love, which helps you to grow where you were already growing, "to live where as yet I had languished"' (1299).[11] And this is precisely the kind of love she believes she will come to feel for Haresh – not the kind that 'merely excites,

---

Golden Gate, Seth's 1986 novel in verse. 'Passion's a prelude to disaster,' one character declares while proposing to our heroine, Liz. 'It's something else that makes us sure / Our bond can last five decades more.' In the end, Liz acquiesces to this logic, deciding that instead of marrying a man she loves passionately, 'she'd far rather / Marry a man who's a good father' (244–45).

10 In this passage, Lata is referring to one of the novel's other major plotlines, which involves the volatile relationship between Maan Kapoor, her brother-in-law, and Saeeda Bai, a Muslim courtesan.
11 In its entirety, the stanza Lata is quoting reads as follows: 'There are two different kinds, I believe, of human attraction: / One which simply disturbs, unsettles, and makes you uneasy, / And another that poises, retains, and fixes and holds you. / I have no doubt, for myself, in giving my voice for the latter. / I do not wish to be moved, but growing where I was growing, / There more truly to grow, to live where as yet I had languished. / I do not like being moved: for the will is excited; and action / Is a most dangerous thing; I tremble for something factitious, / Some malpractice of heart and illegitimate process; / We are so prone to these things, with our terrible notions of duty' (Clough).

unsettles, and makes you uneasy' (1299), but the kind that will develop over time into something solid and reliable and enduring (like a pair of Goodyear Welted shoes).[12]

As suggested above, there is a clear correspondence between Lata's rather muted matrimonial desire, the 'desire' of the narrative itself, and our readerly desire for the full and final predication of meaning that traditionally accompanies narrative closure. Allow me to clarify what I mean by this, and to do so by citing Peter Brooks. For Brooks, all narratives possess an internal energy that drives them forward, 'connecting beginning and end across the middle and making of that middle – what we read *through* – a field of force' (*Reading* 47). This energy, he argues, is ultimately produced by the 'dynamic of desire' (38) within the narrative: 'the desire to wrest beginnings and ends from the uninterrupted flow of middles, from temporality itself; the search for that significant closure that would illuminate the sense of an existence, the meaning of life' (140). Indeed, Brooks writes, one could 'analyze the opening paragraph of most novels and emerge in each case with the image of a desire taking on shape, beginning to seek its objects, beginning to develop a textual energetics' (38). This is certainly true of *A Suitable Boy*, whose inaugural image of desire could not be clearer. 'You too will marry a boy I choose,' Mrs Rupa Mehra tells her daughter in the opening sentence, thus activating the 'textual energetics' that will sustain the novel for a thousand-odd pages. So the narrative is obviously not *without* desire – if it were, it would be unable to sustain itself in this way – but it is a particularly diluted species of desire, one that allows for delayed gratification, for the endless 'obstacles, stoppages, [and] deviations' that impede the onward 'flow of the discourse' (Barthes, *S/Z* 75). And as I have observed, this also influences the way in which we read the novel. According to Brooks, citing Barthes, what animates us as readers of narrative is '*la passion du sens*, which [he would] translate as both the passion *for* meaning and the passion *of* meaning: the active quest of the reader for those shaping ends that, terminating the dynamic process of reading, promise to bestow meaning and significance on the beginning and the middle' (*Reading* 19). In other words, the desire for meaning is, above all, a desire for the end, for the sense of unity and plenitude that the termination of (readerly) discourse provides. Yet here, too, *A Suitable Boy* demonstrates its aversion to any kind of emotional intensity. By creating so many detours and delays, by

---

12 If you refer to the preceding footnote, you will see that Lata has slightly misremembered this phrase.

elongating the discourse to such a large degree, the novel forces us to renounce (or at least moderate) our own readerly desire for meaning and closure. Of course, we do not entirely *lose* our desire for the end – if we did, we would simply stop reading – but we do learn to control this desire, to subordinate it to the 'reality principle' that the discourse so actively promotes. In this way, then, Lata's sublimated matrimonial desire could be said to serve as an intradiegetic correlative for the narrative's own sublimated desires, and for those of the reader, who is obliged to tolerate (and even enjoy) over a thousand pages of 'imposed delay' (Brooks, *Reading* 107).

If you remember, in his description of the hermeneutic code, Barthes identifies two contrasting forces: one that moves the story forward, propelling it ever closer to its conclusion, and another that uses various dilatory strategies to oppose 'the ineluctable advance of language' (*S/Z* 75). As we have just noted, *A Suitable Boy* places a particular emphasis on the second of these two forces – the one that moderates both the narrative's desire for closure and the reader's 'passion for meaning.' In order to understand this dynamic, and its broader affective significance, it may be useful to approach the subject from a neurological perspective. Like a narrative, the body's autonomic nervous system is divided in two. There is the sympathetic nervous system (SNS), which is responsible for the physiological arousal that we associate with emotions such as anger or fear (an increase in heart rate and blood pressure, enhanced muscle tone, accelerated breathing, etc.). And then there is the parasympathetic nervous system (PNS), which, as Bessel van der Kolk writes, 'triggers the release of acetylcholine to put a brake on arousal, slowing the heart down, relaxing muscles, and returning breathing to normal.' Together, these two systems play a vital role in 'managing the body's energy flow, one preparing for its expenditure, the other for its conservation' (77). Turning once more to the literary narrative, we find a similar tension between two opposing 'systems.' On the one hand, we have an SNS that generates the necessary energy to keep the narrative moving forward, while on the other, we have a PNS that regulates or conserves this energy so that it can be sustained for an appropriate length of time. Although their relative preponderance may fluctuate depending on the circumstances, both of these regulatory systems are essential to the survival of any narrative. If there is too much emphasis on the SNS, the narrative faces the danger of a premature discharge of energy. But conversely, if there is too much emphasis on the PNS, it could easily lapse into a state of terminal quiescence, having lost the energy to attach one signifier to another.

As is the case with any successful narrative, *A Suitable Boy* manages to sustain an acceptable, homeostatic balance between the SNS and the PNS until the very end; but the fact that the narrative is required to cover so many pages along the way, and to quell so many internal crises as it progresses, inevitably brings its parasympathetic tendencies to the fore. At the narratological level, of course, this is exactly what Barthes is talking about when he discusses the various 'obstacles, stoppages, [and] deviations' that constitute the hermeneutic code; and at the broader sociopolitical level, this is also what Nehru is talking about when he describes the renunciation of strong feeling, the rejection of 'hatred [and] anger,' as his 'supreme objective.'

So what happens, then, when we do finally reach the novel's long-awaited conclusion? After persisting for more than a thousand pages, the reader is entitled to expect a particularly gratifying discharge of meaning (and emotion) when the narrative draws to a close. But the conclusion that we are eventually offered on page 1335 is anything but gratifying. Instead of choosing to marry the romantic Kabir, or even the charming Amit, Lata decides to spend the rest of her life with Haresh, the least engaging of her three suitors. The motivation behind this decision is never made entirely clear to the reader. On page 1295, out of the blue, as it were, she simply writes to Haresh, 'accepting with gratitude … his often repeated offer of marriage.' More significantly, however, it soon becomes apparent that even Lata herself does not fully understand why she has made this decision – why she has perversely abandoned the man she loves in favour of a man with whom she has 'nothing at all in common' (1295). When she is interrogated on the subject by her friend Malati, in Chapter 18.21, she is unable to explain the logic of what she has done ('I'm not at ease,' she confesses, 'I hardly know who I am or what I'm doing' [1299]); and this is the case, I would argue, because it was a decision that she did not ultimately make. Rather, it was made *for her* by the discourse itself, which chose to intervene at this late stage in order to prevent the efflorescence of feeling – strong feeling, *dangerous* feeling – that a more gratifying conclusion would have provided. In the end, that is to say, Lata loses her 'autonomy' as a character and is obliged to marry the 'suitable boy' who has been chosen for her by the discourse she occupies.[13] And that is why both Malati and Lata herself

---

13 In his analysis of Balzac's 'Sarrasine,' Barthes describes a similar moment of discursive intrusion. One evening as he is leaving the Teatro Argentina, the eponymous hero of the story is cautioned against pursuing his infatuation with the singer La Zambinella. 'Be on your guard, Frenchman,'

are so mystified by the decision she finally makes – because at this stage she is no longer obeying the internal logic of the story (the contingencies of plotting or the psychology of her 'character') but *the external logic of the discourse itself*. According to Jonathan Culler, all narratives obey a 'double logic': the logic of story and the logic of discourse. It is only natural, Culler writes, to assume that story precedes (and in many ways determines) discourse, yet this premise is 'frequently questioned in narratives themselves, at moments when the hierarchy of narrative is inverted' (*Pursuit* 191).[14] At the end of *A Suitable Boy*, when Lata decides to take Haresh as her husband, we witness precisely this kind of inversion, as the novel's discourse suddenly takes precedence over the story it has been charged with telling. And it does so, I believe, for a very simple reason. Only by intervening in this way is it able to prevent a final discharge of meaning and significance that would otherwise prove far too gratifying, far too pleasurable, for the reader – and thus undermine the climate of affective moderation that it has gone to so much trouble to create.

In order to make itself last as long as it does, the discourse is obliged to insert a great deal of unnecessary 'filler' between the initiation of the novel's central hermeneutic sequence on page 3 and its ultimate resolution on page 1335. Not everything that separates these two critical episodes can carry significance; in fact, the more dilatory space a narrative creates, the more *insignificant* material it requires to fill that space. By making this point, I am really distinguishing between two different types of narrative function. On the one hand, we have what Barthes calls *nuclei* (those occurrences that 'constitute [the] real hinge points of [a] narrative'), while on the other, we have what he refers to as *catalyzers* (those occurrences that 'merely "fill in" the narrative

---

    a stranger whispers in his ear. 'This is a matter of life and death ...' (Balzac qtd. in Barthes, *S/Z* 241). At this point, Sarrasine would seem to have a choice: he could either heed the stranger's warning or ignore it. But this 'choice' (and the agency it implies) is ultimately illusory, for if he were to heed the warning and 'refrain from pursuing his adventure, there would be no story.' In other words, as Barthes observes, '*Sarrasine is forced by the discourse* to keep his rendezvous with La Zambinella' – the character's 'freedom' being dominated, at this particular juncture, by the discourse's 'instinct for preservation' (*S/Z* 135).

14 The point Culler is making here emerges out of the classic narratological distinction between story (what is told) and discourse (the way it is told). For more on this double logic, see Culler, *Pursuit* 188–208.

space separating the [nuclei]') ('Introduction' 265).[15] Needless to say, a narrative the size of *A Suitable Boy* requires a large number of inessential catalyzers, or 'subsidiary notations' (Barthes, 'Introduction' 265), whose primary function is to fill empty space – and, in so doing, to delay the predication of the narrative sentence for as long as possible. In this particular case, though, the novel's catalyzers also serve a secondary purpose, having been put there to ensure the ongoing stability of the discourse (through the careful regulation of its affective economy). On page 45, we find a paradigmatic example of this secondary function. While browsing in a local bookstore, Lata picks up a book at random and reads a rather cryptic paragraph:

> It follows from De Moivre's formula that $z^n = r^n (\cos n + i \sin n)$. Thus, if we allow complex number z to describe a circle of radius r about the origin, z^n will describe n complete times a circle of radius r^n as z describes its circle once. We also recall that r, the modulus of z, written $|z|$, gives the distance of z from O, and that if $z' = x' + iy'$, then $|z - z'|$ is the distance between z and z'. With these preliminaries we may proceed to the proof of the theorem.

Although this passage carries no real significance for Lata, she finds it soothing to read: 'What exactly pleased her in these sentences she did not know, but they conveyed weight, comfort, inevitability ... The words were assured, and therefore reassuring: things were what they were even in this uncertain world, and she could proceed from there' (45–46). This is also the function that such inessential passages serve in the novel as a whole. They are there not only to fill the pages, but also to create a general atmosphere of stability and composure – reassuring us that things are what they are, and that they will always be that way. From time to time, the placid surface of the narrative is still disturbed by a sudden irruption of strong feeling; and such feelings, when they do appear, are often associated with the emergence of a vital nucleus

---

15 For a function to qualify as a nucleus, Barthes argues, 'it is enough that the action to which it refers open (or continue, or close) an alternative that is of direct consequence for the subsequent development of the story, in short that it inaugurate or conclude an uncertainty ... Between two [nuclei] however, it is always possible to set out subsidiary notations which cluster around one or other nucleus without modifying its alternative nature ... These catalyzers are still functional, insofar as they enter into correlation with a nucleus, but their functionality is attenuated, unilateral, parasitic' ('Introduction' 265–66).

Affective Disorders

(the acceptance of a marriage proposal, for instance, or the death of a beloved spouse). But it never takes long for the excitement generated by these isolated nuclei to subside, once more, into the reassuring banality of the superfluous, that 'very necessary thing.'[16]

A less obvious example of the dual function served by such catalyzers can be found in Chapter 9.5, which describes in some detail a long train journey that Lata makes from Calcutta to Kanpur. On page 558, we learn that '[t]he train departed on time'; and on page 560, it duly arrives at its destination. In the intervening pages, however, nothing of any real significance takes place. 'A sickly smell of molasses [rises] from a sugar-cane factory.' A woman in a burqa 'roll[s] out a small prayer-rug and beg[ins] to pray.' An egret flies over an adjacent field. At one point, 'for no particular reason,' the train stops at a small, unidentified station where some beggars ply their usual trade. After a few minutes, the train begins moving again, and eventually it crosses the Ganges. Lata reads for a while; then she buys some samosas and a cup of tea, before drowsing off for an hour or so. When she wakes, she finds that her neighbour, an old woman in a white sari, has been keeping the flies off her face. And so it goes – one insignificant thing after another, for over three pages. At a basic structural level, the primary function of these catalyzers is to transform the train journey into a narrative, to separate the moment of departure from that of arrival. If there was no filler here at all, there would be no story. The beginning of the journey would simply collapse into the end, leaving no room whatsoever for any intervening narrative 'substance.' But at a secondary level, once again, these details could also be said to represent the general principle of normality. Everything is fine, they seem to be insisting; everything is as it should be. There is no anger here, no hatred, no violence – just a long, boring train journey full of '[d]ust and flies' (559).[17]

---

16 I am quoting from the first of the novel's two epigraphs here, which itself is taken from line 22 of Voltaire's *Le Mondain* (1736): 'Le superflu, chose très-nécessaire' (296).
17 Of course, at some level, it is possible to recuperate any narrative detail, to ascribe functionality, however limited, to even the most inconsequential of utterances. One could argue, for instance, that at the level of connotative meaning this passage demonstrates the sociocultural diversity of postcolonial India, as Lata travels from the cosmopolitan urban centre of Calcutta, through 'the green and moist countryside of Bengal,' the 'dusty fields and poor villages' (558) of Uttar Pradesh, and the sacred cities of Banaras and Allahabad, to the Raj-era settlement of Kanpur. Or from another perspective, one could claim that her journey

At times, moreover, the characters themselves contribute to this atmosphere by exchanging the verbal equivalent of superfluous catalyzers. In a number of key scenes, they are allowed to saturate the discourse with a 'sociable noise' (Seth, *Suitable* 432) whose ultimate purpose is not to convey a specific message or to move the plot forward, but to sustain the semantic tension of the narrative while also reinforcing its dominant tone of civility and benevolence. The function I am describing here, to use a term first employed by the anthropologist Bronislaw Malinowski, is one of 'phatic communion' (from the Greek *phatos*, or 'spoken'). In a 1923 essay entitled 'The Problem of Meaning in Primitive Languages,' Malinowski discusses at some length the bonding function of 'free, aimless social intercourse' (313). Such utterances, he observes, whether they occur 'among savage tribes [or] in a European drawing room' (313), typically involve 'purposeless expressions of preference or aversion, accounts of irrelevant happenings, [or] comments on what is perfectly obvious' (314). In other words, the literal meaning of a phatic utterance carries no inherent value; what matters is the 'atmosphere of sociability' (315), the communal bond, that it generates. And this is precisely the function that such empty phrases serve in *A Suitable Boy*, where they do little more than fill the air – and the page – with inane pleasantries. In Chapter 7.11, for instance, we accompany Lata as she circulates among the guests at a party held by the Chatterjis. It is a splendid occasion, and she is 'quite amazed by the glitter and glory of it all.' Everyone is talking as loudly as possible, and as she moves from place to place, Lata feels as if she is 'swimming in a sea of language' (399), surrounded on all sides by innocuous banalities such as the following one:

> 'Ever since the year 1933 I have been drinking the juice of bitter gourds. You know bitter gourd? It is our famous Indian vegetable,

---

takes on a broader symbolic significance – emphasizing the difficulties that Nehru will face unifying a country of this magnitude and diversity, while at the same time providing a metaphor for such unity in the form of the journey itself, which arguably serves as a 'picaresque *tour d'horizon*,' bringing these various locales together within a 'clearly bounded' national space (B. Anderson 30). But the real significance of the passage, I believe, lies elsewhere. Although these catalyzers are still capable of producing a (rather attenuated) degree of meaning at the connotative and symbolic levels, their primary function within the novel remains the same. They are there to substantiate Lata's journey, to separate A from B, and, in so doing, to infuse the narrative with a reassuring sense of the prosaic, the ordinary, and the banal.

Affective Disorders

called karela. It looks like this' – [the guest] gesticulated elongatedly – 'and it is green, and ribbed ... Every week my servant takes a seer of bitter gourd, and from the skin only, mark you, he will make juice. Each seer will yield one jamjar of juice ... Then every morning for my breakfast he will give me one sherry glass or liqueur glass – so much – of this juice. Every day since 1933. And I have no sugar problems. I can eat sweetmeats without anxiety. My dermatology is also very good, and all [my] bowel movements are very satisfactory.' (401)

And then thirty pages later, in a similar fashion, we attend a cocktail party at the Finlays', one that also gives rise to a 'hubbub of chatter' and a 'general mash of sociable noise' (431–32):

Everyone stood around talking about the 'monsoonish' weather, which had struck earlier than usual this year. Opinion was divided as to whether today's tremendous rains were monsoonal or pre-monsoonal. Golf had been quite impossible this afternoon, and though the races at Tollygunge were very rarely cancelled owing to the weather ... if the rains were as heavy tomorrow as they had been today, the ground might be complete slush and the going too difficult for the horses. English county cricket too played a large part in the conversation, and Lata heard more than she might have wished to about Denis Compton's brilliant batting and his left arm spinners ... (431)

Here, as elsewhere, the characters do everything they can to fill the intervening space between page 3 and page 1335 with an 'atmosphere of polite, social intercourse' (Malinowski 316). By trading these banalities, they ensure both the continuity of the narrative, when nothing much else is happening, and its affective stability – allowing it to steer a middle course between the palpable animosity of the verbal dispute and the 'strange and unpleasant tension' that people feel 'when facing each other in silence' (Malinowski 314).

In a recent study, Franco Moretti has argued that narrative 'filling' of this kind came to serve a similar purpose during the late nineteenth century. It was, he says, 'a mechanism designed to keep the "narrativity" of life under control; to give it a regularity, a "style"' (*Bourgeois* 72). In 1800, such catalyzers were still a rarity, but 'a hundred years later they [were] everywhere' (79); and for Moretti, it is particularly significant that their growing ubiquity as a narrative device should have coincided with the rise of the European bourgeoisie. 'Why fillers, in the nineteenth century?' he asks.

> Because they offer *the kind of narrative pleasure compatible with the new regularity of bourgeois life*. They are to story-telling what comforts are to physical pleasure: enjoyment pared down, adapted to the daily activity of reading a novel … [S]mall things become significant, without ceasing to be 'small'; they become *narrative*, without ceasing to be *everyday* … [F]illers *rationalize the novelistic universe*, turning it into a world of few surprises, fewer adventures, and no miracles at all. They are a great bourgeois invention, not because they bring into the novel trade, or industry, or other bourgeois 'realities' (which they don't), but because through them the logic of rationalization pervades *the very rhythm of the novel*. (81–82)

As we have seen, the fillers in Seth's novel serve an identical purpose. Simply put, they are there to emphasize the systematic regularity of the characters' lives and to minimize the disruption caused by those critical episodes in the narrative that Barthes would describe as nuclei. Things certainly happen in *A Suitable Boy* – there are a few surprises and adventures that are caused by, or give rise to, strong feelings of one kind or another – but the catalyzers surrounding these episodes of affective intensity are always quick to reassert themselves, to submerge such disruptive emotional energy beneath the unstimulating quiescence of the everyday.

The length of the novel testifies to the general efficacy of this strategy; however, there are some places where the simple accumulation of catalyzers is not enough to quell the upsurge of disruptive feeling. At such times, when the stability of the narrative is particularly endangered, the discourse is obliged to deploy other, more radical protective measures. A notable example of this can be found in Chapter 5.3, where we witness the following episode of communal violence (provoked by the construction of a Hindu temple alongside a mosque):

> No one knew how the men who were gathering in the narrow alleys of the Muslim neighbourhood … became a mob. One moment they were walking individually or in small groups through the alleys towards the mosque for evening prayer, then they had coalesced into larger clusters, excitedly discussing the ominous signals they had heard. After the midday sermon most were in no mood to listen to any voice of moderation. A couple of the more eager members of the Alamgiri Masjid Hifaazat Committee made a few crowd-rousing remarks, a few local hotheads and toughs stirred themselves and those around them into a state of rage, the crowd increased in size as the alleys joined into larger alleys, its density and speed and

sense of indistinct determination increased, and it was no longer a collection but a thing – wounded and enraged, and wanting nothing less than to wound and enrage. There were cries of 'Allah-u-Akbar' which could be heard all the way to the police station. A few of those who joined the crowd had sticks in their hands. One or two even had knives. Now it was not the mosque that they were headed for but the partly constructed temple just next to it. It was from here that the blasphemy had originated, it was this that must be destroyed. (235)

I would contend that it is not only the temple that is being threatened with destruction in this passage, but the discourse itself – or at least the climate of affective moderation it has so carefully created. As indicated above, the judicious insertion of a few catalyzers here (a flying egret, say, or a woman in a white sari) would not be enough to protect the narrative from the crowd's overflowing rage, and so the discourse is obliged to take more radical measures. Earlier, I suggested that Lata's decision to marry Haresh was ultimately determined by certain discursive imperatives; and here, too, the discourse suddenly intervenes, taking precedence over the story it has been charged with telling, in order to protect itself from these dangerous dysphoric energies. In this case, however, it chooses another accomplice, the young district magistrate, Krishan Dayal, whose only real function in the novel is to restore order as quickly as possible. As the crowd approaches the temple, he positions his men on either side of a large alleyway, and waits:

> The mob was less than a minute away. He could hear it screaming and yelling; he could feel the vibration of the ground as hundreds of feet rushed forward.
> At the last moment he gave the signal. [His] men roared and charged and fired.
> The wild and dangerous mob, hundreds strong, faced with this sudden terror, halted, staggered, turned and fled. It was uncanny. Within thirty seconds it had melted away. Two bodies were left in the street: one young man had been shot through the neck and was dying or dead; the other, an old man with a white beard, had fallen and been crushed by the retreating mob. He was badly, perhaps fatally, injured ...
> The DM looked around at his men. A couple of them were trembling, most of them were jubilant. None of them was injured. He caught the head constable's eye. Both of them started laughing

with relief, then stopped. A couple of women were wailing in nearby houses. Otherwise, everything was peaceful or, rather, still. (237–38)

In *S/Z*, Barthes claims that all literary characters could be regarded as willing accomplices of the discourse by which they have been constituted – and it is certainly difficult to argue otherwise.[18] But this complicity is usually concealed by the characters' ostensible autonomy and by the agency they appear to demonstrate. Only at certain critical junctures, when the very survival of the discourse is threatened, does their complicity become more pronounced. In this episode, for instance, the district magistrate is quite clearly intervening *on behalf of* the discourse when he delivers the order to fire, protecting it from the untrammelled rage of the crowd and from the dysphoric energy that such anger inevitably generates.

Much later in the novel, we are given some intimation of what might have happened to the discourse had he not intervened in this way. In Chapter 18.33, a character by the name of Rasheed suffers an emotional crisis and, in doing so, brings the narrative itself to the verge of a complete discursive collapse:

> Rasheed walked along the parapet of the Barsaat Mahal, his thoughts blurred with hunger and confusion.
> Darkness, and the river, and the cool marble wall.
> Somewhere where there is nowhere.
> It gnaws. They are all around me, the leaders of Sagal.
> No father, no mother, no child, no wife.
> Like a jewel above the water. The parapet, the garden under which a river flows.
> No Satan, no God, no Iblis, no Gabriel.
> Endless, endless, endless, endless, the waters of the Ganga.

---

18 'From a critical point of view,' Barthes writes, 'it is as wrong to suppress the character as it is to take him off the page in order to turn him into a psychological character (endowed with possible motives): *the character and the discourse are each other's accomplices*: the discourse creates in the character its own accomplice: a form of theurgical detachment by which, mythically, God has given himself a subject, man a helpmate, etc., whose relative independence, once they have been created, allows for *playing*. Such is discourse: if it creates characters, it is not to make them play among themselves before us but to play with them, to obtain from them a complicity which assures the uninterrupted exchange of the codes: the characters are types of discourse and, conversely, the discourse is a character like the others' (*S/Z* 178–79).

> The stars above, below ...
> Peace. No prayers. No more prayers.
> To sleep is better than to pray.
> O my creature, you gave your life too soon. I have made your entry into Paradise unlawful.
> A spring in Paradise.
> O God, O God. (1315–16)

It is difficult to understand exactly what is happening here; only later do we learn that Rasheed has actually committed suicide at the end of this chapter (which concludes with the final line given above). But before he does so, the emotional turmoil he creates very nearly brings about the demise of the narrative itself – certainly the demise of the readerly values it has privileged over the preceding thousand-odd pages: clarity, order, logic, rationality, and so on. Here, suddenly, the disruptive forces the narrative has worked so hard to control appear to be gaining the upper hand. And it is only by bringing the chapter to a premature close *before* Rasheed's suicide takes place, only by actively repressing this particular nucleus, that the discourse is able to save itself. Or to put it another way, there is a very good reason why Chapter 18.33 should be the shortest chapter in the entire novel. If the narrative were to represent Rasheed's suicide directly, in the form of a mimetic 'scene,' the negative energy released by this event could easily bring about its discursive collapse. So instead it is necessary to approach the subject obliquely, retrospectively, in the form of diegetic 'reportage.'[19] Only thus can the discourse hope to reassert the supremacy of its own emotional regime – one that both adheres to and actively promotes the guiding principles of the Nehruvian secular state.[20]

---

19 Twenty-four pages later, during Lata's wedding, we learn in passing of 'that fellow Rasheed's suicide' (1340).

20 It is, however, worth acknowledging the fact that the novel's secular principles – like those of Nehru himself – are largely confined to the public sphere. As Nehru wrote in 1961, secularism does not mean the 'absence of religion, but putting religion on a different plane from that of normal political and social life' (*Anthology* 331). And this is a distinction that is also emphasized in *A Suitable Boy*, where the anti-sectarianism advocated in the public sphere does not quite extend to the 'private' issue of intercommunal marriage.

IV

In this chapter, I have discussed some of the ways in which *A Suitable Boy* internalizes the affective moderation advocated by Jawaharlal Nehru during the late forties and early fifties. It does so, I have argued, by delaying the resolution of its central hermeneutic sequence for as long as possible (thus diminishing our readerly desire for the full and final predication of meaning), by saturating the intervening thousand-odd pages with an abundance of 'parasympathetic' filler, and by allowing the discourse itself to intervene directly whenever the stability of the narrative is threatened by a dangerous upsurge of feeling. These measures all serve to reinforce the narrative's governing emotional regime, so that any dysphoric energy released by the characters *within* the story is safely contained, at the extradiegetic level, by the discourse they have been made to occupy. Of course, there are places where this discursive control reveals its vulnerability – during episodes of communal violence, for instance, or in the scene where Rasheed prepares to end his life. And at such junctures the connection between the affective stability of the narrative and its *generic* stability becomes particularly pronounced. Confronted by these challenges to its core aesthetic values (clarity, order, rationality, etc.), the narrative is forced to contemplate a radical shift in generic allegiance – and even the possibility of discursive collapse. But in every case, as I have suggested, the aesthetic values of literary realism and the political values of Nehruvian secularism are able to reassert themselves, ensuring that when we finally bid farewell to our heroine and her 'suitable boy' on page 1349 of the novel, we are able to do so in a state of relatively untroubled equanimity.

It is the morning after their wedding, and Lata and Haresh have just boarded a train bound for Calcutta. After an hour or so, the train comes to a halt at a provincial railway station, where Lata notices a small group of monkeys searching for food. She takes out a musammi, 'peel[s] the thick green skin with care, and beg[ins] to distribute the segments' among the monkeys. Only later, as the train is leaving the station, does she notice an old monkey sitting by himself at the end of the platform. She quickly reaches into her bag for another musammi and throws it in his direction. In the last sentence of the novel, we are told that the old monkey 'moved towards [the piece of fruit], but the others, seeing it roll along, began running towards it too; and before [Lata] could see what had become of it, the train had steamed out of the station' (1349). It is a curious, rather enigmatic way to conclude the novel, but also entirely appropriate – for what we are being offered here is simply the last in a long line of inessential catalyzers. Lata could have noticed anything at this particular station (another flying egret, say, or a woman in a white sari) as such 'subsidiary notations' are ultimately interchangeable. Alter or delete a nucleus and you have a different story; alter or delete a catalyzer, on the other hand, and you have the same story told in a different way.[21] By definition, then, such catalyzers have no influence whatsoever over the underlying structure of the narrative. Their principal function is to fill empty space, and to convey, at a secondary level of meaning, not only the reality of what we are reading, but also its profound *ordinariness*, its compatibility with the mundane substance of our own daily lives. And that, I would argue, is precisely what the monkeys are doing on page 1349 of *A Suitable Boy*. They are not there to 'symbolize' anything, to alter anything, or to destroy anything; they are simply there to replicate the reassuring banality of the everyday and to protect the narrative – even at this late stage – from the sudden irruption of strong feeling.

---

21 I am paraphrasing Barthes here: 'A nucleus cannot be deleted without altering the story,' he writes, 'but neither can a [catalyzer] without altering the discourse' ('Introduction' 267).

CHAPTER THREE

Jealousy
Joaquim Maria Machado de Assis'
Dom Casmurro

A jealousy of a particular date in which a subject historicizes himself in relation to a certain woman signifies, for the one who knows how to interpret it, the total relation to the world by which the subject constitutes himself as a self.

Jean-Paul Sartre, *Being and Nothingness*, 1943

[I]t was all real, at least in appearance.

Roberto Bolaño, *2666*, 2004

I

In the early nineteenth-century Bildungsroman, as Franco Moretti observes, the narrative typically establishes a clear distinction between 'illusion' and 'reality,' with the former occupying the level of story and the latter occupying the level of discourse.[1] We see this quite plainly in Stendhal, where the protagonist's ignorance and immaturity are the subject of frequent narratorial asides; but the distinction is even more

---

1 The term 'discourse,' in this instance, refers to 'the narrative statement, the oral or written [utterance] that undertakes to tell of an event or a series of events,' while the term 'story' is being used to describe 'the succession of events, real or fictitious, that are the subjects of this discourse' (Genette 25).

Affective Disorders

pronounced in Balzac, where the aphoristic quality of the discourse serves to distance it from the very substance of the story it is telling.[2] In Balzac, as Moretti argues, the maturity that constitutes the ultimate generic objective of the Bildungsroman, the enlightened realism that we expect our hero to achieve, has shifted from the world of the story to that of the discourse. Maturity, he writes, 'refuses to mingle with life and direct it: those maxims that in *Wilhelm Meister* [1795–96] imparted wisdom to the dialogue *among characters*, in Balzac are found only in the disembodied world of the *narrator's* discourse.' No longer the 'crowning of growth, nor "wisdom" generated directly from the story, Balzacian maturity is founded on a rupture: on its *estrangement* from the narrative universe' (*Way* 140–41). In the novel I shall be discussing in this chapter, Joaquim Maria Machado de Assis' *Dom Casmurro* (1899), it is possible to identify a similar conflict between illusion and reality, only in this case the dynamic is inverted – the underlying story or 'narrative universe' being associated with reality, while the discourse, so astute and judicious in Balzac, here assumes a delusional or illusory quality. What we are offered, in other words, is a reverse Bildungsroman, in which the discourse consistently misrecognizes the reality of the story it is narrating and, in so doing, serves as a linguistic correlative for broader social disjunctures and ideological incongruities. If Balzac chose to subject his youthful heroes to the moderating influence of a mature and knowledgeable narratorial voice, Machado moves in the opposite direction, obliging his characters to occupy a narrative in which the story is *disfigured* by the discourse – and as I shall argue here, it is entirely appropriate that this should be the case.

Set in Rio de Janeiro during the reign of Dom Pedro II (1831–89), *Dom Casmurro* follows a fairly straightforward narrative trajectory. Writing at the turn of the century, our narrator, Bento Santiago, describes his childhood romance with his neighbour, Capitu, their ensuing marriage, and the eventual dissolution of that marriage in circumstances that have been the subject of some critical debate. According to Bento himself, he had discovered irrefutable evidence of an affair between

---

2 Consider, for example, the following adages from *Old Goriot*: 'Though the human heart may have to pause for rest when climbing the heights of affection it rarely stops on the slippery slope of hatred' (48); 'The desire to conquer is as quickly aroused by the easiness of a triumph as by its difficulty' (159); and 'Women are always true even when their actions appear most equivocal, because they are yielding to some natural impulse' (177).

Capitu and his good friend Escobar (who is unable to defend himself, having recently drowned in Guanabara Bay). For many years, this assessment was accepted at face value by the critics, and it is only since the publication of Helen Caldwell's *The Brazilian Othello of Machado de Assis* in 1960 that the dominant reading of the novel has shifted in Capitu's favour – suggesting that she may be the victim of a husband whose pathological jealousy leads him to interpret perfectly innocent gestures as evidence of deception and infidelity. In what follows, I shall be exploring the sociogenic nature of this jealousy while also discussing some of its more significant discursive consequences.³ Although Brazil's independence was formally recognized in 1825, it continued to be ruled by members of the Portuguese royal family, and many of the socioeconomic structures that were established during the colonial period (1500–1822) remained unchanged and unchallenged. Slavery would not be abolished until 1888; and even after the proclamation of the republic the following year, which spelled the end of Dom Pedro II's fifty-eight-year rule (known as the *Segundo Reinado*), Brazil would continue to function as an agrarian oligarchy whose primary form of social mediation was patronage and favour. As the Brazilian critic Roberto Schwarz has noted, these structural continuities came into direct conflict with the imported ideologies of European liberalism, to which the majority of the élite subscribed, and this in turn created a peculiar dissonance within nineteenth-century Brazilian society.⁴ On

---

3 It may be useful, at this stage, to distinguish between the related (and often intertwined) feelings of jealousy and envy. In her discussion of the subject, Melanie Klein is particularly careful to do so, defining envy as a dyadic and covetous emotion and jealousy as a triadic and possessive one. Whereas envy is an 'angry feeling' directed at someone who 'possesses and enjoys something desirable,' she argues, jealousy 'involves a relation to at least two [other] people [and] is mainly concerned with love that the subject feels is his due and has been taken away, or is in danger of being taken away, from him by his rival' (181). In this chapter, too, jealousy will be understood as a triadic (and thus inherently social) emotion, which arises out of the fear that what one 'possesses' may be appropriated by a rival, whether imaginary or real. More precisely, the word 'jealousy' will be used here to designate the belief or suspicion that a particular person 'has formed or may form a relationship with a rival, and the belief or suspicion that this relationship (or this possible relationship) threatens, is in competition with, or may lead to the loss of [our] existing relationship [with that person]' (Goldie 225).
4 This chapter is deeply indebted both to Schwarz's analyses of imperial Brazil (particularly the 1977 essay 'Misplaced Ideas: Literature and Society

the one hand, the élite 'wanted to be part of the progressive and cultured West, at that time already openly bourgeois' (Schwarz, *Master* 24); yet on the other hand, and in reality, they were the privileged beneficiaries of an archaic slave-owning economy. In this chapter, I shall be discussing both slavery and patronage, arguing that the jealousy that dominates *Dom Casmurro* emerges out of these two local realities, and out of the ideological incongruities to which they give rise. I will also explore the various ways in which this jealousy influences the narrative's production of meaning. Simply put, I would like to suggest that the contradiction between such anachronistic social practices and the guiding principles of European liberalism (free labour, the autonomy of the individual, equality before the law, etc.) creates a corresponding disjuncture between story and discourse – one that replicates the more general ideological dissonance that characterized Brazilian society during the *Segundo Reinado*. In Machado's novel, the falsity, the artificiality, the very *discursivity* of the discourse is consistently emphasized, forcing the reader to acknowledge, on almost every page, the profound disparity between the (literary) signifier and the (social) signified, between Bento's narration and the 'implied' story it generates. As Schwarz writes, 'slavery and favour twisted the ideas of the times,' producing a sense of radical incongruity that can still be felt today: 'the impression that Brazil gives of ill-assortedness – unmanageable contrasts, disproportions, nonsense, anachronisms, outrageous compromises …' ('Misplaced' 25). And this, I would argue, is precisely what we find in *Dom Casmurro*, where the protagonist's jealousy (an emotion that is itself typically disproportionate) can be seen as one of the primary affective consequences of living in a society that is always dimly aware of its own impropriety, its fundamental betrayal of the liberal values to which it ostensibly adheres.[5]

---

    in Late Nineteenth-Century Brazil,' which first drew my attention to the significance of slavery and patronage during the *Segundo Reinado*) and to his seminal work on Machado. In the latter case, I will be quoting more than once from *A Master on the Periphery of Capitalism*, which establishes a causal connection between the scandal of slavery and the stylistic volubility and irreverence of *The Posthumous Memoirs of Brás Cubas* (1880).

5 Over the course of his career, Machado would return to the subject of jealousy on more than one occasion. In his first novel, for instance, entitled *Resurrection* (1872), the protagonist becomes convinced that he is being betrayed by his fiancée, and this all-consuming paranoia in many ways anticipates the pathological jealousy that Bento experiences in *Dom Casmurro*. 'Félix's love had a bitter taste,' we are told in the

II

Although Brazil banned the importation of slaves in 1850, a thriving interprovincial slave trade continued until 1888, when the *Lei Áurea* (or Golden Law) was passed, definitively abolishing slavery throughout the country. For much of the nineteenth century, however, slavery remained integral to the Brazilian economy. In 1872, for instance, a population of 341,576 slaves was living in the province of Rio de Janeiro, with 48,939 located in the capital itself (G. Daniel 26). And in 1887, only a year before Abolition, the province of Rio de Janeiro contained an estimated 162,000 slaves, the second highest number in the country after the neighbouring province of Minas Gerais (Fausto 116). During this period, as I have suggested, it was virtually impossible for the élite to reconcile the sordid reality of slavery, on which their economic prosperity depended, with the liberal principles that were so closely associated with European modernity. From the practical perspective, to quote Schwarz, 'slavery was a *contemporary* necessity; from the emotional perspective, a *traditional* presence; and from the ideological perspective, an *archaic* disgrace – all of them contradictory attributes, but real in the light of the historical experience of the [Brazilian] ruling class' (*Master* 21). In an effort to resolve these incongruities, the élite were obliged to misrecognize or simply disregard the true source of their own socioeconomic privilege, choosing to see liberty, equality, and fraternity where there was none. And in a city such as Rio de Janeiro, where by 1872 roughly 37 per cent of the population were slaves, this was not always easy to do.

In *Culture and Imperialism*, Edward Said offers what he describes as a 'contrapuntal reading' of Jane Austen's *Mansfield Park* (1814).[6] According

---

earlier novel, 'ridden with doubt and suspicion ... A smile, a look, a gesture, anything was enough to stir his soul. The young woman's very thoughts were subject to his suspicions. If at any moment he discovered thoughtful languor in her gaze, he would begin to speculate [about] her reasons, recalling a gesture from the previous day, a poorly explained look, an obscure, ambiguous sentence ... and from all of this was born, authentically and luminously, the young woman's treachery' (75).

6 As the reader may know, Said uses this term to describe a practice of reading that acknowledges the presence, within such narratives, of 'intertwined and overlapping histories' (*Culture* 18) – even if one of these histories may have been deliberately suppressed or 'forcibly excluded' (67) by the discourse.

to Said, this critical strategy enables one to trace the connection between a colonial sugar plantation on the Caribbean island of Antigua, referred to only half a dozen times over the course of the novel, and the affluence and privilege of the English country estate that serves as its primary setting. Antigua, Said writes,

> is both incidental, referred to only in passing, and absolutely crucial to the action. How are we to assess Austen's few references to Antigua, and what are we to make of them interpretatively? My contention is that by that very odd combination of casualness and stress, Austen reveals herself to be *assuming* ... the importance of an empire to the situation at home. Let us now calibrate the signifying power of the references to Antigua in *Mansfield Park*; how do they occupy the place they do, what are they doing there? According to Austen we are to conclude that no matter how isolated and insulated the English place (e.g., Mansfield Park), it requires overseas sustenance. Sir Thomas's property in the Caribbean would have had to be a sugar plantation maintained by slave labor (not abolished until the 1830s): these are not dead historical facts but, as Austen certainly knew, evident historical realities. (89)

Mansfield Park, Said argues, is a novel 'based in an England relying for the maintenance of its style on a Caribbean island.' And it is precisely because 'Austen is so summary in one context [yet] so provocatively rich in the other,' precisely because of this 'imbalance,' that the critic is able to 'move in on the novel, [to] reveal and accentuate the interdependence scarcely mentioned on its brilliant pages' (96).[7] Turning to *Dom Casmurro*, we see the same imbalance or disparity, whereby the reality of slavery, which was simply unavoidable in nineteenth-century Rio, is relegated to the background of the novel, while the prosperity and 'culture' it enabled occupies almost the entire field of representation. Any references to slaves that we do encounter are notable for their brevity, as demonstrated by the following examples:

> One of my oldest memories is of seeing [Uncle Cosme] every morning mounting the [mule] given him by my mother ... The slave who had

---

7 In *Atlas of the European Novel*, it is worth noting, Franco Moretti chooses to emphasize both the narratological and symbolic function served by the colonies in *Mansfield Park*. Sir Thomas goes to Antigua because his absence makes the narrative itself possible – and he goes to the Caribbean *specifically* so that the 'link between the wealth of the élite and the "multitude of labouring poor" of contemporary England can be easily severed' (27).

gone to get it from the stable held the reins while he lifted his foot and placed it in the stirrup. (13–14)

[Capitu] was speaking low; she took my hand and put a finger to my lips. A slave woman, who came from inside the house to light the lamp in the corridor, seeing us like that, almost in the dark, laughed sympathetically and murmured, loud enough for us to hear it, something that I did and didn't understand. (78)

It was the morning of a beautiful day. The slave-children were whispering to each other; the women came to take their blessing. (99)

Like the island of Antigua in *Mansfield Park*, however, these slaves are 'both incidental, referred to only in passing, and absolutely crucial to the action,' for the socioeconomic privilege of the Santiago family, their elevated position within Rio society, and the 'style' in which they are accustomed to living are all dependent on the wealth generated by the slave trade. Until the age of two, Bento had lived on a sugar plantation in Itaguaí (a small town roughly sixty-five kilometres west of Rio). Then, when his father died, Bento's mother 'sold the old plantation and the slaves, bought some more that she sent out to work or hired out, bought a dozen buildings and a quantity of government bonds, and settled down in [Rio]' (15). The slave economy is what enables the family to live in the way that it does; but it is also what makes the novel itself possible, for without this economic substructure our narrator would not have had the leisure to produce the 'memoir' we are reading (to 'put down on paper the reminiscences that [came] into [his] head' [7]). And just as the family relies on slavery for the maintenance of its privileged lifestyle, so the narrative relies on this system for the maintenance of its *discursive* style, whose prodigious erudition offers thinly encoded evidence of the very same privilege. Over the course of the novel, to provide just a few examples, there are references to Goethe's *Faust* (6), Tacitus (78), the *Iliad* (114), Lucian's *True History* (121), Montaigne's *Essays* (128), José de Alencar (136), *Othello* (226–27), Wagner (178), Camões' *Lusiads* (183), Victor Hugo's 'Tristesse d'Olympio' (199), João de Barros (203), Dante's *Purgatorio* (219), Plato's *Phaedo* (228), and so on. To recall Said, then, the imbalance between Machado's passing references to slavery and his careful delineation of the economic (and cultural) privilege it enables, this 'odd combination of casualness and stress,' serves to 'reveal and accentuate the interdependence' between the two – but only to the attentive reader, not to Bento himself, who does everything he can to ignore the anachronistic social realities underlying his liberal values, his socioeconomic status, and his profound immersion in European culture.

Instead, he chooses to focus on Capitu, and on the growing sense of jealousy that she provokes. It all begins when the family *agregado* (or 'retainer'), José Dias, describes Capitu's eyes as being 'a bit like a gypsy's, oblique and sly' (48). And then not long afterward, while visiting Bento in the seminary, he reports that she has been 'as happy as ever [during his absence]; she's a giddy little thing. Just waiting to find some local beau to marry her …' This comment inspires in Bento, for the first time, 'a cruel, unknown feeling, pure jealousy' (117) – a feeling that will become increasingly pathological as the novel progresses. Even after he leaves the seminary and they are married, Bento grows intensely jealous if a man so much as glances in Capitu's direction (136), or if she wears short sleeves in public (183), or if her mind wanders while her husband is delivering a lecture on astronomy (184–87). In short, as he himself concedes, he becomes completely consumed by this irrational feeling:

> [I]t's natural for you to ask me if, having been so jealous of her [when I was younger], I didn't go on being so in spite of my son and the passing years. Yes, sir, I did. I went on being so, to such a point that the least gesture alarmed me, the tiniest word, any kind of insistence on a point; often mere indifference was enough. *I came to be jealous of everything and everyone.* A neighbor, a waltz partner, any man, young or old, filled me with terror or mistrust. (196; my italics)

Finally, when his friend Escobar dies, Bento decides that he and Capitu had been conducting an illicit affair, and that his son, Ezequiel, was in fact a product of this liaison. Refusing to listen to reason, and absolutely certain of the boy's filial resemblance to his dead friend, Bento takes both mother and child to Europe, where he establishes them in Switzerland before returning, alone, to Brazil. Some time later, we learn parenthetically of Capitu's death in exile ('I don't think I've said that she was dead and buried' [239]), and after a brief visit to Rio as a young man, Ezequiel also dies, having contracted typhoid during an archaeological dig in Palestine. To the very end, however, Bento is unswayed and unforgiving – utterly convinced that his 'first love and [his] best friend, both so affectionate and so beloved … ended up joining together and deceiving [him]' (244).

As with the anger that dominated *Midaq Alley*, the curiously overdetermined and undermotivated nature of Bento's jealousy encourages us to look elsewhere for its ultimate source – and to consider the possibility that the ostensible causes we find on the surface of the narrative may in fact be concealing something far deeper and far more troubling. Or to put it another way, when we encounter a disproportionate emotion of this kind ('I came to be jealous of everything and everyone'), we may be inclined to search for a more plausible motivation, one that would restore a measure of proportionality to the feeling in question and allow us to make sense of the narrative's governing affective logic. In this particular instance, as suggested above, I would identify the practice of slavery as one of the underlying social causes of Bento's pathological jealousy. If you remember, the conflict between the liberal principles of the élite and their status as the direct beneficiaries of the last slave-owning economy in the Western world compelled them to misrecognize or ignore the true nature of their own social reality. We see this quite clearly in *Dom Casmurro*, where the slaves, who are essential both to the survival of the family and to the very existence of the novel itself, are relegated to the periphery of the narrative, subjected to a deliberate process of erasure so that the ideological contradiction they represent will also be eliminated. At one level, then, we could regard Bento's jealousy as an emotional analogue for the collective distortion of reality that occurred during the *Segundo Reinado* – this inability (or refusal) to acknowledge the mutually incompatible nature of slavery and modernity. At another level, however, one could argue that Bento is subliminally aware of this contradiction, this collective misrecognition of reality, and that this too contributes to the displaced feeling of jealousy he experiences. In other words, Bento may very well suspect that there is something happening in front of him – or just around the corner – that he simply cannot see, a fundamental betrayal of everything he values. But because this 'something' remains opaque to him, the anxieties provoked by this vague intimation of betrayal, of concealment, of duplicity, migrate from the public sphere to the private, where they resurface in the form of the pathological jealousy that we have been discussing.[8]

Along with slavery, another one of the colonial continuities that

---

[8] Such duplicity would eventually become proverbial. In 1831, the Brazilian government, under international pressure to respect an earlier Anglo-Brazilian treaty (1826), introduced a law that banned the importation of slaves and declared free any slave entering the country after that date (Bethell and Carvalho 62). Within Brazil, however, it was generally understood that this law would not be enforced; and it has since given rise to the common Brazilian expression, *para inglês ver* ('for the English to see'), which is used to describe something that has been done for the sake of appearances but in reality changes nothing (Holloway 6).

survived well into the *Segundo Reinado* was that of patronage, which ensured the ongoing dependence of the subordinate classes on the 'benevolence' of the élite.[9] As a consequence, during this period, the principle of favour infiltrated even the deepest recesses of society. 'Under a thousand forms and names,' Roberto Schwarz writes,

> [it] formed and flavoured the whole of the national life, excepting always the basic productive relationship [of slavery] which was secured by force. Favour was present everywhere, combining itself with more or less ease to administration, politics, industry, commerce, the life of the city, the court, and so on. Even professions, such as medicine, or forms of skilled labor, such as printing, which in Europe were on the whole free of favour, were among us governed by it. As the professional depended on favour to exercise his profession, so the small proprietor depended on it for the security of his property, and the public servant for his position. ('Misplaced' 22)

Like slavery, such patronage was fundamentally incompatible with the principles of European liberalism. Yet in this case, through a kind of ideological sleight of hand, the élite were able to reconcile the two, using the latter to justify or 'endorse' the former. As Schwarz notes, this strategy would also bring about a collective distortion of reality, one that in many ways replicated the delusional qualities of pathological jealousy:

> Once the European [ideologies] took hold, they could serve, and very often did, as a justification, nominally 'objective,' for what was unavoidably arbitrary in the practice of favour. Real as it was, the antagonism vanished into thin air ... Liberalism, which had been an ideology well grounded in appearances, came to stand for *the conscious desire to participate in a reality that appearances did not sustain* ... In this way ... the test of reality and coherence did not seem to be decisive ... [O]ne could methodically call dependence independence, capriciousness utility, exceptions universality, kinship merit, privilege equality, and so on. By linking itself to the practice of what, in principle, it should criticize, liberalism caused thought to lose its footing. ('Misplaced' 23–24; my italics)

In *Dom Casmurro*, evidence of such favour, whether requested or granted, can be found everywhere ('These are the favors of worthy people' [50]; 'I

---

9 For a detailed analysis of the connection between patronage and politics in nineteenth-century Brazil, see R. Graham.

still had another promise owing and a favor pending' [68]; 'It was a great favor, and not the only one' [178], etc.). But the character who serves as the most obvious representative of favour in the novel – indeed, as the very personification of this anachronistic social principle – is José Dias, the Santiago family's *agregado*.[10] The figure of the *agregado* occupied a curiously ambivalent position within nineteenth-century Brazilian society. They were not slaves, not quite, but they were not entirely free either. They would often spend their lives working for the same family, yet they received no formal wages for their labour – depending, instead, on the more arbitrary and unreliable patronage of their employers.[11] Many *agregados* would develop close ties with these families, becoming 'honorary' members of the household; and yet, even so, they could be dismissed at any time and were obliged to show complete deference to those they served.[12] We see this in the case of José Dias too. 'He had lived with us as a dependent for many years,' Bento says, 'accept[ing] food and lodging with no … stipend, other than what [we] might be pleased to give him on festival days … He had the gift of making himself amenable and indispensable; when he wasn't there, it was almost as if a member of the family was missing.' And as the years passed, we are told, 'he acquired a certain authority in the family: or at least, people would listen to what he had to say; he didn't overdo it, and knew how to give his opinion submissively' (11–12).

As we have established, then, favour achieved a certain ubiquity during the *Segundo Reinado*, making its presence felt at almost every level of Brazilian society; and as a consequence, I would like to suggest, jealousy became one of the dominant structures of feeling within the

---

10 The term *agregado* (often translated as 'retainer') is actually an abbreviation of the formal phrase, used by the patron, *agregado à minha família* ('attached to my family') (R. Graham 20).

11 In 1870, for instance, one such employer said that her *agregada*, a young widow with a seven-month-old baby, 'live[s] by [my] favor because I took pity when I saw her poverty, but … only as long as she behaves well and works at something that makes it worth giving her some salary besides [her] food' (qtd. in S. Graham 92).

12 Machado's father, Francisco José de Assis, was himself an *agregado* and the son of freed slaves. He and his wife, a woman of Portuguese origin who worked as a washerwoman, served a wealthy family in the Morro do Livramento district of Rio. In due course, the female head of the family, Dona Maria José de Mendonça Barroso Pereira, would become Machado's godmother – 'underscoring,' as Lília Moritz Schwarcz writes, 'how bonds of dependency were formed and favors were exchanged' (14).

Affective Disorders

empire ('caus[ing] thought to lose its footing').¹³ In any society based on a system of patronage, competition among those vying for favour is inevitable, and even once such favour has been granted, there is always a fear that it may be withheld or offered to some other party instead. Needless to say, this competitive quality is also a defining feature of jealousy. As the philosopher Aaron Ben-Ze'ev observes, jealousy involves 'specific, not general, competition with a third party.' It 'stems from the desire to be "favored" in some respect and [from] the suspicion that it is not merely the case that one is not favored, but that another person is being favored more.' In short, when we feel jealous, 'we are afraid of losing our present favorable position to someone else and of ending up in an inferior position' (41). A number of characters in *Dom Casmurro* demonstrate such competitive tendencies, but none more so than José Dias. Whenever possible, he denigrates the family's neighbour, Capitu's father, Pádua, who has also been obliged to compete for the Santiagos' favour; and this animosity becomes particularly pronounced on the day of the Eucharistic procession (described in Chapter XXX). Both José Dias and a young Bento have decided to accompany the procession, and so they make their way to the Church of Santo Antônio dos Pobres:

> [Pádua] saw us [in the church] and came over to greet us. José Dias gave an irritated gesture, and barely replied with one brief word: he was looking at the priest, who was washing his hands. Then, as Pádua was talking to the sacristan in a low voice, he went nearer; I did the same thing. Pádua was asking the sacristan if he could carry one of the poles of the canopy. José Dias asked for one for himself:
> 'There's only one available,' said the sacristan.
> 'That one then,' said José Dias.
> 'But I'd asked first,' ventured Pádua.
> 'You asked first, but you came in late,' retorted José Dias. 'I was already here. You carry a candle.'
> Pádua, for all he was afraid of José Dias, insisted that he wanted the pole, all this in a low, muted voice. The sacristan found a way of contenting both rivals, taking it on himself to ask one of the other carriers of the poles to give up his to Pádua ... He did so, but José Dias upset this arrangement too. No, since there was another pole

---

13 Not that this feeling was necessarily unique to the *Segundo Reinado*. After visiting Rio in 1819, for example, one traveller wrote, rather disapprovingly, that jealousy 'obtain[ed] unbounded influence over the minds of many ... Brazilians, and operate[d] in some instances to such a degree that its victims [were] degraded much below the savage' (Henderson 77).

available, he asked for it to be given to me, a 'young seminarist,' who had a better right to this honor. Pádua went as pale as the candles ...
  'Very well, I give way to our Bentinho,' [he] sighed. (56)

What really motivates José Dias in this scene is the overriding principle of favour and the competitive impulse – the jealousy – that it generates. The 'special distinction' that attaches to the canopy '[comes] from the fact that it cover[s] the priest and the Sacrament,' whereas 'anyone could carry a candle' (56). So by securing the canopy poles for himself and Bento, José Dias has demonstrated his superior position within the hierarchy of patronage, leaving poor old Pádua to 'gnaw his candle with bitterness' – '[a] metaphor, no doubt,' Bento concedes, 'but [he] can think of no better way of conveying [his] neighbor's pain and humiliation' (57).

If you recall, I suggested several pages ago that Bento's sense of betrayal migrates from the public sphere (where it arises out of certain ideological incongruities) to the private sphere (where it becomes personalized, attached to neighbours or waltz partners or 'any man, young or old' [196]). In the case of patronage and favour, we are able to trace an identical trajectory, one that also defies the boundary separating the public sphere from the private. If we turn to the *Oxford English Dictionary*, we find jealousy described as 'a state of mind arising from the suspicion, apprehension, or knowledge of rivalry,' and this definition is divided into two additional subcategories. We have the kind of jealousy that relates to 'success or advantage': the fear of 'losing some good through the rivalry of another; [or] resentment or ill-will towards another on account of advantage or superiority, possible or actual, on his [or her] part.' And then we have jealousy 'in love': the fear of 'being supplanted in the affection ... of a beloved person, esp[ecially] a wife, husband, or lover.' The former definition would seem to relate to the public sphere (where one is more likely to encounter such competition and rivalry), while the latter obviously relates to the private sphere (the realm of love, romance, and sexuality). In *Dom Casmurro*, however, we witness a slippage between these two categories, a rupture of the traditional boundary separating *casa e rua*.[14]

14 As Sandra Lauderdale Graham has pointed out, the distinction between the private space of the 'house' (*casa*) and the public space of the 'street' (*rua*) carried particular significance during this period. 'Threaded through all the concerns of domestic living [in nineteenth-century Rio],' she writes, 'were the contrasting images of *casa e rua*, or house and street, by which contemporaries located and, by locating, interpreted everyday actions

Affective Disorders

As a consequence of Brazil's archaic social configuration during the *Segundo Reinado*, jealousy became a dominant structure of feeling within society at large, one that emerged out of the widespread competition for patronage. We see this most clearly in the case of José Dias, who jealously competes for the favour of his superiors (indeed, one could argue that it is an essential part of the 'emotional labour' that he is obliged to perform as an *agregado*).[15] So it is not particularly surprising, given the ubiquity of this feeling in the public sphere, that Bento should also experience jealous impulses. But as he has no need for patronage or favour, as he already occupies a privileged position within Brazilian society (albeit one that must be 'jealously' guarded), these impulses are displaced into the private sphere, where they eventually resurface in the form of romantic jealousy – the unsubstantiated conviction that he has been betrayed by his first love and his best friend.

III

We have thus far been discussing the contradiction between the anachronistic social realities of nineteenth-century Brazil (namely, slavery and patronage) and the liberal principles associated with European modernity. I have suggested that this dissonance, along with the competitive nature of patronage, gives rise to the pathological jealousy that Bento, the narrator of *Dom Casmurro*, experiences. But how does this jealousy in turn influence the narrative's production of meaning? What are the primary discursive consequences of this particular 'affective disorder'? Under certain circumstances, feelings of jealousy may well be justified; more often, though, it is an emotional state that very quickly becomes disproportionate and may also involve a distortion of reality. In a 1922 essay on the subject, Freud divided jealousy into three different categories: normal, projected, and delusional. 'Although we may call it normal,' he wrote of the first category, 'this jealousy is by no means completely rational, that is,

---

and encounters. House signified a secure and stable domain. To house belonged the enduring relationships of family or blood kin. To street belonged uncertain or temporary alliances in which identity could not be assumed but had to be established. Street was suspect, unpredictable, a dirty or dangerous place' (4). For more on the fundamental distinction between *casa e rua*, see Freyre 35–37.

15 For more on the subject of emotional labour, or the commodification of feeling, see Hochschild.

derived from the actual situation, proportionate to the real circumstances and under the complete control of the conscious ego,' for it is 'rooted deep in the unconscious' and arises out of the 'earliest stirrings of the child's affective life' ('Some' 223).[16] In the case of *Dom Casmurro*, I have located the source of Bento's jealousy elsewhere, yet it certainly demonstrates the irrational and disproportionate qualities that Freud describes here (and, remember, this is his definition of *normal* jealousy). As the novel progresses, moreover, the pathological jealousy that emerges out of the aforementioned contradiction between slavery and liberalism creates a corresponding disjuncture between the story (i.e., the signified) and the discourse (the signifier) – one that ultimately serves as a discursive correlative for the ideological dissonance that plagued Brazilian society during the *Segundo Reinado*. In the nineteenth-century Bildungsroman, as we saw earlier, a strong sense of illusion often characterizes the level of story (where our heroes struggle to identify the basic principles governing the society in which they hope to find a place for themselves), while an air of confidence, maturity, and realism dominates the discourse. In *Dom Casmurro*, by contrast, the reader gradually comes to realize that this dynamic has been inverted. Here, the underlying story is associated with reality ('what really happened'), while the discourse (what Bento believes to be true) assumes an increasingly delusional and distorted quality.

Before going any further, I should probably clarify my understanding of the relationship between story and discourse. It is a matter of some critical convenience, and essential to our readerly pleasure, that story should be seen to precede (and therefore determine) discourse. But

---

16 According to Freud, jealousy is 'one of those affective states, like grief, that may be described as normal. If anyone appears to be without it, the inference is justified that it has undergone severe repression and consequently plays all the greater part in his unconscious mental life' ('Some' 223). *Projected jealousy*, on the other hand, is to be considered neurotic, for it is 'derived in both men and women either from their own actual unfaithfulness in real life or from impulses towards it which have succumbed to repression' and subsequently been projected onto their partner. *Delusional jealousy* also 'has its origin in repressed impulses towards unfaithfulness; but the object in these cases is of the same sex as the subject.' In other words, Freud argues, this form of jealousy is 'what is left of a homosexuality that has run its course, and it rightly takes its position among the classical forms of paranoia. As an attempt at defence against an unduly strong homosexual impulse it may, in a man, be described in the formula: "*I* do not love him, *she* loves him!"' (224–25).

as we noted in Chapter 2, this is not always so. Every narrative is in fact a product of a 'double logic' – the logic of story and the logic of discourse – with neither category being consistently privileged over the other. At certain times, the course of a narrative may be determined by the logic of the story; yet at other times, this priority is challenged when the imperatives of the discourse itself come to the fore, definitively influencing the narrative's trajectory. As Jonathan Culler observes, it is impossible to synthesize these two competing forces as they stand in 'irreconcilable opposition' (*Pursuit* 208) to one another, 'each work[ing] by the exclusion of the other' and 'each depend[ing] on a hierarchical relation between story and discourse which the other inverts' (195). In the opening pages of *Dom Casmurro*, a straightforward mimetic relationship between story and discourse is established; but over time, this superficial alliance comes under increasing pressure, and we begin to suspect that the 'natural' correspondence between the two categories may be deceptive. So when Bento finally accuses his wife of infidelity on page 230, for example, or describes her eyes as 'sly [and] oblique' for the third time on page 244, we are no longer inclined to believe what we are being told.

Given the fact that Bento is the narrative's sole focalizing figure, though, one might wonder how it is possible to distinguish between story and discourse in this way – particularly if we are associating the former with reality and the latter with illusion. In order to address this issue, I would like to refer, just briefly, to the linguist Paul Grice's cooperative principle. Writing in 1967, Grice argued that every conversational exchange is governed by four separate categories of rules and subrules (regarding Quantity, Quality, Relation, and Manner). Under the category of Quality, for instance, he included the rules 'Do not say what you believe to be false' and 'Do not say that for which you lack adequate evidence' (27). Yet even if a speaker appears to be violating one of the rules that fall within these four categories, it is still possible to make sense of his or her utterance – and to assume that he or she is not violating the cooperative principle itself – if we recognize the 'implicature' that such a statement generates. (Irony, of course, is one rhetorical device that operates in this way, creating a recognizable discrepancy between the literal and intended meanings of an utterance.) As Mary Louise Pratt has suggested, it is also possible to apply this principle to literary discourse, in which case it becomes 'hyperprotected' – thus guaranteeing that even if the narrator violates one of these rules and thereby jeopardizes the cooperative principle, 'the jeopardy is almost certainly only mimetic' as the narrative's 'cooperation' can ultimately 'be restored by [discursive] implicature' (215). More specifically:

> [W]hen a fictional speaker [violates the cooperative principle], it will usually be the case that the [discourse] is implicating things in addition to what the fictional speaker is saying or implicating ... In [such instances], it is not only the experiences reported which are unusual and problematic, but the report itself. The verbal version the speaker offers fails to elicit our understanding of events or our agreement with the speaker's interpretation of events. The fictional speaker thus produces a lack of consensus, and the [discourse] implicates that *this lack of consensus is part of what [it] is displaying*, part of what [it] wants us to experience, evaluate, and interpret. (Pratt 199; my italics)

This, I would argue, is precisely what occurs in *Dom Casmurro*. In those places where Bento could be said to violate the cooperative principle, by misinterpreting or distorting the substance of the story he is telling, the primacy of the principle is restored by the discourse itself, so that the disparity – the 'lack of consensus' – between story and discourse becomes the very message we are expected to receive. Although the story we are told emerges out of the discourse (as every story does), in this case it ultimately serves to undermine, *by way of implicature*, the credibility of its own discursive framing. In other words, to paraphrase Grice, what is said in *Dom Casmurro* may be false; but what is implicated is almost certainly true (39). And this, finally, is what enables us to distinguish between story (what is implicated) and discourse (what is actually said), with the former falling under the category of the real and the latter being associated with illusion, with our narrator's tragic misrecognition of his actual diegetic circumstances.[17]

By now the connection between these narratological issues and the ideological dissonance that characterized nineteenth-century Brazilian society ought to be clear. During the *Segundo Reinado*, we also find a convergence of opposing 'logics' – one archaic, the other contemporary – which could not be adequately synthesized as 'each work[ed] by the exclusion of the other' and 'each depend[ed] on a hierarchical relation ... which the other invert[ed]' (Culler, *Pursuit* 195). During these years, we

---

17 I should note here that Pratt herself offers *Dom Casmurro* as an example of a narrative that violates the cooperative principle (194–98). And for a reading of Machado's *Posthumous Memoirs* that also discusses this principle, see Scott, *On Lightness* 39–63.

Affective Disorders

can also identify a 'lack of consensus' between the true nature of the country's economic substructure and the way in which it was perceived by its primary beneficiaries. And during these years, we also encounter a reality that served to undermine the credibility of its own (ideological) framing. Allow me to clarify, if I may, this last correspondence. In nineteenth-century Brazil, the principles of European liberalism obviously served to delegitimize the practices of slavery and patronage (for those who were willing to recognize such an incongruity). But as Roberto Schwarz quite rightly indicates, the reverse was also true. 'Since they are necessary to the organization and identity of the new state and of the élite,' he writes, the principles of liberalism

> represent progress. [Yet] they express *nothing* of the reality of actual labor relationships, which these liberal ideas either reject or fail to recognize *in principle*, not that this prevents the élite from living with them quite congenially. From this stems a special kind of modus operandi that has no obligations to the cognitive and critical duties of liberalism, all of which undermines the latter's credibility and gives it, along with its enlightened side, an aura of the *gratuitous*, the *incongruous*, and the *iniquitous*. (*Master* 21–22)

In short, during this period of Brazilian history, there was a clear contradiction between the archaic modes of production on which the economy was based and the 'modern' values to which the élite ostensibly subscribed. And the fact that these imported ideologies could be made to accommodate the practice of slavery, the fact that they could happily coexist with such a moral scandal, rendered them at once gratuitous, incongruous, and iniquitous. If we return to *Dom Casmurro*, we will be able to identify a similar dynamic – for not only does the growing disparity between story and discourse serve to invalidate the latter, revealing the unreliability of our delusional narrator, but *the discourse itself also assumes a heightened degree of discursivity* and, in so doing, forces us to question the veracity (and legitimacy) of the very narrative we are reading.[18]

One could accumulate numerous examples of the way in which the novel, at the representational level, consistently emphasizes its own

---

18 When I use the term 'discursivity,' I am referring to two basic characteristics of narrative discourse: (1) the various qualities that distinguish discourse from story (semiotic codes, linguistic structures, rhetorical strategies, etc.), and (2) the degree to which any given narrative emphasizes or acknowledges these discursive qualities.

discursivity. In Chapter CXXIX, for instance, Bento directly addresses Escobar's widow, assuming that she is still alive at the time of writing. 'Dona Sanchez,' he says,

> I ask you not to read this book; or if you've read it thus far, drop the rest. All you need to do is shut it; better still, burn it, to avoid the temptation of opening it again. If, in spite of the warning, you go to the end, it's your fault; I can't answer for the harm that may be done. (218–19)

But I am more interested in the formal or structural consequences of the ideological dissonance we have been discussing, and of the pathological jealousy to which it gives rise. Before concluding, then, I would like to offer two examples of the way in which 'what is told' in *Dom Casmurro* comes to be distorted or disfigured by 'the way it is told'; and in order to do so, I shall be employing some of the narratological categories that have been delineated, with such precision and subtlety, by Gérard Genette.

A story, as we have defined it, always follows a chronological trajectory, yet it is often the case that discourse, in the 'retelling,' will rearrange this chronology – thus creating a distinction between 'story time' and 'discourse time.' As Genette notes, such a distinction implicitly assumes 'the existence of a kind of zero degree that would be a condition of perfect temporal correspondence between [discourse] and story'; however, this 'point of reference is more hypothetical than real' (36). In fact, almost every narrative employs what Genette calls *anachronies*: 'various types of discordance between the two orderings of story and [discourse]' (36). So rather than being a question of whether or not a narrative makes use of such anachronies, it is really a question of degree – a question of frequency and salience. Although *Dom Casmurro* follows a largely linear trajectory, whenever the discourse does produce an anachronic sequence, it proves particularly disruptive and only serves to reinforce a lingering sense of narratorial unreliability. At the end of Chapter CXXX, for example, we are offered a rather strange apology:

> I beg your pardon, but this chapter should have been preceded by another, recounting an incident that happened a few weeks earlier ... I'll write it now; I could insert it before this one, before I send the book to the press, but it's a great nuisance to alter the page numbers; [so] I'll leave [it] as it is, and then the narration will go straight on to the end. (220)

Affective Disorders

This passage is followed by a brief, analeptic chapter (entitled 'Before the Previous One'), which takes us back to the beginning of 1872. And on pages 144–46, we find a corresponding episode of internal prolepsis that is also explicitly acknowledged.[19] 'Here,' Bento says,

> I come to a point that I hoped would come later, so much so that I was already considering at what point I should dedicate a chapter to it. Really, I should not have said now what I only ... discovered later; but since I have touched on the matter, it's better to be finished with it. (144)

In *Dom Casmurro*, then, the number of anachronies may fall within the average range, but when they do appear, they are foregrounded to such a degree that we are left to ponder the more general credibility of our poor, confused narrator – and of the narrative he produces, which never quite manages to 'naturalize' its own chronology.

Another disparity that typically distinguishes story time from discourse time is that of duration or tempo. Once more, we have a 'hypothetical reference zero,' whereby a narrative would maintain an unchanging tempo that corresponds perfectly with that of the story. Yet as Genette observes, it is rather hard to imagine such a narrative, one that would 'admit of no variation in speed' (88). Instead, we inevitably encounter *anisochronies*: variations in tempo, ranging from descriptive pauses to ellipses (in which a period of story time is completely elided), with two contrasting intermediaries – scenes (or mimetic sequences) and summaries (diegetic sequences). In the latter case, it should be noted, the narrative tempo can vary widely; and in *Dom Casmurro*, this is precisely what it does. Although Bento's narration maintains a fairly steady pace for much of the novel, oscillating between mimetic scenes and diegetic summaries, on page 172 he suddenly discovers that he has made a grave miscalculation:

> This should have been the middle of the book, but my inexperience has let my pen run away with me, and I have come almost to the end of the paper, with the best of the story still to tell. There's no way for it now but to take it in great strides, chapter after chapter, with few corrections, not much reflection, everything in resumé. This chapter

---

19 In *Narrative Discourse*, Genette divides analepses (retrospective sequences) and prolepses (anticipatory sequences) into 'two classes, external and internal, depending on whether the point to which they reach is located outside or inside the temporal field of the [primary] narrative' (61).

already covers months, others will cover years, and so we will get to the end.

Bento, we soon realize, is as good as his word. The following chapter covers five years in total, summarizing his life from the age of eighteen to twenty-two in just a few sentences. At the beginning of Chapter CVIII, Ezequiel has not yet been conceived, but by the time it concludes he is already 'Christian and Catholic' (190). And the subsequent chapter, entitled 'An Only Son,' takes no more than half a page to 'bring him up to the age of five' (190). This sudden acceleration of narrative tempo not only serves to emphasize the disparity between story and discourse, but also encourages us to question the judgement of our narrator, his ability to distinguish between what carries genuine significance and value within the narrative and what should be considered mere filler.

As we saw in Chapter 2, Roland Barthes uses the term 'nuclei' to describe those episodes that 'constitute [the] real hinge points of [a] narrative,' and the term 'catalyzer' to label those occurrences that 'merely "fill in" the narrative space separating the [nuclei]' ('Introduction' 265). In literary narratives, a correspondence is typically established between the importance of the episode and the quantity (or tempo) of the discourse. When the narrative encounters an episode of some significance, in other words, it will decelerate, ensuring that this critical nucleus receives a share of the discourse that is directly proportionate to its 'hinge' value within the story as a whole. Consequently, the pacing of any given narrative, the story-discourse ratio, will usually provide the reader with a reasonably accurate sense of what carries significance within the narrative and what can be safely regarded as catalytic filler. In novelistic discourse, as Genette argues, the contrast of tempo 'between detailed scene and summary almost always reflect[s] a contrast of content between dramatic and nondramatic, the strong periods of the action coinciding with the most intense moments of the narrative while the weak periods [are] summed up with large strokes and as if from a great distance.' The typical literary narrative thus alternates between 'nondramatic summaries, functioning as waiting room and liaison, [and] dramatic scenes whose role in the action is decisive' (109–10).

Once the discourse accelerates on page 172 of *Dom Casmurro*, however, it becomes apparent to the reader that Bento is no longer capable of distinguishing between those episodes that serve a decisive function within the narrative (nuclei) and those that carry only limited value (catalyzers). Simply put, as a consequence of his pathological jealousy, the narrative's story-discourse ratio loses its proportionality, and it too becomes increasingly unbalanced. Many years before, when he and Capitu were still young, a sweet-seller would pass through Matacavalos, singing a mournful refrain:

> Cry, little girl, cry,
> Got no money to buy ... (37)

In the latter stages of the novel, Bento becomes obsessed by this memory, and by the fact that Capitu can no longer remember the song. He acknowledges that it is a 'trivial subject, and ... not worth the trouble of one chapter, let alone two' (198); but that is exactly what he dedicates to this inconsequential matter.[20] Elsewhere, similarly, he describes in (relative) detail an occasion on which he did *not* end up poisoning some stray dogs (194). Yet when Capitu eventually dies, this tragic event, which should really dominate the conclusion, is only afforded a parenthetical sentence or two. And the description we are given of Ezequiel's death, a couple of pages later, is equally concise: '[He] died of a typhoid fever,' we learn, 'and was buried in the vicinity of Jerusalem' (242). These misjudged anisochronies – whereby an episode of minimal significance, or none whatsoever, is afforded a disproportionate share of the discourse, while a crucial occurrence (such as Capitu's premature demise) is passed over as quickly as possible – provide compelling evidence of Bento's deteriorating psychological state. Like the aforementioned anachronies, they also serve to emphasize the discursivity of the narrative, and the extent to which that discourse has misrecognized, and ultimately distorted, the reality of the story it is telling. But these anisochronies do something else as well. They demonstrate quite clearly the way in which the discourse has internalized many of the qualities that Roberto Schwarz associates with the liberal values that were so thoroughly discredited during the *Segundo Reinado*. If you remember, as a consequence of their incompatibility with the social reality of the period, these ideologies assumed, in Schwarz's words, 'an aura of the *gratuitous*, the *incongruous*, and the *iniquitous*' (*Master* 22). And precisely the same thing could be said of

---

20 It is particularly ironic that Bento should belabour this issue given his own tendency, as narrator, to defy the convention of the 'perfect memory' (Romberg 98) – thus undermining still further his narratorial credibility. '[T]here is only one way of putting one's essence onto paper,' he says in Chapter LXVIII, 'and that is by telling it all, the good and the bad ... For example, now that I have recounted a sin, I would happily tell the story of some good deed done at that time, if I could remember one, but I can't; [so] it can wait for a better opportunity' (128–29).

Jealousy

the discourse in *Dom Casmurro*. When it describes the non-poisoning of a stray dog, it becomes gratuitous. When it dedicates two whole chapters to a song that has not been heard for forty years, it becomes incongruous. And when it reduces the death of this unjustly maligned woman to a single declarative utterance ('she was dead and buried'), it becomes deeply iniquitous.

IV

At the beginning of this chapter, I described some of the characteristic features of the early nineteenth-century Bildungsroman. According to Franco Moretti, many such narratives establish a tangible distinction between illusion and reality, with the former occupying the level of story and the latter occupying the level of discourse. In the pages that followed, I suggested that *Dom Casmurro* reverses this dynamic – reality being associated with the world of the story, while the discourse (i.e., Bento's narration) assumes an increasingly delusional quality. Having reached the end of the chapter, I would like to return, for a moment, to the subject of the Bildungsroman. As the classic Bildungsroman concludes, the hero typically manages to reconcile the competing imperatives of self and society, autonomy and interdependence, the private and the public – and it is this moment of reconciliation, or synthesis, that completes his or her transition from youth to maturity. In early examples of the genre, Moretti argues, a state of maturity could be achieved within the world of the story; but by the time we reach Balzac, in the 1830s, this traditional generic objective is no longer available to the characters themselves, having migrated instead to the 'disembodied world of the *narrator's* discourse' (*Way* 140). And what of Machado's *Dom Casmurro*? In this case, unfortunately, we can find no 'maturity' at all, either in the world of the story or that of the discourse; for if such maturity is to be associated with the repudiation of illusion and the reconciliation of opposites, if it involves a 'formative encounter with reality' (Moretti, *Way* 93), then it is clearly something that Bento has failed to achieve.[21]

---

21 We could usefully compare Bento, in this regard, to one of Stendhal's heroes. During the Bourbon Restoration (1814–30), France, like imperial Brazil, was a place of contradiction and incongruity. Everything, Moretti writes, was 'divide[d] in two, each value [was] opposed by one of equal importance.' And as a consequence of these sociocultural circumstances,

101

The evidence of this failure can be easily summarized. For a start, at the very foundation of the social structure, we have the conflict between the deplorable reality of slavery and the liberal ideologies to which the élite 'officially' subscribe. In order to live with this fundamental contradiction, they are obliged to render the true source of their privilege invisible – and this distortion of reality in the public sphere, I have argued, eventually penetrates the private sphere, where in *Dom Casmurro* it takes the form of a pathological 'romantic' jealousy. Here, too, we encounter acute discrepancies between reality and representation, ontology and epistemology; and these discrepancies, these irreconcilable opposites, ultimately infiltrate the structure of the narrative itself, creating a corresponding disjuncture between story and discourse. The two narratological examples I gave of this disjuncture – the strategies of anachrony and anisochrony – allow our argument to trace a full circle, for in this regard the discourse comes to resemble the 'illegitimate' liberal principles we discussed at the very beginning. On the one hand, that is to say, we have the social reality of the story itself, while on the other, we have a discursive structure that rapidly assumes 'an aura of the *gratuitous*, the *incongruous*, and the *iniquitous*' (Schwarz, *Master* 22).

In the classic Bildungsroman, as mentioned above, the hero is eventually able to reconcile these various incongruities and, in so doing, achieve a state of maturity – but not our Bento. Here, the maturity that serves as the primary generic objective of the Bildungsroman does not simply migrate from the world of the story to that of the discourse, as it does in Balzac (and arguably in Stendhal); *it abandons the narrative altogether*. And so we are left at the end of the novel with a proliferation of unresolved opposites: social reality versus liberal ideology, domestic fidelity versus pathological jealousy, and the logic of story versus the logic of discourse. Furthermore, the fact that none of these disparities have been resolved (or even recognized) by Bento constitutes another departure from the trajectory of the classic Bildungsroman, which typically follows the hero as he or she moves from a state of individual ignorance to one of social knowledge. In the final pages of *Dom Casmurro*, however, it becomes clear that our protagonist is just as deluded as he ever was (if not more so), and rather than finding his place in society,

---

Stendhal abandoned 'any idea of [dialectical] synthesis.' Instead of 'toning down the discordances and resolving the dilemmas' of Restoration society, he chose (like Machado) to 'accentuate the contradictions and even ... the absurdity of [his] subject matter' (*Way* 76).

like the hero of a traditional Bildungsroman, he has retreated into a state of almost complete isolation. 'I live alone,' he says, and 'go out little'; and on those rare occasions when he does leave the house, he 'seldom converse[s]' (4–6) with anyone. In short, we are told, Bento now 'live[s] at a distance' from the world and has 'tried to make people forget [him]' (238). But why should he have chosen to live like this? Why has he suddenly developed these agoraphobic tendencies? It is, I would argue, yet another way of avoiding or disregarding reality – a strategy that allows him to nullify the various discrepancies that we have addressed in this chapter. By retreating into silence and solitude, by rejecting the company of others, Bento is able to ignore the true nature of his social, domestic, and diegetic circumstances. He is able to turn away from the fundamental incongruities of his age, from the pathological jealousy that has destroyed his own life, and from the profound disparities that have disfigured the very narrative he has just finished writing.

CHAPTER FOUR

Boredom
Upamanyu Chatterjee's
English, August: An Indian Story

The only obligation to which in advance we may hold a novel ... is that it be interesting.

       Henry James, 'The Art of Fiction,' 1884

What seems beautiful to me, what I should like to write, is a book about nothing.

    Gustave Flaubert, Letter to Louise Colet, 16 January 1852

I

In the first chapter of Flaubert's *Sentimental Education* (1869), the novel's protagonist, Frédéric Moreau, takes a leisurely boat trip up the Seine. 'At every bend of the river,' we are told, 'the same curtain of pale poplars came into view. The countryside was deserted. Some little white clouds hung motionless in the sky, and a vague sense of boredom seemed to make the boat move more slowly and the passengers look even more insignificant than before' (17). As Peter Brooks has observed, this is hardly the most auspicious of opening sequences, for 'we as readers expect that voyages will lead somewhere, and that the voyagers who fare forth on them will make not only their goal but their experience along the way the source of significance.' Indeed, '[t]o be told that we are scarcely advancing, in the company of the insignificant, makes us wonder why we are to bother at all with a five-hundred-page novel'

(*Reading* 178). At certain junctures, readers of Upamanyu Chatterjee's *English, August: An Indian Story* (1988) may be inclined to ask themselves the same thing. Insofar as it could be said to 'do' anything at all, the novel chronicles the experiences of a young civil servant, Agastya Sen, who has been posted to the provincial town of Madna for a year's administrative training. But if the reader is expecting anything to *happen* during this purgatorial year in the provinces, if they are anticipating the usual pleasures of an unfolding narrative, they are likely to be sorely disappointed. Right from the outset, we are informed that '[t]he district life that [Agastya] lived and saw was the official life, deadly dull' (28). In the words of another civil service employee, 'It's sick [here], there's no one to talk to, no place to go, nothing to do, just come back to your room after office, get drunk, feel lonely, and jerk off' (88–89). And this is precisely what our hero does for one calendar year and 322 pages: masturbate, smoke marijuana, read Marcus Aurelius, and lie in bed 'staring blankly up at the ceiling' (77). Granted, he completes his training too, but these bureaucratic duties also turn out to be 'ineffably dull' (63) and inconsequential – stifling whatever proairetic possibilities the narrative may inadvertently generate as it inches toward its conclusion.

So where does all this leave us as readers? What are we supposed to make of a novel with such pronounced 'anti-proairetic' tendencies, one that gives absolute precedence to the boredom and banality of the non-occurrence? Where do these tendencies originate, and what impact do they ultimately have on the narrative's production of meaning? These are some of the questions that I shall seek to address in the present chapter. I will begin by arguing that the bureaucratic procedures of the Indian Administrative Service (IAS) are primarily responsible for generating the novel's entropic tendencies. This entropy, I would like to suggest, eventually leaks into the structure of the narrative itself, provoking a crisis of meaning and disruption of desire that very nearly brings it to the point of total collapse. Typically, as Leo Bersani writes, realism is supposed to do everything it can to achieve a 'commanding structure of significance' (53) and a full and final predication of meaning; but the leakage of negative affect in this case threatens to undermine both of these traditional generic imperatives. As the energy that drives the narrative forward dissipates, Agastya enters into a 'purely iterative existence … where the direction and movement of plot appear to be finished' (Brooks, *Reading* 122). Under these circumstances, to narrate one day is to narrate every day, and to narrate every day is to narrate the same day innumerable times – thus giving rise to the threat of interminability and the infinite deferral of meaning. In other words, I shall argue, by replicating the dilatory drag of bureaucratic procedure, the narrative itself internalizes many of the qualities that we tend to associate with the IAS: inefficiency, repetition, redundancy, interminability, and, above all, a uniquely bureaucratic combination of the 'bewildering and [the] boring' (Chatterjee 35).

II

At the time of independence in 1947, there was considerable debate in India as to whether the colonial bureaucratic apparatus, known as the Indian Civil Service (ICS), should be replaced by a central or provincial civil service. Many political representatives from the provinces favoured a decentralized bureaucracy that would allow for greater regional autonomy.[1] However, Vallabhbhai Patel, the country's first deputy prime minister, was convinced that a uniform administrative structure would discourage 'provincial susceptibilities' and provide a necessary counterbalance to the centrifugal forces that were believed to be threatening national unity. He therefore proposed that an 'all-India administrative service' should be established, one that would be 'efficient, impartial, and free from local or communal bias, party allegiance or political influence' (qtd. in Tummala 36). And so, in November 1949, having been ratified in Article 312 of the Indian Constitution, the IAS officially came into being.

Despite Patel's promises, however, the IAS would soon become notorious for its petty corruption, inefficiency, and 'rule-bound incompetence' (Nandy, 'Culture' 68) – a reputation it carries, with some justice, to this day. As one Indian government report issued in 2008 observes,

> For the common man [in India], bureaucracy denotes routine and repetitive procedures, paper work and delays. This, despite the fact that the Government and bureaucracy exist to facilitate the citizens in the rightful pursuit of their legal activities. Rigidities of the system, over-centralization of powers, highly hierarchical … functioning with a large number of intermediary levels delaying [the]

1 In 1946, for instance, Sir Khizar Hayat Khan, the premier of Punjab, declared that 'Punjab is one of those provinces which would prefer to have a superior service of their own instead of an all-India administrative service' (qtd. in Maheshwari 298).

finalization of any decision, divorce of authority from accountability and the tendency towards micromanagement have led to a structure in which form is more important than substance and procedures are valued over end results and outcomes. (Government of India 365)

The key sentence here, for our purposes, is the first one, which could also serve as a useful summary of Chatterjee's novel. Routine, repetitive procedures, and delays – these are the bureaucratic features around which *English, August* is structured and out of which the narrative's organizing quality of feeling emerges. For a start, everybody in the novel seems to be waiting for something. Whenever Agastya enters a government building, his eyes are drawn to the lines of people waiting patiently outside: 'On the left, [he could see] the old and shabby office buildings that had ignored all the decades of an undramatic history. The flags, patient in the heat … The people who waited for Government to be kind to them, in white dhoti, kurta and napkin' (54). Then there are the government employees themselves, many of whom, 'if posted away from home,' are simply biding their time until they are 'transferred to a [more] congenial place' (28). And of course, like everybody else, Agastya is also waiting: sitting through interminable meetings, staring blankly up at the ceiling, reading his Marcus Aurelius, and killing time until his year of training is complete.

The German term for boredom, *Langeweile* (literally, 'long while'), nicely encapsulates the sense of temporal 'elongation' that is typical of this particular affective state. 'In boredom,' Heidegger writes, 'the *while* [*Weile*] becomes *long* [*lang*] … The lengthening of the while is the *expansion of the temporal horizon*, whose expansion does not bring Dasein liberation or unburden it, but precisely the converse in *oppressing* it with its expanse' (*Fundamental* 152–53). Although we may feel this 'lengthening of the while' under a range of circumstances (such as attending a faculty meeting or listening to John Cage's 4'33"), it is most commonly associated with the experience of waiting. In his 1929–30 lecture series at the University of Freiburg, entitled 'The Fundamental Concepts of Metaphysics,' Heidegger structured his discussion of boredom around the following scenario:

> We are sitting … in the tasteless station of some lonely minor railway. It is four hours until the next train arrives. The district is uninspiring. We do have a book in our rucksack, though – shall we read? No. Or think through a problem, some question? We are unable to. We read the timetables or study the table giving the various distances from this station to other places we are not otherwise acquainted with

at all. We look at the clock – only a quarter of an hour has gone by. Then we go out onto the local road. We walk up and down, just to have something to do. But it is no use. Then we count the trees along the road, look at our watch again – exactly five minutes since we last looked at it. Fed up with walking back and forth, we sit down on a stone, draw all kinds of figures in the sand, and in so doing catch ourselves looking at our watch yet again – half an hour – and so on. (*Fundamental* 93)

This example of boredom could well have been taken from the pages of *English, August*, for the novel itself is really just one long description of waiting, of the oppressive 'expansion' of time and its various affective consequences.[2] As the days drift by, Agastya gradually lapses into a state of debilitating apathy and indifference: 'When he woke up he hardly heard the sounds of the morning. On some afternoons he couldn't leave the bed even to roll a smoke ... He wanted nothing, it seemed – only a peace, but that was too pompous a word' (152). Although he occasionally contemplates suicide, even 'looking for that kind of a cessation' (153) requires more energy and motivation than he currently possesses. For Agastya, in this lethargic state, nothing seems capable of carrying meaning or value, and as a consequence, it becomes increasingly difficult for him to take an interest in anything at all. The world, as Reinhard Kuhn writes in his classic study of ennui in Western literature, has been 'emptied of its significance. Everything is seen as if filtered through a screen; [and] what is filtered out and lost is precisely the element that gives meaning to existence' (12).[3] In a word, Agastya is bored, terribly bored, and this affective quality will have a profound influence over the narrative in which he figures – draining it too of its meaning, its energy, and its desire.

2 For more on the connection between waiting, 'prolonged time,' and boredom, see Majumdar 121–23; and for an insightful ethnographic analysis of waiting as a social, cultural, and political practice among the middle classes in Uttar Pradesh, see Jeffrey.
3 Kuhn is not alone in emphasizing the deprivation of meaning that we experience when we are bored. In her cultural history of the relationship between boredom and European modernity, for example, Elizabeth S. Goodstein describes boredom as 'an experience without qualities, [a] quotidian crisis of meaning' (1); and in his philosophical analysis of the subject, Lars Svendsen argues that boredom can be understood as 'a discomfort which communicates that the need for meaning is not being satisfied' (30).

Affective Disorders

If you remember, we have discussed the subject of narrative desire before, in Chapter 2, where I argued that *A Suitable Boy* forces the reader to renounce (or at least moderate) his or her desire for meaning and closure. In order to make this argument, I cited Peter Brooks, whose *Reading for the Plot* explores the way in which narratives both 'arouse and make use of desire as [a] dynamic of signification' (37). According to Brooks, every narrative possesses an internal energy that drives it forward, 'connecting beginning and end across the middle and making of that middle – what we read *through* – a field of force' (47). This energy, he suggests, is ultimately generated by a 'dynamic of desire' (38): 'the desire to wrest beginnings and ends from the uninterrupted flow of middles, from temporality itself; the search for that significant closure that would illuminate the sense of an existence, the meaning of life' (140). In *English, August*, however, as Brooks notes of *Sentimental Education*, 'there seems to be a problem of will,' an inability on the part of 'the hero to invest the world and his career with coherent and sustained desire' (175). Indeed, to an even greater degree than Frédéric Moreau, Agastya has lost the capacity to feel desire for *anything*, so deeply boring does he find his life in the provinces. It is not unusual that this should be the case, either, for as Patricia Meyer Spacks observes, boredom is a feeling that by its very nature 'opposes' desire:

> More precisely than repulsion, the negative form of desire, [boredom] constitutes desire's antithesis, assuring its victim of the utter impossibility of wishing for anything at all. The sufferer from boredom finds it impossible to invest fully in any action, to believe any action worth the effort of involvement ... Why bother? The hope of something new may dimly remain ... But a sense of futility precedes and forestalls endeavor. (259)[4]

As Chatterjee's novel progresses, this absence of desire gradually enters the narrative itself, inhibiting its progress, making of its middle not a field of force but a field of entropy and indolence. Or to put it another way, if we agree that boredom is the absence of desire (as Schopenhauer, for one, does), then *English, August* could be described not as a boring novel so much as a *bored* one – lacking the desire to

---

4 Similarly, in a 1934 essay, the psychoanalyst Otto Fenichel defined boredom as 'an unpleasurable experience of a lack of impulse' (292); and in a lecture delivered at the Collège de France in February 1980, Roland Barthes described it as 'a state without hate and without love, a loss of drive' (*Preparation* 271).

move toward its own conclusion, to engineer its own closure, and thus achieve a final discharge of meaning.[5] In fact, at various junctures, the narrative almost comes to a total standstill. Take the following passage, for example, in which Agastya arrives back in Madna after a brief trip to Delhi:

> [H]e unpacked slowly. He put back on the shelf the *Gita*, Marcus Aurelius, and his diary. He had hardly remembered them on his holiday ... He trimmed his beard slowly, with care. The lizards seemed to have multiplied greatly in his absence. The late-afternoon sun touched the cassettes on the table. He browsed through his diary. Now he had nothing to record. He picked up the *Madna District Gazetteer* from beside his canvas shoes on the bottom shelf. He read a paragraph or two, but the words didn't register. He then lay down to watch the ceiling. (200)

Agastya has nothing to record here; and nor, it would seem, does the novel's narrator. At this point, the narrative has almost completely stalled, lapsing into a series of insignificant micro-occurrences ('He trimmed his beard ... He browsed through his diary ... He picked up the *Madna District Gazetteer*,' etc.). Although each of these actions keeps the narrative alive, as it were, by sustaining its semantic tension, they do very little to carry it forward – never quite generating enough energy to move beyond the self-enclosed, self-foreclosing parameters of the paratactic utterance.[6]

In *S/Z*, Roland Barthes uses the term 'proairetic' to describe the logical sequences of action and behaviour that structure literary narratives (18–20). According to Barthes, the proairetic code is responsible (along with the hermeneutic code) for maintaining our interest in a story, for creating a kind of epistemophilia, a desire to know what the outcome of any narrative sequence will be. If a character does something (writes a love letter, say, or goes on a journey), the proairetic code determines that this action will have consequences of some kind, and one of the

5 '[L]ife,' Schopenhauer writes, 'swings like a pendulum to and fro between [desire] and boredom' (312).
6 One may be reminded here of Jean-Paul Sartre's stylistic analysis of Albert Camus' *The Stranger*, in which he argues that '[e]ach sentence refuses to exploit the momentum accumulated by preceding ones. Each is a new beginning. Each is like a snapshot of a gesture or object' ('Camus' 35). In other words, Sartre writes, 'the sentence has frozen ... Instead of acting as a bridge between past and future, it [has become] a small, isolated, self-sufficient substance' (39).

reasons we continue reading is to find out what these consequences might be, to find out just how the narrative sequence initiated by this action will ultimately be resolved. Needless to say, things do happen in *English, August*, narrative sequences are initiated, but these actions and the consequences they produce very rarely coalesce into anything resembling a 'plot' – and thus, like the remote locality to which Agastya has been posted, the narrative itself eventually assumes the 'enduring contours of underdevelopment' (278). In the passage cited above, for instance, Agastya initiates a proairetic sequence that we might label 'unpacking,' and in due course this sequence reaches its conclusion, but it does so almost imperceptibly, generating very little interest or narrative 'desire' in the reader, and discharging a minimal degree of meaning or significance within the narrative. We simply do not care about the outcome of such sequences, and in this respect, one could argue, the proairetic code has failed in its plot-making duties – or more precisely, perhaps, it has been subject to a process of attenuation that severely impedes the novel's teleological trajectory, its linear progress toward a 'desirable' and revelatory ending.

Over the course of the novel, Agastya's life becomes increasingly dominated by routine, further disrupting the narrative's trajectory. Everything he does, he does repeatedly, ritually, day in and day out, until it is not just the energy of the narrative that comes under threat but its very *narratability* – for as Barthes observes, 'to repeat excessively is to enter into loss, into the zero of the signified' (*Pleasure* 41).[7] Early in the novel, we are offered an entirely iterative account of Agastya's daily routine, as if the narrator were compressing a year of diary entries into a single chapter of twelve pages (75–86). Here are just a few examples:

> On most days, the [official] jeep would come for him between eleven and twelve … The driver of the jeep … was usually unable to

---

[7] With reference to *Madame Bovary*, Mikhail Bakhtin describes a similar kind of provincial 'chronotope' associated with 'cyclical everyday time.' In the provincial town or village, he writes, 'there are no events, only "doings" that constantly repeat themselves. Time here has no advancing historical movement; it moves rather in narrow circles: the circle of the day, of the week, of the month, of a person's entire life. A day is just a day, a year is just a year – a life is just a life. Day in, day out the same round of activities are repeated, the same topics of conversation, the same words and so forth … Time here is without event and therefore almost seems to stand still. Here there are no "meetings," no "partings." It is a viscous and sticky time that drags itself slowly through space' (247–48).

differentiate one district office from another. So, for almost an hour on some of the (good) days, he would drive Agastya around the town, just trying to *locate* an office. (82)

[During the afternoon] he could doze a little ... daydream, fantasize, think of his past, reorganize it, try to force out of it a pattern, masturbate without joy, sometimes smoke some marijuana, read a little Marcus Aurelius, or just lie down and think of the sun shrivelling up the world outside. (84–85)

On most nights that he didn't eat with the Collector, dinner was early, at about eight, because Vasant liked to sleep early. (85)

In Madna [Agastya] could never take sleep for granted. He would repeat the activities of the afternoon, thinking that for more than twenty years he had always slept well, except for one or two nights when excitement had kept him awake ... But in Madna he seemed to have appalled sleep. When he finally dropped off, it was out of a weariness even with despair. (86)

'Thus,' the chapter concludes, 'he played out, in one day, one kind of life of the lonely' (86). At this point, the narrative has lapsed, like Agastya himself, into a purely iterative state.[8] Every act that is narrated carries an implied *et cetera*, indicating its status as plural, gesturing toward the infinite series of (largely identical) occurrences that lies behind it. Under these circumstances, as I suggested earlier, to narrate one day is to narrate every day, and to narrate every day is to narrate the same day innumerable times – for there is no way of distinguishing between these quotidian episodes, no flashes of significance or uniqueness that will allow us to identify one day as being antecedent or subsequent to any other day. Ordinarily, as Gérard Genette points out, 'iterative sections are almost always functionally subordinate to singulative scenes, for which the iterative sections provide a sort of informative frame or background ... Like description,

---

8 The distinction I am making here, following Gérard Genette, is between *singulative* narration ('where the singularness of the narrative statement corresponds to the singularness of the narrated event' [114]) and *iterative* narration ('where a single narrative utterance takes upon itself several occurrences together of the same event' [116]). Genette offers the statement 'Yesterday, I went to bed early' (114) as an example of the former; and to demonstrate the latter, he invokes the famous opening line of Proust's *In Search of Lost Time*: 'For a long time I would go to bed early' (Proust 1).

in the traditional novel the iterative narrative is *at the service* of the narrative "as such," which is the singulative narrative' (116–17). In *English, August*, by contrast, the iterative dimension of the narrative is consistently foregrounded – and in places even actively privileged over the singulative. Furthermore, although iterative passages are usually to be found embedded within larger singulative narratives, in this case the reverse is true. Here, as Genette writes of Proust, 'the singulative itself is to some extent *integrated* into the iterative, compelled to serve and illustrate it, positively or negatively, either by respecting its code or by transgressing it, which is another way of manifesting it' (140). In this early chapter of Chatterjee's novel, then, we find the singulative embedded anecdotally within the iterative – liberating the latter from its functional dependence on the former, reducing the capacity of the narrative to move beyond the 'always,' the 'every day,' the 'usually,' and thus replicating, once more, the dilatory and entropic qualities of the bureaucratic apparatus.

I have been arguing so far that the incorporation of these bureaucratic features into the structure of *English, August* leads to the diminution of the narrative's proairetic code and the privileging, in places, of the iterative over the singulative. Like Agastya, that is to say, Chatterjee's novel appears to have run out of energy – not the energy to continue but the energy to conclude, to achieve 'full predication of the narrative sentence [and] final plenitude of meaning' (Brooks, *Reading* 314). And it is this entropic quality, I would like to suggest, this failure to move forward, that ultimately creates the threat of interminability in the novel, giving rise to the very real possibility that it may never achieve the retrospective significance that traditionally accompanies narrative closure.[9]

For Barthes, every narrative produces a 'dilatory area' (*S/Z* 75), a zone filled with delays and stoppages, through which we must proceed in order to reach the end; but in *English, August*, this area seems to be extended indefinitely, perpetually deferring the final discharge of meaning. Indeed, the novel itself demonstrates no real desire to achieve closure, as 'looking for that kind of a cessation' also involves 'too much effort' (153). Hence the threat of interminability,

---

9 As Wolf Lepenies observes, such interminability is also a typical attribute of the boring. 'When we are bored,' he writes, 'time grows long – it cannot be filled or used up; and finally, time is "killed" when we notice that it seems endless. Consequently, boredom appears to be eternal monotony, always the same, a gaping void' (87).

the threat that the narrative we are reading may be incapable of summoning the energy required to terminate itself and will instead drift on endlessly, oblivious to our need for resolution, like the bureaucratic procedures it replicates. At various junctures throughout the novel, Agastya appears to sense this threat of interminability. More than once, for instance, he cites the following line from the *Bhagavad Gita*: '[M]any-branched and endless are the thoughts of the man who lacks determination' (153).[10] And in one of the novel's more mystical passages, he describes his life as being characterized by '[m]ovement without purpose, an endless ebb and flow, from one world to another.' Although he struggles to impose order and patterns of meaning onto this existence, Agastya finally recognizes the futility of longing 'for repose through the mastering of chaos' (311) – understanding, perhaps, that the narrative he occupies is simply not equipped to provide this kind of quiescence.

As readers, of course, we are always aware that the threat of linear interminability will never be realized, for the novel is quite clearly finite: we can see the end approaching as we turn the pages. But the possibility of *circular* interminability does surface in two specific places within the narrative, creating a genuine threat of discursive rupture. The novel's opening lines read as follows: 'Through the windshield they watched the wide silent road, so well-lit and dead. New Delhi, one in the morning, a stray dog flashed across the road, sensing prey' (5). Some time later – 164 pages, to be precise – Agastya hears one of Tagore's songs playing on the stereo, and he is reminded of that long-ago night in Delhi: '[T]hey had sat in the car outside Dhrubo's flat, watching the wide silent road through the windshield at one in the morning; a stray dog had at one moment flashed across the road, sensing prey' (169). This recollection is significant, for by beginning to narrate once more the novel we are reading, by repeating its opening lines, Agastya inadvertently raises the spectre of interminability – the possibility that he may simply *continue* narrating, rehearsing the story we have already read, until he reaches the point of recollection a second time and is forced to start over again from the beginning. The danger represented by this narrative circularity is perhaps best articulated by Borges in his justly celebrated analysis of *The Arabian Nights*:

10 The line Agastya is quoting here comes from *shloka* (verse) 41 of Chapter 2, which reads in its entirety: 'The follower of this path has one thought, and this is the End of his determination. But many-branched and endless are the thoughts of the man who lacks determination' (13).

> The necessity of completing a thousand and one sections obliged the copyists of the work to make all manner of interpolations. None is more perturbing than that of the six hundred and second night, magical among all nights. On that night, the king hears from the queen his own story. He hears the beginning of the story, which comprises all the others and also – monstrously – itself. Does the reader clearly grasp the vast possibility of this interpolation, the curious danger? That the queen may persist and the motionless king hear forever the truncated story of the *Thousand and One Nights*, now infinite and circular. (195)

To identify such a danger in *English, August* would leave one vulnerable to the charge of over-reading were it not for the fact that Agastya himself raises this very possibility just prior to the recollection described above. In the novel's opening pages, on the train to Madna, he had been rudely interrogated by another passenger: 'Agastya? What kind of name is Agastya? ... You are IAS? You don't look like an IAS officer ... You don't even look Bengali' (9). And during a brief visit to Delhi some time later, he is tormented by the possibility that his return to Madna will replicate every last detail of this inaugural journey: '[I]n nine days he would be packing again and saying bye to his uncle,' and then 'someone on the train would again ask him to categorize himself, would not believe that he was what he was, and would never have heard of the name Agastya' (160). What we have here is not a simple case of *déjà vu*, but something far more disconcerting: the possibility of *déjà vécu* – an encounter with the 'already lived.' In other words, the threat of interminability has shifted from the level of the discourse (the telling of the story) to the intradiegetic world created by the discourse (the 'living' of the story); and that is what makes it possible for a character located within this universe to have some intimation, however vague, of the ontological danger he faces.

Over the years, as the government itself concedes, such interminability has come to be regarded as another typical feature of Indian bureaucracy. Near the end of the novel, Agastya is sent for further training to a remote 'tribal' locality, where he quickly recognizes the strategic value of procrastination and delay. As Block Development Officer for the district, he is required to accept or reject all manner of '[p]etitions, applications, [and] requests' (279); and those he is unable to resolve one way or the other are simply directed elsewhere by his subordinates: 'Agastya could see these rejected petitions moving from one ignorant official to another unhelpful one, the black creases on each petition marking its tortuous journey' (277). Although this all seems mystifying at first, over time he comes to understand the bureaucratic logic, the 'psychology of evasion' (Dwivedi and Jain 209), informing such procedures.[11] 'Eventually,' we are told,

> he learnt to see the pattern, how an incomprehensibility in the post became, in a few weeks (things moved even more slowly in Jompanna than in Madna), an incomprehensibility in a file – the passage of a petition, or a request for redress, from desk to desk, gathering around it, like flesh around a kernel, comment and counter-comment, and irrelevant comment, till it was fat enough to be offal for the rats in the office cupboards. (281)[12]

This last passage provides a good example, in miniature, of the way in which the dilatory tendencies of the bureaucratic process gradually enter into the very tissue of the narrative. In this particular case, the representation of interminability is re-enacted formally through the steady accretion of subordinate clauses, so that the sentence itself, like the petition it describes, takes on additional layers of unnecessary commentary as it progresses. And by the time it finally achieves full predication and closure, we as readers have been made to endure a similarly 'tortuous' journey along the corridors of the Collectorate, gaining experience of these superfluities, hindrances, and delays through their various syntactical correlatives. In an especially incisive

---

11 In the article from which this phrase is derived, O.P. Dwivedi and R.B. Jain offer a fierce critique of 'bureaucratic morality' in India, arguing that the IAS is characterized by 'excessive self-importance, indifference towards the feelings or the convenience of individuals and by an obsession with the binding and inflexible authority of departmental decisions, precedents, arrangements or forms, regardless of how badly or with what injustice they work in individual cases' (208).
12 According to Matthew S. Hull, writing on Pakistani bureaucracy, the circulation of files is a strategy by which the individual functionary is able to avoid taking responsibility for any given case. 'The circulation of the file,' he writes, 'precipitates a multiparty interaction through which authorship and therefore agency ... is distributed over a larger and larger network of functionaries. The achievement of movement up and down the chain of command and laterally to other departments produces on the note sheet a representation of collective agency' (138). By adopting these circulatory practices, Hull concludes, 'functionaries try to maximize the mediations of their actions and writings, transforming the procedures designed to specify responsibility into the means to disperse it' (150). For a discussion of the role of the form, the file, and the register in Indian bureaucratic life, see Gupta 144–49.

reading of *Bleak House* (1852–53), D.A. Miller has suggested that Dickens' representation of the Court of Chancery reproduces, in its length and complexity, some of the salient characteristics of the emerging Victorian state bureaucracy. The novel's 'suspension of teleology,' he argues, is exemplary of an entire 'social sphere that seems to run on the principle of a purposiveness without purpose' (*Novel* 86).[13] Indeed, for Miller, the Victorian novel as a whole typically 'establishes a little bureaucracy of its own, generating an immense amount of paperwork and both physically and mentally sending its readers here, there, backward and forward, like the circumlocutory agencies that Dickens satirizes' (88–89). To some degree, I believe, the same thing could be said of *English, August*, which also makes of itself a 'little bureaucracy' and operates on a principle of 'purposiveness without purpose.' (Remember that phrase: '[m]ovement without purpose' [Chatterjee 311].) Moreover, as Miller suggests, in the process of reading such a novel we are inevitably familiarized with the affective consequences of bureaucracy and schooled in the 'appropriate' response to its procedures. We learn to wait patiently – to suspend teleology and desire, to tolerate perpetually deferred outcomes, and to reconcile ourselves to the 'lengthening of the while' (Heidegger, *Fundamental* 93). In short, like Agastya, we learn to be bored.

But this is a dangerous strategy for any narrative to employ, one that gives rise to a formidable discursive challenge. How is the author to make the boring interesting enough to keep us reading, but not so interesting that it should destroy the verisimilitude of the uninteresting? In order for *English, August* to succeed as a novel, it is crucial that we maintain some interest in its outcome and derive some degree of readerly pleasure from its diachronic unfolding; for as Miller observes of *Bleak House*, 'were the novel itself ever to become as dreary [as the world it depicts], were it ever to cease *making itself desirable*, it would … by the same token cease to be read' (*Novel* 85). Given its generic affinities, however, Chatterjee's narrative is also compelled to convey the reality of the bureaucratic existence – the interminable meetings, the unnecessarily complicated and repetitive procedures, the endless paper trail of signatures and countersignatures – and by pursuing this objective, it inevitably diminishes its own readability. But not fatally so.

13 By using this phrase, Miller is of course evoking Kant, who, in the *Critique of Judgement*, claimed that the aesthetic category of the beautiful has as its basis 'a merely formal purposiveness, i.e., a purposiveness without a purpose' (73).

Chatterjee, I would argue, ultimately manages to accommodate these conflicting imperatives by bringing *English, August* as close as possible to 'the absolute minimal condition of [the] interesting' (Ngai, 'Merely' 791), yet without completely destroying its 'desirability' as a narrative – doing just enough to keep us turning the pages, just enough to ensure the survival of the (realist) discourse, and no more.[14]

III

As I have suggested, the threat of interminability in literature is above all the threat of non-meaning, the threat that the narrative we are reading will fail to deliver the significance and coherence we traditionally expect from fictional discourse. 'Meaning,' the anthropologist Victor Turner writes, 'is connected with the consummation of a process – it is bound up with termination … The meaning of any given factor in a process cannot be assessed until the whole process is past' (97). Or to quote Peter Brooks once more,

> The very possibility of meaning plotted through sequence and through time depends on the anticipated structuring force of the ending: the interminable would be the meaningless, and the lack of ending would jeopardize the beginning. We read the incidents of narration as 'promises and annunciations' of final coherence … [A]cross the bulk of the as yet unread middle pages, the end calls to the beginning, transforms and enhances it. (*Reading* 93–94)

Simply put, it is primarily through endings, both anticipated and realized, that we seek to understand beginnings and middles. And that

---

14 Although the danger of boredom is particularly acute in this case, it is an affective state that underlies the production (and consumption) of all literature, however 'interesting' it may be. 'The ideal dynamic between writing and reading,' Patricia Meyer Spacks notes, 'depends in part on boredom as displaced, unmentioned, and unmentionable possibility. The need to refute boredom's deadening power impels the writer's productivity and the reader's engagement. In the best of all possible arrangements, an author's energy and a reader's reciprocate, establishing a "dialectics of desire" … But the implicit contract between creator and responder – the promise "I will interest you" corresponding to the demand "you will interest me" – remains, like other contracts, subject to default. The writer may fail to engage the reader's interest [or] the reader may refuse to be interested' (1–2).

at least partially explains the 'curious danger' (Borges 195) of narrative interminability; for a novel with no ending would never be able to achieve final plenitude of meaning, would never be able to produce the 'commanding structure of significance' (Bersani 53) that distinguishes the narrated from the unnarrated or the unnarratable.

Throughout *English, August*, Agastya struggles to derive some kind of meaning from his life in the provinces – a semblance of order that would make everything he experiences, all the disconnected trivialities and absurdities of bureaucratic existence, somehow converge and cohere. But of course it is not to be. Time and again, he is forced to confront, in Jonathan Culler's words, 'the discrepancy between meaning and experience' (*Flaubert* 24). Nothing in his life makes sense, nothing matters, nothing satisfies – and so it is not particularly surprising that he should contemplate ending it all. 'Sometimes,' we learn,

> he would lie in bed and remember Prashant, his schoolfriend who had been perfectly ordinary and likeable, but who had opted out, one June afternoon five years ago, by stepping into the path of a truck, to be minced into the melting tar of the VIP Road, leaving behind only a note saying that he was sorry. (153)

For Agastya, suicide represents the 'ultimate release, the profoundest renunciation of one's sentience' (251–52). And that, I would contend, is precisely what he is hoping to achieve here: a total quiescence that would defy interminability and bestow retrospective significance on everything that has gone before. (On this subject, too, he cites his beloved Marcus Aurelius: 'O, the consolation of being able to thrust aside and cast into oblivion every tiresome and intrusive impression, and in a trice be utterly at peace' [153].[15]) Agastya's suicidal tendencies are to be understood, then, both existentially and narratologically – for by terminating his own life, by achieving the 'ultimate release,' he would also terminate and give meaning to the novel we are reading. But apparently even this kind of conclusion requires 'too much effort' (153); and so, like the words in his diary, the narrative continues to 'trail aimlessly across the page' (218), without any sense of direction or urgency.

Needless to say, Chatterjee's novel does eventually run out of pages, but the ending, when it finally arrives, could hardly be considered an ending at all. Although the novel itself obviously comes to a conclusion

---

15 This line can be found in *Meditations* 5.2 (78).

Boredom

on page 322, in doing so, as we shall see, it refuses to provide the 'complex of narrative summations that would match ... the external termination of [the] discourse with its internal closure' (Miller, *Novel* 90). It fails, in other words, to ensure that termination coincides with closure, that what finishes the narrative also resolves it. Furthermore, just when we are expecting the novel's proairetic code to achieve a degree of resolution, however diminished or meagre, the discourse strives to jettison proairesis altogether by 'externalizing' it, by projecting it beyond the spatial and temporal parameters of the text we have before us.

I suggested earlier that something does keep us reading Chatterjee's novel, something prevents us from simply giving up on it, and that something is the question of whether the narrative will sustain its anti-proairetic qualities to the end, or whether there will be a late flurry of action that retrospectively 'energizes' everything that has gone before. Essentially, the question we ask ourselves as we read is not what will happen in the end but whether anything will happen at all – whether the novel's starved proairetic code will be capable of adequately resolving itself and thus producing a final discharge of meaning. But even this question does not generate too much suspense; and it is fairly predictable that it should turn out to be answered in the negative. Something does happen at the end of *English, August*, but it happens to someone else, somewhere else, and as readers we are offered only a fleeting, anecdotal glimpse of the kind of 'endings' taking place outside the spatial frame of the narrative. While visiting a remote village, Agastya hears some disturbing news about one of the novel's peripheral characters, a forestry service officer who had recently been posted to another 'very boring' (294) location in the hinterland. 'He abused the honour of the tribal woman who cooked for him,' Agastya is told. 'The men of her village were very angry. They visited [him] three nights ago, and surprised them both. In revenge, and as punishment, they cut off his arms' (290). Thus, the most exciting event in the entire novel, indeed its most overtly *novelistic* event, is dispensed with in a mere two or three sentences, leaving us with the distinct impression that we may have been reading the wrong novel all along – or that the narrative has inadvertently taken the wrong character as its protagonist, and while we have been following Agastya's trivial activities, something genuinely interesting and significant has been happening just around the corner. But it is obviously too late to do anything about it. This momentary glimpse of uninhibited proairesis soon fades, and before long we are back where we started, immersed in the quotidian banalities of our

121

hero's life: 'The rest of the months in Jompanna passed [with] the same routine, office and Rest House, two vegetarian meals a day, exercise on the three feet of jute carpet between bed and desk, in the evening [reading] files in his room to the music from the stalls' (301).

And what of Agastya himself, how does his story conclude? Well, in this case the proairetic is projected beyond the narrative's *temporal* frame, so that the novel closes by anticipating an event that has yet to occur, one that will take place only after the discourse itself has been terminated. We last see Agastya in a train on his way to Calcutta, where he will be staying with his father while he tries to decide what to do with his life. The novel's final sentence reads as follows: 'He watched the passing hinterland and looked forward to meeting his father' (322). This moment of external prolepsis is particularly significant, for it ensures that the closure both Agastya and the reader have been seeking must once more be deferred, once more projected into the future.[16] That the novel's last sentence should anticipate something else, something located outside its chronological field, means that the termination of the discourse precedes (and thus precludes) closure – giving rise, yet again, to the threat of interminability. One might be reminded here, too, of Flaubert's *Sentimental Education*, which also concludes by transgressing its own temporal boundaries. In the novel's final scene, Frédéric Moreau and Deslauriers are reminiscing about a (frustrated) visit to a brothel they had made some years previously. 'That was the happiest time we ever had,' Frédéric says. 'Yes,' his friend replies, 'perhaps you're right. That was the happiest time we ever had' (419). And there the narrative concludes, invoking an event that, as Peter Brooks observes,

> does not fall within the normal chronology of the novel, a moment presented at the very end that in fact predates the beginning. This striking analepsis ... seems to say that everything we have read in this very long novel is somehow secondary to the unrecorded moment of three years before it began. It is as if the novel suddenly discovers that it began too late ... Closure here also uncloses, suggesting that novels, like [psycho]analyses, may in essence be interminable. (*Reading* 211–12)

---

16 As mentioned in Chapter 3, Genette divides prolepses (or anticipatory sequences) into 'two classes, external and internal, depending on whether the point to which they reach is located outside or inside the temporal field of the [primary] narrative' (61).

As indicated above, the final sentence of *English, August* is also significant in that it serves to project the faltering proairetic code beyond the parameters of the narrative we have before us. Something may still happen, that is to say, but it will not be happening in this novel – not yet, not here. And this specific instance of deferral could be seen as emblematic of the narrative's more general procrastinatory tendencies. In the traditional Bildungsroman, as we noted in Chapter 3, the hero eventually manages to find a place for himself in the world, and he does so by reconciling the competing imperatives of self and society, autonomy and interdependence. But not here. In Chatterjee's novel, our hero never quite achieves this kind of equanimity, never manages to find 'repose through the mastering of chaos' (311). Instead, the narrative constantly frustrates or defers Agastya's 'coming of age,' so that even in the final pages it is clear that he has made almost no progress toward this traditional generic objective. He has simply decided to take a year off to think about what he *might* like to do. But what exactly will that achieve? And what has he been doing during his year in the provinces anyway, if not idly contemplating his future? This deferral of 'maturity,' then, not only denies the narrative the possibility of closure, but also deprives it of the capacity for initiating change – leading us to believe that even if it *were* to continue indefinitely, what followed would merely repeat what had gone before. And this, of course, destroys the linear trajectory of the Bildungsroman by exposing the narrative, at the very moment it expires, to the renewed threat of circularity and eternal recurrence.

Here, too, Chatterjee's novel could be said to resemble the bureaucratic processes it so accurately describes. As we have seen, the IAS is notorious for 'delaying [the] finalization of any decision' (Government of India 365) and for consistently valuing procedures over outcomes. In this world, '[e]verything is static' (Chatterjee 231), endlessly deferred, 'bewildering and boring' (35). So it is not too surprising that the novel itself should have internalized many of these entropic qualities, that its own energies should have been dissipated by the dilatory drag of IAS procedures. Only thus, I have argued, are we able to make sense of the narrative's abbreviated proairetic code, its tendency to privilege the iterative over the singulative, and its pronounced aversion to anything that might constitute closure. But it would be unwise to overstate this case, for there is something in the very nature of *English, August* that militates against grand gestures and critical certainties. Jonathan Culler has suggested, rather provocatively, that 'interpretation is interesting only when it is extreme' (*Literary* 167); yet

Chatterjee's novel refuses to accommodate or endorse such extremes and, in so doing, effectively subdues (bores?) whatever critical discourse it might generate. Overinterpretation may well be more 'interesting and intellectually valuable than "sound," moderate interpretation' (Culler, *Literary* 168), but to make the narrative too interesting, too stimulating or 'productive,' would be to disregard its essential *ordinariness*, its commitment to the banality of the bureaucratic experience.

Allow me to explain what I mean by this. To begin with, I have argued that the novel actively pursues 'non-meaning,' but this state is something it only partially achieves – for as Barthes notes, 'everything in [a narrative] signifies ... Even were a detail to appear irretrievably insignificant, resistant to all functionality, it would nonetheless end up with precisely the meaning of absurdity or uselessness' ('Introduction' 261). Take the passages describing Agastya's daily routine, for instance. However 'meaningless' and inconsequential these descriptions may be, they still manage to produce a secondary layer of signification representing the principle of banality itself. This gesture is banal, they say to the reader; this action is boring and repetitive. Similarly, although the threat of interminability surfaces from time to time in the narrative, it is never fully realized, remaining perpetually mired in the subjunctive: 'if [the novel] *were* to continue indefinitely, what followed *would* merely repeat what had gone before.' And in this respect, the narrative's dominant structure of feeling takes on additional significance. After all, boredom is an emotion that also abjures extreme states of being, occupying the same temperate zone as alienation, indifference, and apathy. Indeed, one could describe boredom as the *absence* of feeling, certainly the absence of desire, for when we are bored we lose the capacity to feel strongly, one way or the other, about anything. ('He wanted nothing, it seemed – only a peace, but that was too pompous a word' [Chatterjee 155].) Boredom de-intensifies our lives, leaving us, as Heidegger writes, 'equally distant from despair and joy' (*Introduction* 2), and for this reason it has always been considered one of the 'weaker' and less prestigious dysphoric states. Unlike the pity and fear described in Aristotle's *Poetics*, boredom is 'explicitly *a*moral and *non*cathartic, offering no satisfactions of virtue, however oblique, nor any therapeutic or purifying release' (Ngai, *Ugly* 6).[17] And this 'greyness,' this tendency to avoid extremes or intensities, could be regarded as the last of the novel's bureaucratic qualities. For the bureaucratic world is also a world of half-measures and compromise – a world in which we are bored but

---

17 See Aristotle, *Poetics* 10.

never quite bored enough to leave (or stop reading), a world in which meaning recedes but never quite disappears, a world in which the end terminates but never quite closes.

IV

What, then, are we to make of these realist narratives that seem to contravene their own governing generic principles by resisting closure, suspending meaning, and deprivileging the proairetic? What are their commonalities, and what do they tell us about the relationship between bureaucracy, boredom, and narrative? As noted earlier, realism is expected to do everything it can to achieve an overarching significance and a full and final predication of meaning. In other words, the primary obligation of the realist novel is to locate the 'interesting' in the everyday, the meaningful in the mundane, and to make of that reality something *worth narrating*. But of course bureaucracy complicates this imperative, for any attempt to practise Erich Auerbach's 'serious treatment of everyday reality' (491) in the age of the IAS would also require that the uninteresting be treated seriously; and to do so would bring two of the central aesthetic impulses of literary realism into direct conflict – namely, the commitment to verisimilitude and the desire to fill the world with significance. As Theodor Adorno observes, 'telling a story means having something *special* to say, and that is precisely what is prevented by the administered world, by standardization and eternal sameness' ('Position' 31). Or to put it another way, how is it possible for the realist writer to deliver something (significance, meaning, 'interest') that the reality to which he or she is beholden simply refuses to yield? For Adorno, this contradiction ultimately invalidates realism as a mode of representation in the bureaucratic age. 'The more strictly the novel adheres to realism in external things,' he writes, 'to the gesture that says "this is how it was," the more every word becomes a mere "as if," and the greater becomes the contradiction between this claim and the fact that it was not so' (33). The only way out of this impasse, Adorno concludes, is for the novel to abandon the 'lie of representation' (34) and defy the 'epic precept of objectivity and material concreteness' (32).

Narratives such as *Bleak House*, *Sentimental Education*, and Chatterjee's *English, August* would seem to controvert Adorno's stance, however, for in each case they are able to accommodate this underlying contradiction without entirely abandoning their governing generic principles. Although the Jarndyce and Jarndyce suit in *Bleak House* is never adequately

Affective Disorders

resolved – simply 'laps[ing] and melt[ing] away' on page 901 of my edition – the novel itself does eventually provide the kind of closure denied by the Court of Chancery. *Sentimental Education* also manages to negotiate the conflicting imperatives of realism and reality by asserting that the failure of meaning can itself be considered 'interesting,' and thus transformed into an object of readerly desire. And as we have seen, Chatterjee's novel is only ever partially successful in its pursuit of non-meaning and insignificance, always managing to create just enough interest and energy to keep the narrative going and the reader reading. In this way, all three narratives generate a kind of 'tenuous readability' (Brooks, *Reading* 171) – hovering uncertainly between the interesting and the boring, meaning and non-meaning, significance and inconsequentiality. And it is this tenuous quality, this threading together of contradictory impulses and imperatives, that brings these examples of literary realism closer to Adorno's 'anti-realistic' ('Position' 32) ideal than may, at first glance, appear to be the case. Moreover, such ambivalence implies that realism as a mode of representation may be a good deal more agile than is oftentimes allowed – that it may be capable of accommodating (and even encouraging) significant ruptures of meaning, and capable, too, of challenging the very aesthetic principles to which it 'officially' adheres.

CHAPTER FIVE

Fear
Michael Ondaatje's *Anil's Ghost*

I comprehend in this word *fear*, a certain foresight of future evil.

> Thomas Hobbes, *Philosophical Rudiments Concerning Government and Society*, 1651

The tradition of the oppressed teaches us that the 'state of emergency' in which we live is not the exception but the rule.

> Walter Benjamin, 'On the Concept of History,' 1940

I

During the Sri Lankan Civil War, which lasted from 1983 until 2009, an estimated 60,000 to 100,000 people disappeared (Amnesty, *Only* 7). Of course, they did not simply 'disappear'; they were arrested or abducted, often tortured and mutilated, and then almost certainly killed. According to an Amnesty International report published in 1990, none of the parties responsible for such atrocities made any effort to conceal what they had done:

> Piles of bodies were dumped openly by roadsides, in fields and in cemeteries; others were thrown into rivers ... Many bodies dumped in Sri Lanka were mutilated or burned beyond recognition, often on pyres of rubber tyres. In November and December [1989], the

> mutilated bodies of [Janatha Vimukthi Peramuna] suspects, many of them apparently captives at the time of their killing, were reported to have been left hanging at central points in Kandy ... while in surrounding villages severed limbs were hung from trees as part of a macabre and terrifying warning to communities considered sympathetic to the JVP. (*Sri Lanka* 13)

In this case, the perpetrators were the Sri Lankan government forces, although the other two sides in what was essentially a three-way conflict – the Liberation Tigers of Tamil Eelam (LTTE), who were fighting for an independent Tamil homeland in the north of the island, and the aforementioned JVP, a revolutionary left-wing party, which was mainly composed of young Sinhalese – were responsible for similar atrocities.[1] Altogether, by the time a ceasefire was finally declared in 2009, at least 100,000 people had been killed (Kingsbury 142).[2] One of the primary objectives of this violence was to terrorize the civilian population, to create a climate of fear that would reinforce the political and military dominance of the party in question – whether it be the Sri Lankan government, the LTTE, the JVP, or even the Indian peacekeeping force that was deployed in the country from 1987 to 1990. Despite their obvious differences, then, all three major parties (along with their

---

1 To be more precise, the war can be divided into three main phases: the period between 1983 and 1987, when the government and the LTTE were the primary adversaries; the period between 1987 and 1990, when the JVP entered the fray (along with an Indian peacekeeping force); and the period after 1990, when the largely bilateral conflict between the government and the LTTE resumed. By establishing an independent state, the LTTE sought to protect the minority Tamil community (which comprises roughly 15 per cent of the population) against discrimination on the part of the majority Sinhalese community (which comprises about 75 per cent). As for the JVP, it sought to overthrow the government of President J.R. Jayewardene and establish in its place a revolutionary socialist state based on the principles of radical Sinhalese nationalism. In the words of Jayadeva Uyangoda, the JVP's 'self-understanding during this period was that it was the sole patriotic force with the historical mission ... to liberate the "motherland" from "traitors," "aggressors," and "foreign invaders"' (43).

2 This figure – the most widely cited – is based on an estimate provided by the UN in 2009. In a report published two years later, however, the UN suggested that up to 40,000 civilians may have died in the spring of 2009 alone (during the final assault on the LTTE) (Seoighe 8). If we combine this more recent figure with the 60–100,000 people who 'disappeared' during the civil war, and whose fate has yet to be confirmed, it would seem that a total estimate of 100,000 casualties is decidedly conservative.

affiliates and allies) employed identical tactics of intimidation and terror. During the war, as Darini Rajasingham-Senanayake notes, 'ethnic' violence became 'organized, routinized, and systematized through disappearances, torture, rape, checkpoint searches, and massacres of entire villages in remote areas' (58). And as a consequence of this widespread and deeply traumatizing violence, fear became a dominant structure of feeling within Sri Lankan society, giving rise to a large number of related pathologies. 'The vast majority of ordinary people,' Jagath P. Senaratne writes, 'could not keep track of either the killers or those killed, and [therefore] retreated into cowed silence, fearful of venturing out of their homes' (146). By the late eighties, the country had become 'paralysed' by this feeling of terror; and for the first time, '[p]hrases such as "fear psychosis" [and] "fear syndrome" ... began to be commonly used' (145). Indeed, this particular phase of the conflict would come to be defined by the terror it generated, and in common parlance it is still known as the *beeshana kalaya* – the 'time of great fear' (Wickramasinghe 260).

In the novel I shall be discussing in this chapter, Michael Ondaatje's *Anil's Ghost* (2000), we can find traces of such fear on almost every page. 'Everyone's scared,' one character observes. 'It's a national disease' (53). And there is a good reason why this should be the case. The novel is set in the late eighties and early nineties – a time of 'continual emergency' (42), of suicide bombings and mass graves and torture. Anil Tissera, a forensic anthropologist, has returned to Sri Lanka after many years to investigate the 'organized campaigns of murder on the island' (16). In order to do so, she has been paired with a local archaeologist, Sarath Diyasena; and when they discover a modern skeleton hidden in the Bandarawela caves, a national archaeological preserve, Anil hopes that she can use this evidence to prove that the security forces have been committing extrajudicial killings. The need to identify the skeleton (which they name Sailor) constitutes the narrative's primary motivating force – not only because it will allow Anil to hold the government accountable for this specific crime, but also because it will provide, as far as she is concerned, a kind of representative justice for all of the unidentified victims of the civil war. '*One village can speak for many villages*,' she believes. '*One victim can speak for many victims*' (176).

As this quest advances, through a process of incremental repetition, we are given an increasingly strong sense of the fear that has come to dominate the affective lives of many of the novel's characters. 'In her years abroad,' we are told, 'Anil had courted foreignness, was at ease whether on the Bakerloo line or on the highways around Santa Fe ...

Affective Disorders

But here, on this island, she realized that she was moving with only one arm of language among uncertain laws and a fear that was everywhere' (54). As we shall see, this fear achieves a kind of ubiquity that allows it to saturate the representational plane of the narrative while also percolating into its underlying structure, where it creates a number of quite profound generic disturbances. In a fascinating article on the proliferation of supernatural narratives during the civil war, the anthropologist Sasanka Perera argues that the conflict even transformed the Sinhala language itself. According to Perera, as the violence intensified in the late eighties, words such as *beeshanaya* (terror), *wadhakagaraya* (torture chamber), *issuwa* (kidnapped), and *athurudahanwoowo* (the disappeared) acquired 'substantially altered meanings' that were 'specifically marked' by the experience of terror.[3] Having entered both journalistic and popular discourse, these transformed signifiers contributed to a more general 'culture of terror' within the country, a culture that had 'its own vocabulary as well as its own overall structure' (127).[4] In the following pages, I will be exploring the way in which this culture of terror can also influence the production of literature. What, precisely, does such debilitating fear *do* to the literary discourse it generates? What does it make possible and what does it preclude? I shall begin by explaining how an emotion that is usually experienced in a deeply physiological way ('one sweats, one's heart races, one's whole body becomes a space of unpleasant intensity' [Ahmed, *Cultural* 65]) can acquire a decentred, disembodied status that facilitates the type of ubiquity I have been describing.[5] I will then trace the process by which *Anil's Ghost* internalizes

---

3 Similarly, while conducting fieldwork in Sri Lanka in the early eighties, E. Valentine Daniel observed that the 'very words "project," "informants," "information," "interview," "evidence," [and] "description" [had taken on] new and terrifying meanings' (3).

4 It was Michael Taussig who first used the phrase 'culture of terror' to describe the atrocities that were perpetrated along the Putumayo River, a tributary of the Amazon, during the rubber boom of the late nineteenth and early twentieth centuries. '[S]tep by step,' he writes, 'terror and torture became *the* form of life for some fifteen years, an organized culture with its systematized rules, imagery, procedures, and meanings involved in spectacles and rituals that sustained the precarious solidarity of the rubber company employees as well as beating out through the body of the tortured some sort of canonical truth about Civilization and Business' (495).

5 Of all the emotions, fear is perhaps the most canonical and heavily theorized. In the *Rhetoric*, for instance, Aristotle defines it as 'a kind of

this feeling of fear and, in so doing, replicates some of its more salient features – namely, its phobic, non-cathartic, and indefinite qualities. In each case, I would like to suggest, these qualities disrupt the generic imperatives that would typically govern a narrative of this kind, making it impossible to achieve the linearity, the hermeneutic closure, and the 'localization of culpability' that we tend to associate with classic crime fiction. Under these circumstances, I shall argue, in a country where as many as 100,000 people are still missing (presumed dead) and where the language itself has been changed forever, acquiring terrifying new layers of connotative meaning, such reassuring literary palliatives are simply no longer available.

II

We all have the capacity to feel fear, and we all have the capacity to feel it in the same place: the amygdala. Discovered in 1819, the amygdala is a small bundle of nuclei located within each of the anterior temporal lobes of the brain. It is an integral part of the limbic system and primarily responsible for generating the feeling of fear – or more precisely, to quote the neurologist Antonio Damasio, it has the ability to trigger 'the enactment of a body state characteristic of the emotion fear' and to alter 'cognitive processing in a manner that fits the state of fear' (*Descartes' Error* 131).[6] In order to activate this emotion, the 'early sensory cortices [must first] detect and categorize the key … features of a given entity' (e.g., speed, size, proximity, etc.), before

---

pain or disturbance resulting from the imagination of impending danger, either destructive or painful' (153); and in an often-cited passage from the *Poetics*, he argues that the arousal (and subsequent purgation) of both fear and pity are essential to the aesthetic pleasure that we derive from tragedy (10). Writing in the seventeenth century, Thomas Hobbes identified 'mutual fear' as the affective foundation of 'all great and lasting societies' (113). And in 1757, Edmund Burke described fear as 'the ruling principle of the sublime.' No emotion, he claimed, 'so effectually robs the mind of all its powers of acting and reasoning as fear. For fear being an apprehension of pain or death, it operates in a manner that resembles actual pain. Whatever therefore is terrible, with regard to sight, is sublime too, whether this cause of terror be endued with greatness of dimensions or not; for it is impossible to look on anything as trifling, or contemptible, that may be dangerous' (53).

6 For more on the amygdala, see LeDoux 138–78, Plamper 1–4, and Whalen and Phelps.

alerting the amygdala to 'their *conjunctive* presence' (131–32). Once the amygdala receives these signals, it initiates a wide array of autonomic responses (releasing adrenaline, increasing blood pressure, enhancing muscle tone, etc.), which are also registered at the cognitive level, thus allowing the individual a *'flexibility of response based on the particular history of [his or her] interactions with the environment'* (133).[7] This is what Damasio refers to as a primary emotion; but of course it does not describe the full range of our emotional behaviour. There are also secondary emotions, he argues, which occur once we start 'experiencing [conscious] feelings and forming *systematic connections between categories of objects and situations, on the one hand, and primary emotions, on the other'* (134). Rather than being activated at the somatic level, these secondary emotions begin with a cognitive evaluation of the individual's current (or anticipated) circumstances; and rather than being an innate response, they are *acquired* – that is to say, they are based on the individual's 'unique experience,' which 'may be at subtle or at major variance with that of others' (136). Although this evaluative process takes place in the prefrontal cortices, the fear signals it generates are also conveyed to the amygdala, whose autonomic response to such stimuli (involving a diverse range of physiological and neurological changes) is ultimately perceived, at the cognitive level, as the 'feeling' of fear.

From our perspective, the fact that Anil should be fascinated by 'this nerve bundle which houses fear' (Ondaatje 135) is of particular significance. She had first discovered the amygdala, we are told, while studying in London, where her professor had described it as 'the dark aspect of the brain,' a 'place to house fearful memories' (134). And even now, when conducting an autopsy, she always makes a detour to look for this almond-shaped concentration of nerve fibres. It is significant, as well, that this analeptic reference to the amygdala should be immediately followed by a conversation that occurs while Anil and Sarath are driving. 'Is your tape recorder off?' Sarath asks, not once but twice. 'Is your tape recorder off?' And only when Anil replies in the affirmative does he begin to tell her about the detention centres in Colombo and the torture that takes place there. '*I wanted to find one law to cover all of living,*' the narrator says, citing the poet Anne Carson. '*I found fear ...*' (135). But the fear that Sarath demonstrates in this scene is not the innate fear that Damasio would describe as primary; it is a secondary fear that has been conditioned by experience and involves

---

7 For a more detailed description of these autonomic responses, see Rodrigues et al.

a cognitive evaluation of both the situation in which he finds himself *and* its potential consequences. Moreover, although it is object-directed in the sense that he is concerned about the tape recorder (and the danger it represents), the real source of his apprehension is far more indefinite and widely dispersed. In this respect, I would argue, the fear that Sarath is experiencing here displays some of the qualities that we would typically associate with anxiety, thus complicating the traditional distinction between the two feelings.

We find this distinction everywhere. Kierkegaard, for instance, writes that anxiety is 'altogether different from fear and similar concepts that refer to something definite.' Whereas fear is clearly object-directed, he suggests, the 'relation of anxiety to its object' is the relation of 'something' to 'nothing' (42–43). Similarly, for Heidegger, 'anything "fearsome" is always encountered as an entity within-the-world,' while anxiety is caused by something 'completely indefinite' (*Being* 230–31). And from a psychoanalytical perspective, Freud also chooses to distinguish between anxiety (*Angst*) and fear (*Furcht*): 'I will only say that I think "*Angst*" relates to the state and disregards the object, while "*Furcht*" draws attention precisely to the object' (*Introductory* 443). In *Anil's Ghost*, however, the conventional distinction between these two categories is blurred. The fear we find here is still attached to an object, or at least *anticipating* an object of some kind, but the identity and location of that object is unpredictable and always shifting. The ultimate object of this fear could be the government forces (army, navy, air force, police, etc.), or the various pro-government paramilitaries, or the LTTE, or the JVP – or all of the above. And this is what gives the fear in the novel its free-floating, indiscriminate quality: not the fact that the object is nowhere (as is the case with anxiety) but that it is *everywhere*, or at least potentially so. Furthermore, even if this fear is not realized on a particular occasion, even if the fearsome object 'passes them by,' the apprehension that the characters experience will simply be transferred to other occasions and other objects – and as Sara Ahmed notes, this mobility, this slipperiness, only serves to intensify such dysphoric feelings. 'Fear,' she writes,

> is all the more frightening given the potential loss of the object that it anticipates. The more we don't know what or who it is we fear *the more the world becomes fearsome*. In other words, it is the structural possibility that the object of fear may pass us by which makes everything possibly fearsome. This is an important dimension in the spatial politics of fear: the loss of the object of fear renders the world

itself a space of potential danger, a space that is anticipated as pain or injury on the surface of the body that fears. (*Cultural* 69)

This is precisely the kind of fear that we encounter in *Anil's Ghost* – one that is no longer attached to a single entity, or contained within a single object (whether it be a tape recorder or a detention centre), but has become systemic, an atmospheric pathology that inundates the entire narrative.[8] We find the first reference to this emotion on the opening page of the novel ('*There was always the fear, double-edged, that it was their son in the pit, or that it was not their son – which meant there would be further searching*' [5]); and such references only proliferate thereafter – on pages 17, 20, 40, 54, 55, and so on – until finally the discourse itself internalizes this inescapable structure of feeling. And it is the decentred, indeterminate, and 'atmospheric' nature of the feeling in question that allows it to do so. In a way, one could argue, this process replicates the formation of a secondary emotion, as defined by Damasio. At the representational level of the narrative, we have a repository of mental images based on particular patterns of neural firing in the early sensory cortices. These images are evaluated by the discourse using acquired 'dispositional representations that embody [prior] knowledge pertaining to how certain types of situations ... have been paired with certain emotional responses' (*Descartes' Error* 136). Automatically and involuntarily, this (discursive) evaluation is then conveyed to the amygdala (i.e., the underlying structure of the narrative). And once the amygdala receives these signals, it initiates a number of autonomic responses that are registered at both a physiological and cognitive level – thus creating a 'feeling.'[9] Or to complete the analogy, the narrative's

---

8 As such, this structure of feeling shares a number of clear affinities with Ato Quayson's notion of the systemic uncanny, which we discussed in Chapter 1. 'In the face of persistent physical and social violence,' Quayson argues, 'either triggered by acute political chaos or the general collapse of the social order, a process of internalization of these perceived disorders takes place. In such instances, the self is presumed to be constantly under threat, whether this threat ever materializes or not. The internalized translation of disorder does not, however, remain merely internalized, but gets cathected into inchoate senses of guilt, inexplicable terror, or a general sense of disquiet that may or may not be consciously traceable to a direct source' (*Aesthetic* 142).
9 I am using Damasio's terminology here. 'If an emotion is a collection of changes in body state,' he writes, 'connected to particular mental images that have activated a specific brain system, *the essence of feeling an emotion*

limbic system, having received these fear signals, initiates a number of autonomic responses that are subsequently registered at both a formal and representational level – thus ensuring that this feeling infiltrates even the deepest recesses of the discourse. And as I shall argue in the following section, these autonomic responses can be discerned most clearly at the level of genre, where they influence (and unsettle) the entire 'organism.'

III

The fear responses we encounter most often in *Anil's Ghost* are not of the confrontational variety but the evasive – replicating the classic 'phobic' trajectory of this negative feeling. As Sianne Ngai writes, fear can be described as 'dysphoric or experientially negative' in the sense that it evokes 'pain or displeasure'; it can be described as 'semantically' negative in the sense that it is 'saturated with socially stigmatizing meanings and values'; and it can be described as 'syntactically' negative in the sense that it is 'organized by trajectories of repulsion rather than attraction, by phobic strivings "away from" rather than philic strivings "toward"' (*Ugly* 11). There are many examples of such phobic tendencies in the novel, but for our purposes, just a couple should suffice.

Sarath's brother, Gamini, works as a surgeon in the emergency ward of a hospital in Colombo. Every dead body that is discovered in the city eventually finds its way here; and Gamini is required to sign off on it before it can be claimed or cremated. Despite his experience as a surgeon, however, he has developed a strong aversion to these corpses, and does everything he can to avoid direct contact with the bodies themselves:

> Gamini had chosen not to deal with the dead. He avoided the south-wing corridors, where they brought the torture victims to be identified. Interns listed the wounds and photographed the bodies. Still, once a week, he went over the reports and the photographs of the dead, confirmed what was assumed, pointed out fresh scars caused by acid or sharp metal, and gave his signature.

While studying these photos, Gamini covers the faces of the corpses with his left hand ('the pulse in his wrist jumping'). 'He worked better

---

is the experience of such changes in juxtaposition to the mental images that initiated the cycle' (*Descartes' Error* 145).

this way,' we learn, 'and there was no danger of his recognizing the dead' (212–13). For Gamini, it appears, even the photographic representation of these corpses provokes a kind of phobic aversion – a turning 'away from' rather than a turning 'toward.' And as I suggested earlier, this fear at the representational level of the discourse also influences the novel's formal qualities. On one occasion, just as Gamini is completing his weekly duties, another consignment of bodies arrives at the hospital; and as it does so, the discourse undergoes a sudden transition from the literal to the figurative: 'The doors opened and a thousand bodies slid in, as if caught in the nets of fishermen, as if they had been mauled. A thousand bodies of sharks and skates in the corridors, some of the dark-skinned fish thrashing ...' (213). This sudden shift in register could be seen as a phobic reaction on the part of the discourse itself, which turns away from the aesthetic principles that have governed the narrative thus far, and instead takes refuge in a series of oblique metaphorical correlatives. As mentioned in the Introduction, Ato Quayson employs the term 'symbolization compulsion' to describe this kind of evasive strategy – a phobic impulse that drives the narrative toward an 'insistent metaphorical register even when this register does not help to develop the action, define character or spectacle, or create atmosphere.' Ultimately, Quayson argues, such a gratuitous use of figurative language serves as a defence mechanism for the discourse, a way of avoiding or repressing a traumatic experience that 'cannot be named except through symbolized digressiveness' (*Calibrations* 82). So when, on page 213 of *Anil's Ghost*, the discourse suddenly lapses into figurative language that is really only notable for its incongruity, it is reasonable to see it as an evasive response, one that has been activated at the autonomic level of the narrative and has subsequently influenced the entire organism, saturating it with the linguistic equivalent of cortisol, say, or adrenaline.

We witness a similar response, a little earlier in the novel, when the disappearance of one of the characters' wives is described. The passage in question occupies four pages and begins with a detailed account of her daily routine:

> *At six in the morning she dressed, then began walking the mile to the school. A few hundred yards before she climbed the hill, the road narrowed into a bridge, a lagoon on one side, a salt river on the other ... It was always six-thirty a.m. when she reached the bridge. There would be a few prawn boats, a man up to his neck in the water, whose hands, out of sight, would be straightening the nets that had been dropped by his son from a boat during the night ... From here Sirissa would reach the school in ten*

minutes, change in a cubicle, soak rags in a bucket, and begin cleaning the blackboards ... In the evenings during the government curfews she remained indoors, with a lamp and a book in her room. (172–73)

After two and a half pages, this iterative sequence gives way to a singulative description of one morning in particular. '*Sirissa wakes and bathes herself at the well behind the house she is living in*'; then, as always, she dresses and leaves for the school. When she reaches the bridge, however, she discovers a horrific scene: four local teenagers, whom she recognizes, have been decapitated – their heads impaled on stakes. Feeling the presence of something behind her, Sirissa begins to run. She runs across the bridge and up the hill toward the school. '*She keeps running forward*,' we are told, '*and then she sees no more*' (174–75). Once again, then, we have a phobic aversion to violence, and once again the discourse internalizes this fear, bringing the passage to an abrupt conclusion with the line quoted above. By doing so, it ensures that the majority of the passage should be dedicated to the kind of catalytic material that contributes nothing of any real significance or value to the story we are reading – while the implied act of violence that follows, which actually *does* matter, is 'safely' consigned to the interstices of the narrative.[10]

The phobic tendencies we have been exploring here also influence the narrative's overarching trajectory, which is constantly deviating from its (generically) ordained course. As Tzvetan Todorov has argued, the classic detective novel is composed of not one but two narratives. We have the story of the crime and the story of the investigation, with the former obviously preceding the latter as it is the first narrative that makes the second one possible – or necessary – and the second narrative that makes the first one legible. Indeed, the sole purpose of the second narrative is to uncover the first one, the story of the crime, which is only revealed by following the various clues (the 'traces' left behind by the first narrative) back to their original source. Or to put it another way, as Todorov does, we might characterize 'these two stories by saying that the first – the story of the crime – tells "what really happened," whereas the second – the story of the investigation – explains "how the reader (or the narrator) has come to know about it"' (44–45). In the opening pages of *Anil's Ghost*, a scenario of this kind

---

10 Interestingly, in his essay on the subject, Quayson suggests that symbolization compulsion may also take the form of an 'intensification of the quotidian or the everyday' ('Symbolization' 759–60).

is immediately established. We have the mystery of the first narrative (involving Sailor's murder) and the investigation that comprises the second (involving our two detective figures). But things very quickly begin to go awry. Rather than steadily advancing from one clue to another, in a concerted attempt to 'reveal' the first narrative, the discourse assumes an increasingly digressive quality, exploring a wide range of peripheral subtrajectories. On pages 39–40, for instance, we have a lengthy description of the *National Atlas of Sri Lanka* (full of poetic litanies and evocative place names). Not long afterward, there is an interlude of some thirty pages, during which Anil and Sarath visit the latter's elderly mentor in the 'Grove of Ascetics' (86). And on pages 138–40, we are introduced to some of the fundamental principles of Sri Lankan astrology, with particular reference to love and marriage. Needless to say, such digressive passages contribute very little to the novel's primary plotline; and as they continue to accumulate, we eventually realize that there is something else going on here. More specifically, we begin to realize that the discourse has developed a phobic aversion to the very narrative it is supposed to be uncovering (i.e., the 'story of the crime'). Instead of investigating Sailor's murder, as a 'good' detective novel should, it would much rather be expatiating on the subject of native birdlife or prehistoric caves or astrology – or *any* subject, however arcane, that will allow it to turn away from this terrifying act of violence.

Along with its distinctly phobic qualities, the fear we encounter in *Anil's Ghost* is also of the non-cathartic variety. 'In a fearful nation,' our narrator observes,

> public sorrow was stamped down by the climate of uncertainty. If a father protested a son's death, it was feared another family member would be killed. If people you knew disappeared, there was a chance they might stay alive if you did not cause trouble. This was the scarring psychosis in the country. *Death, loss, was 'unfinished,' so you could not walk through it.* There had been years of night visitations, kidnappings or murders in broad daylight ... All that was left of law was a belief in an eventual revenge towards those who had power. (56; my italics)

In Ondaatje's novel, however, such revenge, such closure, never arrives; and as a consequence, the general climate of fear within the country assumes an ongoing, 'unfinished' quality, which in turn removes the possibility of cathartic release. This is the kind of emotion that Antonio Damasio would describe as a 'background feeling': a constant, underlying state of being that may be punctuated, from time to time, by more pronounced and less durable affective impulses. 'When background feelings are persistently of the same type over hours and days,' Damasio argues, 'and do not change quietly as thought contents ebb and flow' (*Descartes' Error* 151), they contribute to a more general mood – which in the present case, of course, is notably dysphoric.[11] And it is this interminable quality that eventually infiltrates the structure of the novel itself, making it almost impossible for the discourse to achieve its primary generic objective: hermeneutic closure. Who killed Sailor? Why? Under what circumstances? Were they ever brought to justice? These are just some of the questions that remain unanswered at the end of the novel. Rather fortuitously, Anil and Sarath do manage to identify Sailor, but this discharge of meaning, when it finally occurs on page 269, carries very little significance within the narrative as a whole and does almost nothing to alter its overall trajectory. The name of the victim may have been Ruwan Kumara, and he may have worked in a plumbago mine. He may have been identified as a 'rebel sympathizer' and subsequently taken into custody. But there is really nothing that we as readers can *do* with this information, and nothing much that the characters can do either. What should have been a pivotal moment in the novel, a moment of resolution and vindication, has become just another inconsequential aside – of no more significance than an endangered bird or a prehistoric cave.

And the reason that the solution to this particular mystery can be so easily disregarded is because it does nothing to contain or dissipate the fear that was generated by the discovery of Sailor's body in the first place. After all, he is just one of many such victims, his murder just one of many such crimes. As a 1989 Amnesty International report put it, 'Violence is now so widespread [in Sri Lanka] that it is often difficult to establish with authority who the agents of specific killings were – or even to identify the victims whose bodies are sometimes grossly mutilated, burned to ashes or transported long distances … before being dumped' (qtd. in Senaratne 146). The overwhelming scale of the

---

11 Elsewhere, Damasio has indicated that background feelings are 'engendered by ongoing physiological processes or by the organism's interactions with the environment or both,' and that they can include 'feelings of tension or relaxation, of fatigue or energy, of well-being or malaise, of anticipation or dread' (*Feeling* 52). 'When asked "how we feel,"' he says, 'we consult this "state of being" and answer accordingly' (*Looking* 44).

violence is made abundantly clear on page 41 of the novel, where we are offered a representative list of unsolved disappearances (including precise times and places):

> *Kumara Wijetunga, 17. 6th November 1989. At about 11:30 p.m. from his house.*
>
> *Prabath Kumara, 16. 17th November 1989. At 3:20 a.m. from the home of a friend.*
>
> *Kumara Arachchi, 16. 17th November 1989. At about midnight from his house.*
>
> *Manelka da Silva, 17. 1st December 1989. While playing cricket, Embilipitiya Central College playground.*
>
> *Jatunga Gunesena, 23. 11th December 1989. At 10:30 a.m. near his house while talking to a friend ... [etc.]*[12]

One could argue that each of these entries initiates a separate hermeneutic sequence, a separate mystery, so what does it really matter if just the one murder is (partially) solved? Under these circumstances, genuine closure, and the justice that ought to accompany it, is simply impossible to achieve. This is what ultimately gives the fear in the narrative its indefinite, free-floating quality – the fact that it cannot be attached to, or contained by, any one object – and this is also what makes it so very difficult to localize culpability in the manner of the classic detective novel. In traditional crime fiction, by solving the crime and identifying the criminal, the narrative serves to 'quarantine' criminality and re-establish a sense of social order. This stability may have been momentarily threatened by the discovery of the crime itself, but by locating (and ultimately punishing) the criminal, the narrative restores the social status quo and reassures us that such disruptive forces can be effectively contained. According to Franco Moretti, the perfect crime, which constitutes the 'nightmare of detective fiction,' is the 'featureless, deindividualized crime that anyone could have committed because at this point everyone is the same.' Classic detective fiction, however, serves to 'dispel the doubt

---

12 As Sophia A. McClennen and Joseph R. Slaughter note, this passage reproduces a list of 'unresolved disappearances' that was first published in a 1992 Amnesty International report and later submitted to the UN Commission on Human Rights in 2005 (10).

that guilt might be impersonal, and therefore collective and social' (*Signs* 135). By concentrating criminality within the figure of the criminal, it absolves society of all responsibility for the crime – thus producing or reinforcing a more general state of social innocence. In *The Novel and the Police*, D.A. Miller makes a similar point with reference to the production of meaning within such narratives. At the beginning of a detective novel, the discourse is saturated with potential significance; anything and everything may carry investigatory value, may constitute a 'clue.' Furthermore, any character (even the narrator in rare cases) may be guilty of the crime that is being investigated. At the end of the novel, though, when the detective offers his or her final summation, all of these 'hypothetical significances … are simultaneously dissolved,' and we discover that only a fraction of the narrative's signifiers carry any real value. Everything and everyone else lapses into a state of irrelevance (which is also, of course, a state of innocence). 'It is often argued,' Miller writes,

> that the detective story seeks to totalize its signifiers in a complete and all-encompassing order. On the contrary, it is concerned to restrict and localize the province of meaning: to guarantee large areas of irrelevance. One easily sees, moreover, what else is guaranteed in such a form. For as the fantasy of total relevance yields to the reality of a more selective meaningfulness, the universality of suspicion gives way to a highly specific guilt. (34)[13]

Yet this is obviously not the case in *Anil's Ghost*. Here, we find an abundance of violent crimes but no specific criminal – leaving society itself to bear the responsibility for such atrocities. In other words, the potential significance (and potential culpability) that saturates the novel at the beginning remains just as unfocused and widely dispersed at the end. Although Anil is given the opportunity to deliver a final summation before an audience of military and police personnel, here too things quickly go awry. She becomes confused and flustered. Her evidence is confiscated. She is interrupted, challenged ('Why do you not investigate the killing of government officers?' [275]), and then finally forced to leave the auditorium, having revealed little and resolved nothing. If, as Miller argues, the objective of the fictional detective is to 'restrict and localize the province of meaning,' to 'guarantee large areas of irrelevance,' then she has quite clearly failed in this endeavour. Anything could still carry

---

13 Some of this material is derived from my discussion of Roberto Bolaño's *2666* (see Scott, 'Roberto'), which touches on similar issues.

Affective Disorders

significance and anyone could still be guilty. By localizing meaning and culpability, the fictional detective also manages to localize fear – attaching it to a specific figure, the criminal, who is subsequently 'brought to justice' and thus neutralized. But as I have suggested, the fear in *Anil's Ghost* is not tethered to a single entity or figure; it cannot be localized in the form of an unidentified corpse, or an LTTE soldier, or a representative of the state. Instead, it moves from body to body, and from place to place, creating a dysphoric atmosphere – or structure of feeling – that permeates every level of the discourse.

IV

According to Tzvetan Todorov, as we have noted, the detective novel is founded on a duality, being composed of not one but two narratives – the story of the crime and the story of the investigation. The significance of the first story is easy enough to understand, but what happens, Todorov asks, in the second? 'Not much. The characters of this second story, the story of the investigation, do not act, they learn. Nothing can happen to them: a rule of the genre postulates the detective's immunity' (44). In this chapter, we have discussed the way in which *Anil's Ghost* internalizes the fear that achieved such ubiquity during the Sri Lankan Civil War. We have also looked at the way in which the discourse replicates some of the more salient features of this emotion (i.e., its phobic, non-cathartic, and indefinite qualities). These qualities, I have argued, in turn give rise to a number of generic disturbances, depriving the narrative of the linearity, the hermeneutic closure, and the 'localization of culpability' that we ordinarily associate with crime fiction. And so it is only fitting, perhaps, that the novel should conclude with one last generic violation, one last example of the way in which certain social realities can have quite tangible discursive consequences. As I mentioned at the beginning of the chapter, an estimated 60,000 to 100,000 people disappeared during the twenty-six years of the civil war. The initial manifestation of these disappearances, Sasanka Perera writes, was the 'mutilated or burned bodies that were scattered around. People soon realized that every time they discovered bodies in places where they were not supposed to be, real people had disappeared from places where they should have been' (166–67). In Ondaatje's novel, the 'first story,' the story of the crime, is initiated by one such disappearance. As we eventually learn, a plumbago miner by the name of Ruwan Kumara, having been identified as a 'rebel sympathizer,' was arrested one day by the security forces and never seen again. In the classic crime novel, this discovery would provide some closure; but not here, and certainly not under these specific circumstances. Typically, to quote Northrop Frye, the detective novel serves a 'balancing and neutralizing' function within society – 'the murderer discovered at the end balancing the corpse that we normally find at the beginning' (137). In *Anil's Ghost*, however, this reassuring symmetry collapses, and our detective figures never even come close to identifying Kumara's killers. Moreover, in the novel's penultimate chapter, the boundary between the story of the crime and the story of the investigation, the one that is supposed to ensure the immunity of the detective, his or her inviolable status, finally ruptures. After leaving the auditorium in Colombo where Anil had been speaking, Sarath is abducted by the security forces, tortured, and murdered – thereby ensuring that the only symmetry to be found here involves the tragic repetition of the novel's inaugural atrocity.

This second murder also activates an autonomic fear response on the part of the discourse, just as the first one had. After leaving the auditorium, Sarath waves down a Bajaj and gives the driver the address of his office: '[S]itting forward, his head in his hands, he trie[s] to lose touch with the world around him as the three-wheeler struggle[s] through the traffic' (282). And that is the last we see of our 'detective,' until his mutilated body is delivered to the hospital morgue some time later. In this case, too, the act of violence is consigned to the interstices of the narrative – surrounded on one side by the deliberately banal description of the Bajaj and the heavy Colombo traffic, and on the other side, eventually, by the intensely poetic scene with which the novel concludes. The scene in question describes in some detail the construction (and reconstruction) of two monumental Buddha statues, a process that is only complete once the *nētra mangala* ceremony has been performed.[14] This ceremony is conducted by Ananda, an artisan who had been helping with the investigation into Sailor's murder; and as you can imagine, it is beautifully depicted. At one point, Ananda

---

14 Earlier in the novel, we are offered a useful description of this ceremony: '*Nētra* means "eye,"' one character says. 'It is a ritual of the eyes. A special artist is needed to paint eyes on a holy figure. It is always the last thing done. It is what gives the image life. Like a fuse. The eyes are a fuse. It has to happen before a statue or a painting in a *vihara* can become a holy thing' (97). For more on the significance of the *nētra mangala* ceremony, see Salgado 139–42 and Farrier 90–91.

assumes the perspective of the statue itself, seeing 'all the fibres of natural history' laid out before him. He can see everything from 'the smallest approach of a bird, every flick of its wing,' to 'a hundred-mile storm coming down off the mountains near Gonagola.' He can feel 'each current of wind, every lattice-like green shadow created by cloud.' And above everything else, he is able to witness the 'great churning' of the weather as it is formed 'in the temperate forests and sea, in the thorn scrub behind him in the southeast, in the deciduous hills, and ... [along] the coast of mangroves, lagoons and river deltas' (307). It is an intoxicating state of omniscience, but it does not last long. In the novel's final line, Ananda feels his nephew's 'concerned hand on his,' a 'sweet touch from the world' (307).

As I say, this is a beautiful piece of writing, and heavily freighted with symbolic resonance – only it has been difficult for critics to agree on its precise meaning.[15] Given everything we have discussed thus far, however, I would be inclined to see it as another instance of 'symbolization compulsion,' as a way of avoiding or repressing a traumatic experience through the use of oblique figurative language. According to Ato Quayson, such phobic impulses often give rise to a semiotic structure whose 'intensity completely obscures its [true] referential locus' (*Calibrations* 90). And that, I would argue, is largely the case here. We have a series of signifiers that have been saturated with connotative value: the ceremony itself, for example, or the panoptic vision of the surrounding landscape, or the 'combustible world of [the] weather' (306), or the faint smell of grass being burned, or the girl moving in the forest below, or the 'great scarred face' (307) of the other statue half a mile away, or the intimate 'touch' of the boy's hand. Every detail has been intensified, accentuated, invested with multiple layers of implied significance (much of which may be

---

15 'The ending of *Anil's Ghost*,' Minoli Salgado writes, 'is contentious partly because it seems to replicate [the novel's more general] interpretative indeterminacy in the very act of presenting an epiphanic insight. Critics have variously praised it as a "healing vision" that offers "a peace that *encompasses* understanding" ... or either attacked it or dismissed it as a literary gloss. In terms that replicate Althusser's formulation of art as an aesthetic resolution of political conflict, John de Falbe has claimed that this epiphany "uses an easy poetic image to evade a problematic conclusion to the novel." Fans have claimed that it is "a tour de force" linked "with the redemptive act of writing," while Qadri Ismail, in a vituperative attack on Ondaatje's "casual racism," has claimed that it indicates that Ondaatje is clearly "on the side of the enemy or Sinhala nationalism"' (138).

perfectly plausible).¹⁶ And this is what makes it so easy to overlook the solitary detail within this passage that gestures toward its invisible referential locus. I am referring to the line on page 305, where we learn that beneath his brocade costume, Ananda is wearing Sarath's cotton shirt – 'the one he had promised himself he would wear for this morning's ceremony.'¹⁷ While everything else in the passage moves us toward a higher plane of paradigmatic meaning (where we may very well discover something of 'thematic' significance), this single, relatively mundane detail takes us to another place altogether. By gesturing toward the 'unutterable traumatic occurrence' (Quayson, *Calibrations* 82) that has precipitated this sudden discharge of symbolic meaning, it creates a pathway into the underlying structure of the narrative. Or to revive my earlier analogy, it moves us away from the narrative's frontal lobes – where higher-order cognitive reasoning takes place – and into the deeper recesses of its limbic system, where the amygdala is located. This is the almond-shaped bundle of nerves, you may recall, that 'creates' the feeling of fear, giving rise to the various physiological processes and behavioural responses that we have learned to categorize in this way. Or in the case of *Anil's Ghost*, as we have seen, it activates a phobic response on the part of the discourse itself, one that is registered most clearly, at the 'cognitive' level, as a series of generic and stylistic incongruities. But this response does not mean that the dead have been forgotten, only that they have assumed another form, another kind of discursive presence; and if we read the novel carefully enough, it is still possible to detect the faint traces of those who have disappeared – whether it be in the guise of the figurative, the mundane, or the symbolic.

16 For Quayson, it is worth noting, symbolization compulsion can in some cases take the form of an 'intensified perceptual sensorium' accompanied by the 'intrusion of the extraordinary into the mundane' ('Symbolization' 764); and it is also interesting that Freud should associate 'increased sensory attention' with the feeling of 'realistic anxiety' (*Introductory* 442).

17 This crucial gesture is anticipated earlier in the novel when we are told that Anil 'used to believe that meaning allowed a person a door to escape grief and fear. But she [now] saw that those who were slammed and stained by violence lost the power of language and logic. It was the way to abandon emotion, a last protection for the self. They held on to just the coloured and patterned sarong a missing relative last slept in, which in normal times would have become a household rag but now was sacred' (55–56).

CHAPTER SIX

Stuplimity
Vikram Chandra's *Sacred Games*

> Ours is indeed an age of extremity. For we live under continual threat of two equally fearful, but seemingly opposed, destinies: unremitting banality and inconceivable terror.
>
> Susan Sontag, 'The Imagination of Disaster,' 1965

> We were interested precisely in those things which are the opposite of the extraordinary yet ... are not the ordinary either.
>
> Paul Virilio, 'On Georges Perec,' 2001

I

Although it is often described as a thriller and demonstrates many of the characteristics that we typically associate with this genre, Vikram Chandra's 2006 novel *Sacred Games* can, in places, be surprisingly unthrilling. For long stretches of time, nothing of any real significance transpires; and much of the narrative serves to impede, rather than facilitate, the progress of its most 'thrilling' plotline. It is certainly true that there is no shortage of spectacle here – whether it takes the form of a brutal gangland massacre, a terrorist bombing, or a police siege. Yet we are also exposed to the routine violence and criminality that, for many people, has become an inescapable feature of everyday life in Mumbai, the Indian city of twenty-two million that serves as the novel's primary setting. In the following pages, I would like to suggest that this conjunction of opposing categories gives rise to a dominant structure of feeling that not only influences the novel at the representational or mimetic level, where all the action takes place, but also penetrates the deeper reaches of form, genre, and style. More specifically, I shall argue that the concurrence of both spectacular and mundane forms of criminality within *Sacred Games* produces an affective state that is equally heterogeneous, combining the categories of the sublime and the stupefying, the astonishing and the boring. And this feeling – which I shall be describing as one of 'stuplimity' (Ngai, *Ugly* 271) – ultimately infiltrates the discourse itself, creating an unsettling slippage between the narrative's more significant episodes (or nuclei) and those that constitute mere filler.

Before we begin, though, it may be worth considering, just briefly, some other crime narratives that have sought to dissolve the boundary between the public sphere and the private, the historical event and the everyday occurrence. In 1987, the Subaltern Studies historian Ranajit Guha published an essay, entitled 'Chandra's Death,' that would go on to acquire a seminal status within the field of postcolonial studies. Based on a fragmentary document he discovered in the archives of Viswabharati University, Guha's essay describes the accidental death of a young woman – a member of the disadvantaged Bagdi agricultural caste – in rural Bengal in the year 1849. The woman in question, Chandra Chashani, had been conducting an 'illicit love affair' (136) with her brother-in-law, and when this transgression led to an unwanted pregnancy, she was offered the choice of either aborting the child or being ostracized from the village in a punishment known as *bhek*. Together with her female relatives, Chandra decided on the former course of action; and with this purpose in mind, they procured 'a herbal medicine which had to be taken thrice a day … [along] with some *horituki* (a wild fruit of medicinal value) and two tablets of *bakhor guli* (a preparation of herbs and rice used to induce abortion) diluted in lime water.' In her subsequent statement, Chandra's sister described the tragic consequences of this decision. 'I prepared a paste of the medicine with my own hands,' she said,

> and administered one dose of it to Chandra at a quarter past the second *pohor* of the night [around 12.45 a.m.] … [As a result, the] foetus was destroyed and it fell to the ground. My mother picked up the bloody foetus with some straw and threw it away. Even

after that the pain in Chandra's belly continued to increase and she died [roughly two hours before sunrise]. Chandra's corpse was then buried near the [river's] bend by my brother Gayaram, his brother-in-law, and my mother's brother Horilal. I administered the medicine in the belief that it would terminate her pregnancy and did not realize that it would kill her. (qtd. in Guha 136)

According to Guha, this document reveals the limitations of traditional historiography, which has been '[d]esigned for big events and institutions' and 'tends to ignore the small drama and fine detail of social existence, especially at its lower depths' (138). Moreover, the fact that the episode has been translated into judicial discourse, in the form of a legal deposition, makes it particularly elusive. Although we are offered a number of statements that constitute 'direct speech,' Guha observes,

> it is speech prompted by the requirements of an official investigation into what is presumed to be a murder … [T]he narrative in the document [thus] violates the actual sequence of what happened in order to conform to the logic of a legal intervention which made the death into a murder, a caring sister into [a] murderess, all the actants in this tragedy into defendants, and what they said in a state of grief into *ekrars* [a legal term for confessions or acknowledgements of guilt]. (139–41)

As a way of challenging these reductive judicial processes, Guha advocates a 'critical historiography' that is capable of 'bending closer to the ground [so as] to pick up the traces of a subaltern life in its passage through time' (138). And in this particular case, he argues, such a methodology would involve recontextualizing the document (and the 'crime' it describes) by situating it within 'the life of a community,' where 'a multitude of anxieties and interventions endowed it with its real historical content,' and by seeing it not as an *ekrar*, not as an admission of legal culpability, but as 'the record of a Bagdi family's effort to cope collectively, if unsuccessfully, with a [personal] crisis' (142).[1]

---

1 Although Guha's masterful essay has been particularly influential within Indian literary studies, it is possible to identify similar tendencies elsewhere too. In 1984, for instance, the South African critic Njabulo Ndebele delivered a lecture in which he argued that the 'history of black South African literature has largely been the history of the representation of spectacle.' According to Ndebele, the sheer visibility of apartheid, the

Affective Disorders

If historiographical discourse has traditionally ignored 'the small drama and fine detail of social existence, especially at its lower depths' (138), and judicial discourse has typically reduced the complexity of crime to 'a set of narrowly defined legalities' (140), then we must look elsewhere for a more complete picture of these historical episodes. In a fascinating aside, Guha identifies one such source in the 'narratives of crime' (*récits de crimes*) that were widely read in France during the nineteenth century. These journalistic descriptions of actual cases, he writes, made it possible for the 'common murder ... to cross the uncertain frontier which separates it from the "nameless butcheries" of battle and make its way into history' (139–40). Guha is quoting Foucault here, and referring, more specifically, to his 1973 essay 'Tales of Murder' (which discusses the case of Pierre Rivière, a Norman peasant who murdered three members of his immediate family in 1835). If we turn to this essay, it is easy to see why Guha favours such popular journalism as an alternative to standard historiographical and judicial discourse. According to Foucault, the purpose of the nineteenth-century *récit de crime* was to

> alter the scale, to enlarge the proportions, to bring out the microscopic seed of the story, and make narrative accessible to the everyday. The first requisite in bringing about this change was to introduce into the narrative the elements, personages, deeds, dialogues, and subjects which normally had no place in [it] because they were undignified or lacking in social importance, and the second was to see that all these minor events, however commonplace and monotonous they may be, appeared 'singular,' 'curious,' 'extraordinary,' unique, or very nearly so, in the memory of man. (204)

---

spectacular nature of its systemic 'violence and brutality,' has given rise to 'a highly dramatic, highly demonstrative form of literary representation' (41). Under the circumstances, of course, this would appear to be a perfectly valid response to the flagrant inequities of apartheid; and Ndebele is careful to acknowledge as much in his lecture. However, he also argues that it is necessary to move beyond this melodramatic emphasis on spectacle by 'rediscovering the ordinary' – by making the 'ordinary daily lives of people ... the direct focus of political [and literary] interest' (57). Responding to Ndebele's lecture some thirty years later, Saikat Majumdar has also emphasized the need for '[n]arratives of postcolonial reality' to situate themselves within the world of the quotidian and the uninteresting, thereby 'reclaim[ing] banality as an aesthetic form' and acknowledging the significance of boredom for the vast majority of people who live their lives 'far from the glare of the spectacle' (178).

Stuplimity

By privileging 'minor events' in this way, Foucault concludes, such narratives were able to 'make the transition from the familiar to the remarkable, the everyday to the historical' (204), and thus served as a crucial 'point of intersection' (205) between these disparate spheres.

In *Sacred Games*, as I have noted, we encounter a similar collision of contraries. On the one hand, over the course of 947 pages, we are made to endure all the banality, repetition, and monotony of crime and criminality in the city of Mumbai, while on the other hand, we find ourselves confronting the periodic *rupture* of the ordinary in the 'spectacular' form of terrorism and communal violence. In what follows, I shall be exploring both sides of this apparent dichotomy. I will begin by discussing the minor crimes to be found within the pages of Chandra's novel – the petty burglaries, the routine corruption, the domestic disputes, and so on. I will then move on to address the episodes of 'exceptional' criminality that also feature here: namely, the destruction of the Babri Masjid in Ayodhya in 1992, the communal violence that took place in Bombay (as it was then known) in 1992–93, and the retaliatory bombings that occurred on 12 March 1993, killing 257 people.[2] For some time, I shall argue, our hero – the police inspector Sartaj Singh – oscillates from one extreme to the other, from the banal to the extraordinary, the boring to the spectacular, before finally reconciling these traditional antitheses. The emotion that Sartaj experiences as a consequence of this dialectical intermingling could best be described by invoking Sianne Ngai's notion of stuplimity (as formulated in her 2005 work *Ugly Feelings*). According to Ngai, classic theories of the sublime fail to account for the 'experience of boredom' that has become 'increasingly intertwined with contemporary experiences of aesthetic awe' (8). 'Stuplimity,' a portmanteau combination of the stupefying and the sublime, is the term she uses to delineate an aesthetic response of this kind, one in which 'the initial experience of being aesthetically overwhelmed involves not terror or pain … but *something much closer to an ordinary fatigue*' (270). And as we shall see, this is precisely the mood that dominates the conclusion of *Sacred Games*, allowing these

---

2 In 1995, the state government of Maharashtra, led by the right-wing Shiv Sena party, officially changed the name of the city from Bombay to Mumbai – thus privileging the language, culture, and history of the city's Marathi majority. (For a particularly illuminating analysis of the identity politics underlying this transformation, see Hansen 1–6.) In this chapter, however, I will be alternating between the two names so as to avoid anachronism.

'opposing' realities – the stupefying and the sublime, the mundane and the spectacular – to infiltrate the very tissue of the narrative we are reading.

II

At a superficial, proairetic level – the level of action and plotting – *Sacred Games* clearly qualifies as a thriller. In the novel's opening pages, Sartaj Singh, the world-weary police inspector mentioned above, discovers the dead body of a local gangster in a nuclear fallout shelter, and at the behest of the Indian security services, he launches an investigation into the case. Why had the legendary *bhai*, Ganesh Gaitonde, returned to Mumbai in the first place, and what was he doing in a bunker that had been designed to withstand a nuclear apocalypse? During his investigation, Sartaj discovers that in recent years Gaitonde had fallen under the influence of a radical Hindu religious figure, Swami Shridhar Shukla ('Guru-ji'), who has managed to smuggle a nuclear bomb into Mumbai with the intention of detonating it in the centre of the city and thereby ushering in a millenarian 'golden age' (838). As one might anticipate, however, Sartaj eventually manages to locate the nuclear device and, in so doing, both ensures the survival of the city he loves and reinforces the generic allegiance of the narrative in which he figures.

But there is a good deal more to *Sacred Games* than the plot I have outlined here. In his classic essay 'Introduction to the Structural Analysis of Narratives,' Roland Barthes draws a useful distinction between nuclei (those occurrences that 'constitute [the] real hinge points of [a] narrative') and catalyzers (those occurrences that 'merely "fill in" the narrative space separating the [nuclei]') (265). According to Barthes, nuclei are 'the risky moments of a narrative' – the places where discoveries are made, disasters averted, and nuclear devices disabled – while the catalyzers 'lay out areas of safety' (266), places where the energy of the narrative dissipates and nothing of any genuine consequence transpires.[3] In the preceding synopsis, needless to say, I have cited only one or two of the novel's most essential nuclei; yet as any reader of *Sacred Games* will know, the space *between* these crucial occurrences is heavily freighted with catalytic detail. On several occasions over the course of the novel, Sartaj becomes trapped in the 'congealed mass' (Chandra, *Sacred* 88) of a traffic jam, the 'compacted

---

3 For more on the distinction between nuclei and catalyzers, see Chapter 2.

clog of rush-hour traffic' (227), and one could argue that these delays serve as an intradiegetic correlative for the rather clogged nature of the narrative itself. Take the following passage, for instance:

> A party of Municipal men were working on a hole in the road. They weren't actually working, they were standing around the hole looking at it, and apparently waiting for something to happen. Meanwhile, a vast funnel of traffic pressed up against the bottleneck. Sartaj was somewhere towards the front, on his motorcycle. He was hemmed in by a BEST bus and two autos, and there was nowhere for anyone to go, so they all waited companionably. The bus was crammed full of office-goers, and the autos were taking college students to their classes. Young boys were working the stalled traffic, selling magazines and water and gaudy Chinese statues of a laughing man with his hands above his head. A pair of maimed beggars went from car to car, tapping their stumps on the windscreens. (945–46)

Of course, a scene like this is not without significance; but any meaning it does generate is inevitably 'attenuated [and] parasitic' (Barthes, 'Introduction' 266).[4] We could remove this passage entirely, or alter every sentence, every detail, and the basic narrative structure would remain unchanged, for none of these magazines or bottles of water or gaudy Chinese statues contribute anything of real value to the story we are reading. Like the traffic jam itself, all these catalyzers do is prevent the narrative from moving forward – forcing us to turn our attention to the inconsequential, the banal, and the boring while we wait 'for something [of significance] to happen.'[5]

---

4 In a perceptive article on the role of waiting (anticipation, deferral, delay, etc.) in the contemporary detective novel, Theodore Martin argues that this particular scene demonstrates the fact that waiting is not merely 'an empty space of disappointment,' an 'absence or a void,' but the 'temporal form of our inchoate, unfolding present.' In other words, the traffic jam gives Sartaj 'a different way to measure present time … Forced, finally, to slow down, [he] is no longer waiting *for* something. The experience of the traffic jam instead hints that [waiting] is the basic condition of everyday life – the time that governs each passing day' (180–81). Although this interpretation is obviously quite legitimate (and provides a good example of the way in which any scene, however banal it may be, is capable of generating symbolic meaning), the traffic jam still carries no 'proairetic' significance within the narrative and does nothing whatsoever to move the plot along.

5 Ross Chambers' description of narrative 'clogging' comes to mind here. 'What is at issue in [the] clogging of narrative,' he writes, 'is a certain

Affective Disorders

We find the same aesthetic strategy employed elsewhere too. Relatively early in the novel, Sartaj and his partner are waiting (once more) to apprehend some gangsters who are suspected of having murdered one of their accomplices; and in order to kill time, and fill space, they begin to trade grievances. Among other things, they complain about the municipality, the price of mangoes, the traffic, collapsing buildings, clogged drains, bad movies, unwatchable television, interstate quarrelling over natural water resources, American interference in subcontinental affairs, the depiction of the police in the aforementioned movies – and, of course, 'the job, the job, and the job.' When you have 'complained enough about everything else,' our narrator says, 'there [is] always the job, with its unspeakable hours, its monotony, its political complications, its thanklessness, [and] its exhaustion' (296). As readers, we are already familiar with the monotony of Sartaj's professional duties – not to mention his fatigue. On page 19, for example, he is assigned to investigate a murder case that we are told, quite candidly, will not be 'especially interesting.' The neighbourhood where the crime occurred, a slum by the name of Navnagar, is 'very poor, and dead bodies there [are] just dead, devoid of any enlivening possibilities of professional praise, or press, or money' (19). And this indeed proves to be true. As far as Sartaj's partner, Katekar, is concerned,

> a Bangladeshi boy had been murdered by his [accomplices], but so what? It was a minor case with minor possibilities, and it could easily be investigated on paper, just like the municipality lorries which on paper ran punctually every morning. Nobody would mind too much if this case was left undetected, and so it was silly to be out here [in Navnagar] suffering [the] odours and the odiousness of these foreigners. (78)

This minor case with minor possibilities, devoid of any larger significance, will eventually be solved; but like so much else in the novel, it hovers on the very edge of tellability and contributes almost nothing

---

reversal of proportion and emphasis between narrative structure, with its reliance on story and its beginning-middle-end grammar of closure, and the paradigmatic or listing dimension of discourse that spins out a narrative enunciation in time, employing devices like description, parenthesis, asyndeton, digression, so that the supposedly secondary comes to occupy the foreground of attention, and the hierarchizing distinction between the relevant and the pointless, on which the story depends, begins to lose its own cogency' (117).

to the primary plotline that we are supposed to be following (the one involving the dead gangster and the threatened destruction of India's largest city).[6] And the same thing could be said of all the other routine crimes that clog the narrative too – the 'everyday matters of blackmail, thievery, [and] murder' (614) that are 'perfunctorily investigated and [almost] never solved' (429).[7]

At the microcosmic level, as we have seen, this inconsequential 'filling' (magazines, bottles of water, gaudy Chinese statues, etc.) has practically no influence over the underlying structure of the narrative. However, when entire scenes assume a largely catalytic function, they create conspicuous deviations in the novel's plot trajectory. To some degree, of course, all plotting involves a series of deviations from a straight line; without these irregularities, these 'anomalies,' there would be no intervening substance to prevent the beginning of a narrative from collapsing prematurely into its end. 'Deviance,' Peter Brooks writes, 'detour, an intention that is irritation: these are [the] characteristics of the narratable ... of *fabula* [story] become *sjužet* [discourse].' The desire we experience as readers, Brooks argues, like the 'desire' of the discourse itself, is ultimately 'desire for the end, but desire for the end reached only through the at least minimally complicated detour, the intentional deviance ... which is the plot of narrative' (*Reading* 104). Such deviations are, then, essential to the diachronic unfolding of any narrative, yet again it is a question of degree; and in the case of *Sacred Games*, these digressive tendencies become one of the novel's governing aesthetic principles. Consider the morgue scene, for instance, which takes place in Chapter 4. In the classic detective novel or police procedural, this scene serves a crucial function. It establishes, in the form of a dead body lying on an autopsy table or a steel refrigerator-tray, a point of intersection between two different narratives: the narrative of the crime, usually

---

6 By 'tellability' I mean, very simply, the quality that makes stories worth telling, the 'prolonged deviance from the quiescence of the "normal"' (Brooks, *Reading* 103) that characterizes all successful narratives. For a useful summary of this concept, see Ryan.

7 In an article on the aesthetics of the 'non-event' in contemporary South Asian literature, Megha Anwer makes a similar observation, arguing that *Sacred Games* 'shrink[s] from climactic moments, evading the event in favour of desultory non-events and the quotidian' (27). Unlike Anwer, however, I shall be exploring the way in which the novel ultimately achieves an amalgamation of the eventful and the non-eventful, the spectacular and the boring, in the form of stuplimity.

Affective Disorders

murder, and the narrative of the investigation.[8] For this reason, the morgue scene typically occupies a privileged position within the narrative, and often provides the detective with something of forensic (and narratological) value – a way of moving the case (and the plot) forward. In *Sacred Games*, however, Sartaj's visit to the morgue to view the dead bodies of Gaitonde and his female companion, Jojo, is ultimately futile, a complete waste of narrative energy. Once more, this is something that Sartaj's partner correctly anticipates: 'The man was dead, Katekar said, and he and the woman would remain dead, so there was no need to go near them now, none at all' (90). Ignoring this advice, Sartaj passes at least half an hour – and five pages – in the morgue, before rejoining his colleague outside. Although he assures the pathologist that seeing the dead bodies has been '[v]ery useful,' on reflection he decides otherwise: 'Now the desire to see the bodies, which only a little while ago had seemed so coherent, seemed bizarre. What had he learnt? Sartaj had no idea. *It had all been a waste of time*' (95; my italics).

It should be pointed out at this stage that I am not simply referring to the odd superfluous scene here; I am actually describing the majority of the novel. For alongside the story of Sartaj's investigation, we are also offered a detailed, analeptic account of Gaitonde's rise to prominence within the Mumbai underworld. This tangential plotline is narrated by Gaitonde himself and occupies at least half of the novel's 947 pages – carrying us from 'A to C' by way of 'L, M and Z' (526). The dead gangster's story is engaging, to be sure, and beautifully told; but for the most part it operates not on the syntagmatic plane of the (primary) narrative, moving the plot forward in a horizontal direction, but on the associative or paradigmatic plane, which always moves sideways, at an oblique angle, bringing us no closer to the final predication of the narrative sentence. In this regard, the trajectory of the novel could be said to resemble the 'squiggle' that Balzac, citing Sterne's *Tristram Shandy*, uses as his epigraph to *The Wild Ass' Skin* (1831):

---

8 I am paraphrasing Tzvetan Todorov here. As we saw in Chapter 5, he famously observed that the classic detective novel 'contains not one but two stories: the story of the crime and the story of the investigation.' According to Todorov, we can characterize 'these two stories by saying that the first – the story of the crime – tells "what really happened," whereas the second – the story of the investigation – explains "how the reader (or the narrator) has come to know about it"' (44–45).

Stuplimity

But why should *Sacred Games* look like this? Why should a novel that is supposed to be a thriller consistently privilege the paradigmatic over the syntagmatic, deviance over directionality? In his incisive reading of Eugène Sue's *The Mysteries of Paris* (1842–43), Brooks provides us with a possible answer to these questions. As the nineteenth century became increasingly 'standardized and boring,' he argues, writers began to explore a new 'urban topography and demography,' one of 'crime and social deviance' (*Reading* 147). In Sue's case, it is clear that he regarded the Parisian underworld, the 'social inferno' (153) in which he chose to situate his *roman-feuilleton*, as 'the last refuge of the narratable' (155). That was where his stories were to be found, among the various reprobates, the prostitutes and thieves, who in those days populated the Cité; and as a consequence, these wayward and degenerate figures came to embody two different types of deviance – one social, the other narratological. As Brooks writes,

> Deviance as a question in social pathology offers an opportunity for tracing its arabesque figure as plot. That 'arabesque' – the figure found in *La Peau de chagrin* [*The Wild Ass' Skin*] – represents the opposite of the straight line: it is the longest possible line between two points, or rather, the maintenance of the greatest possible deviance and detour between beginning and end, depending on the play of retardation, repetition, and return in the postponement and progressive unveiling of the end ... If the wretched of the earth are Sue's preferred subject, it may be first of all because ... they are eminently the stuff of plotted story. (155–56)

In *Sacred Games*, the various criminal figures (and above all Gaitonde himself) also constitute 'the stuff of plotted story.' They, too, embody both social and narratological deviance. Yet as we have observed, the stories they generate in such abundance often contribute very little to the narrative's primary plotline. Instead, these episodes of routine crime and violence assume a catalytic quality, creating paradigmatic subtrajectories that consistently lead us away from, rather than toward, the spectacular conclusion we are anticipating.

III

As I suggested at the beginning of this chapter, however, episodes of 'exceptional' criminality can also be found within the pages of *Sacred Games*. Situated more obviously in the public sphere, these episodes form part of a larger, historical narrative that will already be familiar to many of the novel's readers. In December 1992, the Babri Masjid, a sixteenth-century mosque located in Ayodhya, Uttar Pradesh, was illegally demolished during a rally held by the Vishva Hindu Parishad (VHP), a right-wing Hindu nationalist organization affiliated with the Bharatiya Janata Party (BJP). Constructed on a site that also carries religious significance for Hindus, the mosque had long been 'the pivot for leaping political parties, the target for processions of thousands, [and] the standing sign for ancient wrongs' (Chandra, *Sacred* 383). In the days following the demolition of the mosque, communal violence erupted in urban centres around the country, leading to the death of an estimated 900 people in Bombay alone.[9] The majority of the dead were Muslim, and in many cases they had been killed with the direct complicity of the police.[10] In retaliation for this violence, Dawood Ibrahim, a legendary figure within the Mumbai underworld, organized a series of bombings in the city that took place on 12 March 1993, killing 257 people and injuring roughly 700.[11] As a young police officer, Sartaj had witnessed the 1993 bombings, and he finds it difficult, even years later, to reconcile this 'spectacular' event, this terrifying rupture of the ordinary, with the everyday crimes he typically solves. On one occasion, for instance, while searching for a missing *chokra* (or street kid), he remembers 'that day, that long-ago Friday in 1993,' when he had found himself 'walking on blood, splashing through it,' in the immediate aftermath of the explosions. Although he tries, repeatedly, to '[c]oncentrate on the problem at hand' (the missing *chokra* in the red

---

9 For a vivid description of this violence, see Chandra, *Sacred* 383–87.
10 A 1998 commission of inquiry led by Justice B.N. Srikrishna found that the Bombay police had not only failed to prevent anti-Muslim violence during the 1992–93 riots, but had actually participated in such atrocities by 'shoot[ing] people dead or actively direct[ing] the [Shiv] Sena mobs' (Mehta 81).
11 For a detailed account of Ibrahim's life and career, see Zaidi, *Dongri*; and for more on the subject of the 1993 bombings, see Zaidi, *Black*. In the foreword to the first of these volumes, Vikram Chandra acknowledges that much of *Sacred Games* was based on information provided by Zaidi, who served as his Dantesque 'guide into the underworld' (ix).

T-shirt), he is 'unable to rid himself completely of [these] memories' (519), and of his fear that Mumbai may be about to experience another episode of apocalyptic violence. 'What use was it to be concerned with the everyday matters of blackmail, thievery, [or] murder,' he wonders later in the novel,

> when this enormous fear billowed overhead? It was an abstracted danger, this grim notion of a sweeping fire, it was unreal. But with its cold drip of images, it crowded out the mundane. Sartaj blinked. He was at his desk, in his dingy little office with the weathered benches and untidy shelves. [Another police officer] was hunched over a report. Two constables were laughing in the corridor outside. There was a little pool of sunlight from a window, and a pair of hopping little sparrows on the sill. And all of it was dreamlike, as gauzy as the wafting of early morning. If you let yourself believe in that other monstrous thing, even a little, then this ordinary world of bribes and divorces and electricity bills vanished … It got eaten up. (614)[12]

In this passage, as elsewhere, Sartaj oscillates rapidly from one extreme to another. On the one hand, he experiences an overwhelming fear of nuclear annihilation ('this grim notion of a sweeping fire'), while on the other, he forces himself to concentrate on the mundane reality of his daily life ('this ordinary world of bribes and divorces'). Try as he might, he is simply incapable of accommodating both the exceptional *and* the routine, the spectacular *and* the boring, without one of these categories invalidating or precluding the other. Images of a nuclear apocalypse, we are told, 'crowded out the mundane,' leaving no space whatsoever for the banal substance of everyday life. Or to put it another way, we might say that Sartaj is struggling here to reconcile the nuclear (this time in the narratological sense of the word) with the catalytic – his dingy little office, the weathered benches, the untidy shelves.

12 Sartaj's fear of nuclear annihilation may not be restricted to the specific threat he faces here. In the aftermath of the nuclear tests conducted by the Indian Army in 1998 (codenamed Operation Shakti), Ashis Nandy published a sobering article in which he explored the 'psychopathological' consequences of the Indo-Pakistani arms race. The ideology of 'nuclearism,' he wrote, 'seeps into public consciousness, [creating] a new awareness of the transience of life. It forces people to live with the constant fear that, one day, a sudden war or accident might kill not only them, but also their children and grandchildren, and everybody they love' ('Nuclearism' 14–15).

Of course, there are clear correspondences between this dynamic and the act of reading itself, which also combines the exceptional and the routine, the nuclear and the catalytic. In other words, every narrative fluctuates between episodes of intensity and episodes of relative quiescence (Barthes' 'areas of safety'), where nothing of any real significance seems to be happening; and this shifting dynamic in turn influences our experience as readers – episodes of greater intensity within a narrative typically soliciting more attentive or avid reading than the intervening 'low-intensity' passages. As Barthes observes in *The Pleasure of the Text*, the classic readerly narrative

> bears within it a sort of diluted tmesis: we do not read everything with the same intensity of reading; a rhythm is established, casual, unconcerned with the *integrity* of the text; our very avidity for knowledge impels us to skim or to skip certain passages (anticipated as 'boring') in order to get more quickly to the warmer parts of the anecdote ... we boldly skip (no one is watching) descriptions, explanations, analyses, conversations ... [I]t is the very rhythm of what is read and what is not read that creates the pleasure of the great narratives: has anyone ever read Proust, Balzac, *War and Peace*, word for word? (10–11)

Needless to say, one does feel inclined to read every word of *Sacred Games*, but we may not read every page with the same 'avidity.' And in those passages or scenes that could be described as low-intensity – where the paradigmatic function of the discourse overrides its syntagmatic function, or where the catalytic eclipses the nuclear – we may find ourselves anticipating more eagerly the action that lies ahead. This is, after all, a thriller; and it is a fundamental requirement of the genre that it should privilege the proairetic over all other codes. Yet for long stretches of time, we are obliged to focus our attention on episodes of minimal significance: a two-year sojourn in the Arthur Road jail (450–87, 490–505), a mystical enquiry into 'the nature of the self [and] the universe' (609; 574–605), even the ill-fated production of a Bollywood movie (666–704). And it is during these episodes, as the narrative explores the outer reaches of relevance – the discursive equivalent of weathered benches and untidy shelves – that we first encounter the phenomenon of stuplimity.

In *Ugly Feelings*, if you remember, Sianne Ngai uses the term 'stuplimity' to describe the way in which boredom or fatigue has become 'increasingly intertwined with contemporary experiences of aesthetic awe' (8) – hence her neologistic conjunction of the stupefying and the sublime. Some of the examples she offers, in order to demonstrate this tendency, include Gertrude Stein's 922-page *The Making of Americans* ('an experiment in both duration and endurance' [253]), Samuel Beckett's late fiction (which manages to be '[s]imultaneously astonishing and ... fatiguing' [260]), and the 'exciting [yet] enervating' (264) work of Georges Perec, John Cage, and Gerhard Richter. According to Ngai, such a contradictory aesthetic gives rise to an equally contradictory emotional response, involving a combination of affective states that, in traditional theories of the sublime, have always been regarded as mutually exclusive. She describes this hybrid feeling as a 'concatenation of boredom and astonishment – a bringing together of what "dulls," and what "irritates" or agitates; [a mixture] of sharp, sudden excitation and prolonged desensitization, exhaustion, or fatigue' (271). I am not suggesting, of course, that *Sacred Games* is simply boring, or that it could be easily classified alongside Gerhard Richter's *Atlas* (1997) or the meticulous inventories of Georges Perec. However, I do believe that its governing aesthetic principles can be aligned, in several key ways, with Ngai's notion of stuplimity. For one thing, as we have seen, the narrative of *Sacred Games* is particularly vulnerable to clogging, whether it be in the form of unnecessary catalytic detail (magazines, bottles of water, gaudy Chinese statues, etc.) or equally unnecessary paradigmatic digressions (recall, if you will, the morgue scene, which even our hero describes as a complete 'waste of time' [95]). Such clogging or coagulation is, for Ngai, one of the characteristic features of stuplimity. Although 'repetition, permutation, and seriality figure prominently as devices in aesthetic uses of tedium,' she notes, '[writers] have achieved the same effect through a strategy of *agglutination* – the mass adhesion or coagulation of data particles or signifying units' (263; my italics).[13] In the case of

---

13 One could also relate such agglutination to Sara Ahmed's notion of 'stickiness,' a term she uses to describe the way in which certain objects, bodies, or signs can become 'saturated with affect' (*Cultural* 11), be it positive or negative. According to Ahmed, this accumulation of affective value not only binds objects, bodies, or signs together, but may also create a blockage, preventing them from 'moving [on] and acquiring new value' (92). Stickiness, she writes, 'involves a form of relationality, or a "withness," in which the elements that are "with" get bound together. One can stick by a friend. One can get stuck in traffic. Some forms of stickiness are about holding things together. Some are about blockages or stopping things moving' (91). For more on this subject, see Ahmed, *Promise* 230–31.

Sacred Games, this steady accretion of extraneous material serves to elongate the discourse, ensuring that the space between the beginning and the end should be filled with as much (narratological) deviance as possible; and this, too, is a typical feature of the 'stuplime' narrative. Like the feelings they generate, Ngai argues, such narratives often have a 'remarkable capacity for duration' (7), an ability to fill page after page with particles of meaning whose functionality or value within the narrative as a whole approaches the zero degree.

Over the course of *Sacred Games*, as I have suggested, Sartaj struggles to reconcile the spectacular nature of communal violence and nuclear annihilation with the mundane reality of his everyday life ('this ordinary world of bribes and divorces' [614]). Only at the very end of the novel does he experience a genuine sense of stuplimity – as the sublime finally merges with the stupefying, the spectacular with the boring. It is early evening, and Sartaj and his colleagues have at last managed to locate the nuclear device that has been smuggled into Mumbai. Once they arrive at the scene, a 'two-storey bungalow' (874) in a neighbourhood known as Chembur, the police and the security forces immediately establish a command post some distance from the house itself. And this, we are told, is where Sartaj chooses to stay for the rest of the night, thereby missing the dramatic conclusion of his own narrative:

> Sartaj never saw the bungalow ... He was content to sit in the glow of the laptop screens and watch the [sky] change colour outside the window to the rear. Someone had once told him, he didn't remember who, that the fantastic colours in Mumbai's evening came from all the pollution that floated over the city, from all the incredible millions who crowded into a very small space. Sartaj had no doubt it was true, but the purples and reds and oranges were still beautiful and grand. (875)

Meanwhile, sixty metres away, 'behind a screen of trees' (875), the raid itself is taking place: '[Sartaj heard] a series of pops, and then another, phap-phap-phap, phap-phap-phap-phap. And then a last little boom ... [And] with those little banging sounds far away, apparently the world had been saved' (876–77). After more than eight hundred pages of preliminaries, then, we have finally reached the novel's climactic episode, the spectacular event that will provide the closure we have been seeking for so long, the ultimate discharge of meaning that will justify – or bestow value on – everything that has gone before. Only, when it does eventually transpire, this climactic event, it takes place just beyond the representational range of the narrative we are reading. Instead of witnessing the raid directly, that is to say, we are obliged to join Sartaj in contemplating the colour of the evening sky. And rather than experiencing the 'thrill' that the novel's generic affiliation ostensibly promises, we are subjected instead to our narrator's inexplicable sense of fatigue:

> Sartaj tried to discover some enthusiasm within himself … but he just felt sleepy. He noted his own curious lack of excitement about the prospect of being saved, and thought it was probably just exhaustion … Probably I will feel something tomorrow. But right now I think I will just sit here and feel nothing. (876)

This apathy, this anticlimactic fatigue, is difficult to understand without recourse, once more, to the concept of stuplimity. When we encounter a combination of the sublime and the stupefying, Ngai argues, our 'initial experience of being aesthetically overwhelmed involves not terror or pain … but *something much closer to an ordinary fatigue*' (*Ugly* 270). And this is precisely what Sartaj is experiencing here – not a transcendent state of sublimity, not the kind of tranquillity that we might associate with Kant's notion of sublime *apatheia*, but a much more 'adulterated' feeling, one that combines the overwhelming nature of the spectacular with the deadening qualities of the boring, the sudden irruption of the extraordinary with the inescapable banality of the everyday.[14]

---

14 In *Ugly Feelings*, Ngai is careful to distinguish between the philosophical notion of *apatheia*, as it relates to the Kantian sublime, and the sense of boredom that accompanies the feeling of stuplimity. While *apatheia* signifies the complete absence of emotion, and is therefore experienced by the subject as neither 'pleasurable nor unpleasurable,' boredom 'involves a deficiency of affect that is reflexively felt to be dysphoric – stultifying, tedious, irritating, fatiguing, or dulling' (269). 'Given the *sluggishness* associated with boredom,' Ngai writes, 'the difference between the two types of affective deficiency becomes clearer when Kant … contrasts "affection[s] of the strenuous kind," which merit characterization as aesthetically sublime, with "affections of the languid kind," which are barred from the sublime and, as Kant notes, "have nothing noble in themselves"' (270). For a more detailed discussion of sublime *apatheia*, see Kant 132–33.

Affective Disorders

IV

In Book Two of Stendhal's *The Red and the Black* (1830), the protagonist, Julien Sorel, challenges an aristocrat by the name of Charles de Beauvoisis to a duel. Once his challenge has been accepted, the two men immediately set off for the 'secluded spot' where the duel is to take place. The adversaries, each accompanied by a second, are travelling in the same carriage; and given the purpose of their journey, Julien is rather surprised when the conversation on the way proves to be 'extremely pleasant':

> [Monsieur de Beauvoisis and his second] were talking about some dancers who had had a great public success at the ballet the previous evening. The gentlemen alluded to some spicy details about which Julien and his second, the lieutenant of the 96th, knew nothing whatsoever. Julien was not so stupid as to pretend to know; with a good grace he admitted his ignorance. His candour pleased [de Beauvoisis'] friend – he told them the stories replete with details, and told them very well. (285)

As for the duel itself, the melodramatic focal point of many a nineteenth-century narrative, it 'was over in a moment.' Julien 'received a ball in the arm; they dressed it with handkerchiefs; they damped these with brandy; and the Chevalier de Beauvoisis very politely begged to be allowed to take Julien home in the same carriage by which they had come' (285). In this scene, as D.A. Miller has observed, the discourse undergoes a process of displacement; it moves sideways, like Balzac's dilatory squiggle, gravitating toward the banal periphery of the narrative. Or to put it another way, rather than focusing on the episode's 'nuclear' core (the 'risky moment' of the duel), it allows itself to be distracted by the surrounding catalyzers – those 'areas of safety' (Barthes, 'Introduction' 266) where no one ever gets hurt and the conversation is always pleasing.[15] On the one hand, Miller writes, there is

---

15 Such tendencies are also typical of the digressive mode of writing that Ross Chambers has labelled 'loiterature.' According to Chambers, the classic 'loiterly' narrative constitutes a site of 'endless *intersection*,' its narrator's attention being 'always divided between one thing and some other thing, always ready and willing to be distracted' (9). The loiterly style, he writes, is 'inevitably episodic [and] digressive'; it is 'more concerned with the, often obscure, "coherence" of experience ... than it is respectful of patterns that are more strictly designed and thus "cohesive"' (31).

something like a scenario: a sequence of actions whose order is presumed to be known in advance. Logical expectations are invoked: it is hard to imagine any telling of a duel ... in which the actual shooting would not be the logical climax or ending of the account. Cultural expectations are aroused as well: semantically, a duel would seem naturally to involve motifs of honor, risk, fear, shame, and so forth. On the other hand, narrative attention is distracted from what logically and culturally 'ought' to happen; and it is instead focused on what retards or frustrates the articulation of the scenario, on peripheral details and incidents that the scenario neither demands nor accounts for. The very contours of the scenario run the risk of dissolving under the pressure of so much 'irrelevant' material. (*Narrative* 261)

The correspondences between this episode and the raid scene from *Sacred Games* ought to be clear. In both cases, the discourse defies its own generic imperatives by renouncing the spectacular, the dramatic, and the meaningful, in order to concentrate on their opposites: those 'subsidiary notations' that 'merely "fill in" the narrative space separating the [various nuclei]' (Barthes, 'Introduction' 265). As Miller indicates, this catalytic material not only carries a minimal significance within the narrative as a whole, but it also 'frustrates the articulation of the scenario' itself – very nearly causing what *really* matters (the raid, the duel) to dissolve altogether under the pressure of such irrelevance. Very nearly but not quite; and that is the point I am trying to make with regard to *Sacred Games*. The spectacular may be sidelined here, the raid may be concealed 'behind a screen of trees,' but it is not entirely evacuated from the narrative. Instead, as I have suggested, this shift in narratorial focus ultimately brings about a conflation of these two categories – of the sublime and the stupefying – integrating one into the other, so that the spectacular becomes a constitutive feature of everyday life (no longer 'crowd[ing] out the mundane' [Chandra, *Sacred* 614]), and the everyday in turn merges with the spectacular, creating something that is both extraordinary *and* banal, both astonishing *and* boring.

We see this conjunction quite plainly in the scene described above; but we also see it, operating in a more subtle way, in the novel's final lines. Early one morning, we are told, having arrived at the police headquarters,

Sartaj got off his [motorcycle]. He put his shoes up on the pedal, one by one, and buffed them with a spare handkerchief until they shone. Then he ran a finger around his waistline, along the belt. He patted

Affective Disorders

his cheeks, and ran a forefinger and thumb along his moustache. He was sure it was magnificent. He was ready. He went in and began another day. (947)

And there the novel concludes. On the face of it, this passage would appear to be entirely unremarkable. Sartaj arrives at the police station; then he polishes his shoes and makes sure that everything else is in order, running a 'forefinger and thumb along his moustache,' before going inside. But the fact that these are the novel's final lines gives them an underlying significance that belies their superficial banality. All endings, by virtue of their *being* endings, assume a certain intensity; they demand our attention in the same way that beginnings do. Over the course of a novel, as mentioned earlier, we may read with varying degrees of avidity, but the conclusion will almost always be read as closely as possible, for this is where the final predication of meaning occurs, where the narrative circle is closed (one way or the other), and where the major hermeneutic and proairetic sequences are typically resolved. Even if Barthes is right when he suggests that no one has ever read *In Search of Lost Time* or *War and Peace* word for word, it would be difficult to find someone who had not read their final lines (having made it that far) with due diligence. Endings also typically involve a shift in register, whereby they assume the kind of semantic resonance – often lyrical or contemplative – that we have come to expect from 'last words,' even if what is actually being said at the literal level is quite mundane. This is what Viktor Shklovsky describes as a 'false ending' (56), and it is precisely how Chandra has chosen to bring his novel to a close.[16] Nothing could be more banal than this description of Sartaj arriving at the police headquarters, shining his shoes, carefully grooming himself, and then walking inside to 'beg[in] another day.' But because of the fact that it is situated at the very end of a (947-page) narrative, because this is the conclusion we have been pursuing all along, each one of these catalytic occurrences takes on a 'nuclear' quality – and the passage as a whole assumes the kind of semantic resonance that Shklovsky associates with the 'false ending.' Thus, the extraordinary manages, once more, to infiltrate the everyday; and it is

---

16 According to Shklovsky, such endings are 'usually fashioned from a description of nature or the weather,' but have nothing to do with the actual resolution of the narrative. Instead, they provide the *illusion* of closure by offering us a (vaguely metaphorical) description of autumn leaves, say, or an 'indifferent sky' (56).

entirely appropriate that it should do so, for in contemporary Mumbai it has become increasingly difficult to disentangle these two categories.

During the last half-century, as the anthropologist Vyjayanthi Rao observes, Bombay has been transformed from a 'city of risk' – of 'speculation and entrepreneurial spirit' – to a 'city *at* risk,' one that is 'marked by spectacular [as well as] quotidian violence' (5). The communal violence that erupted in 1992–93, following the destruction of the Babri Masjid, clearly belongs to the first of these categories, as do the many terrorist attacks that have occurred since the so-called Black Friday bombings of 1993.[17] However, it is also important to acknowledge the episodes of 'routine' criminality that may not always make it into the newspapers: the corruption, the domestic violence, the extrajudicial killings (an estimated total of 589 during the years 1993–2003 [Belur 204]), the burglaries, the kidnappings, and so on. Over the course of *Sacred Games*, as we have noted, Sartaj gradually manages to reconcile these antithetical categories and, in doing so, experiences a feeling that could be closely aligned with Sianne Ngai's notion of stuplimity – a counter-intuitive, yet immediately recognizable, combination of the stupefying and the sublime. This feeling in turn infiltrates the narrative itself, so that episodes of 'nuclear' intensity (such as the climactic raid in Chapter 24) merge with catalytic passages of utter insignificance; and purely catalytic sequences (such as the description we are offered in the novel's final lines) are invested with all the intensity, all the prestige, and all the *danger* of the nuclear. For Barthes, if you remember, nuclei constitute 'the risky moments of a narrative,' the places of tension, of potential catastrophe, while catalyzers 'lay out areas of safety' ('Introduction' 266), places where nothing particularly bad can happen because nothing of any consequence can happen there at all. In *Sacred Games*, however, this reassuring binary collapses, allowing danger to merge with safety, the extraordinary with the mundane, the

---

17 In 2003, for instance, two car bombs exploded in the centre of the city, claiming fifty-four lives and injuring 244 people. Three years later, in 2006, the Mumbai suburban railway system was the target of another bombing, this time a series of seven explosions that killed 209 people and injured 700. In 2008, in a coordinated assault that was televised around the world, ten members of the Pakistani terrorist organization Lashkar-e-Taiba subjected the city to four days of shootings and bombings that would ultimately kill 164 people (including the chief of the Mumbai Anti-Terrorist Squad [ATS]) and injure 308. And most recently, in 2011, a series of explosions in three different locations within the city claimed a further twenty-eight lives and left 130 people injured.

spectacular with the boring. And in a narrative of this kind, a narrative where there are no longer any 'areas of safety,' where the nuclear and the catalytic have fused with one another, even an action as banal as shining your shoes or grooming yourself can quite easily bring everything to an end.

Works Cited

Abu-Lughod, Janet. *Cairo: 1001 Years of the City Victorious*. Princeton, NJ: Princeton University Press, 1971.
Adorno, Theodor W. *Aesthetic Theory*. Ed. and trans. Robert Hullot-Kentor. London: Continuum, 2002.
——. 'The Position of the Narrator in the Contemporary Novel.' *Notes to Literature*. Vol. I. Ed. Rolf Tiedemann. Trans. Shierry Weber Nicholsen. New York: Columbia University Press, 1991. 30–36.
Ahmed, Sara. *The Cultural Politics of Emotion*. New York: Routledge, 2004.
——. *The Promise of Happiness*. Durham, NC: Duke University Press, 2010.
Altieri, Charles. *The Particulars of Rapture: An Aesthetics of the Affects*. Ithaca, NY: Cornell University Press, 2003.
Amnesty International. *'Only Justice Can Heal Our Wounds': Listening to the Demands of the Families of the Disappeared in Sri Lanka*. London: Amnesty International, 2017.
——. *Sri Lanka: Extrajudicial Executions, 'Disappearances' and Torture, 1987 to 1990*. London: Amnesty International, 1990.
Anderson, Benedict. *Imagined Communities: Reflections on the Origin and Spread of Nationalism*. Rev. ed. London: Verso, 2006.
Anderson, Perry. 'Modernity and Revolution.' *New Left Review* 144 (1984): 96–113.
Anwer, Megha. 'Resisting the Event: Aesthetics of the Non-Event in the Contemporary South Asian Novel.' *ARIEL: A Review of International English Literature* 45.4 (2014): 1–30.
Appadurai, Arjun. 'Topographies of the Self: Praise and Emotion in Hindu India.' *Language and the Politics of Emotion*. Ed. Catherine A. Lutz and Lila Abu-Lughod. Cambridge: Cambridge University Press, 1993. 92–112.

Affective Disorders

Aristotle. *The Art of Rhetoric*. Trans. Hugh Lawson-Tancred. London: Penguin, 1991.

———. *The Nicomachean Ethics*. Trans. David Ross. Oxford: Oxford University Press, 2009.

———. *Poetics*. Trans. S.H. Butcher. New York: Cosimo, 2008.

Auerbach, Erich. *Mimesis: The Representation of Reality in Western Literature*. Trans. Willard R. Trask. Princeton, NJ: Princeton University Press, 2003.

Aurelius, Marcus. *Meditations*. Trans. Maxwell Staniforth. London: Penguin, 1964.

Bakhtin, Mikhail. 'Forms of Time and of the Chronotope in the Novel: Notes Toward a Historical Poetics.' *The Dialogic Imagination: Four Essays*. Ed. Michael Holquist. Trans. Caryl Emerson and Michael Holquist. Austin: University of Texas Press, 2002. 84–258.

Balzac, Honoré de. *Old Goriot*. Trans. Marion Ayton Crawford. London: Penguin, 1951.

———. *La Peau de Chagrin* [*The Wild Ass' Skin*]. Vol. I. Paris: Charles Gosselin; Urbain Canel, 1831.

Baraka, Magda. *The Egyptian Upper Class between Revolutions, 1919–1952*. Oxford: Ithaca Press, 1998.

Barthes, Roland. 'The Death of the Author.' *Image-Music-Text*. Trans. Stephen Heath. New York: Noonday Press, 1977. 142–48.

———. 'Introduction to the Structural Analysis of Narratives.' *A Roland Barthes Reader*. Ed. Susan Sontag. London: Vintage, 2000. 251–95.

———. *The Pleasure of the Text*. Trans. Richard Miller. New York: Hill and Wang, 1975.

———. *The Preparation of the Novel: Lecture Courses and Seminars at the Collège de France (1978–1979 and 1979–1980)*. Trans. Kate Briggs. New York: Columbia University Press, 2011.

———. *S/Z*. Trans. Richard Miller. New York: Hill and Wang, 1974.

Basu, Aparna. *Mridula Sarabhai: Rebel with a Cause*. Delhi: Oxford University Press, 1996.

Belur, Jyoti. 'Police Shootings: Perceived Culture of Approval.' *Crime and Justice in India*. Ed. N. Prabha Unnithan. Delhi: Sage, 2013. 203–25.

Benjamin, Walter. 'On the Concept of History.' *Selected Writings, Volume 4, 1938–1940*. Ed. Howard Eiland and Michael W. Jennings. Trans. Edmund Jephcott et al. Cambridge, MA: Harvard University Press, 2003. 389–400.

Ben-Ze'ev, Aaron. 'Jealousy and Romantic Love.' *Handbook of Jealousy: Theory, Research and Multidisciplinary Approaches*. Ed. Sybil L. Hart and Maria Legerstee. Oxford: Blackwell, 2010. 40–54.

Berman, Marshall. *All That Is Solid Melts into Air: The Experience of Modernity*. New York: Penguin, 1988.

Bersani, Leo. *A Future for Astyanax: Character and Desire in Literature*. Boston: Little, Brown and Co., 1976.

Bethell, Leslie, and José Murilo de Carvalho. 'Empire: 1822–1850.' *Brazil: Empire and Republic, 1822–1930*. Ed. Leslie Bethell. Cambridge: Cambridge University Press, 1993. 45–112.
Bewes, Timothy. *The Event of Postcolonial Shame*. Princeton, NJ: Princeton University Press, 2011.
The Bhagavad Gita. Trans. Juan Mascaró. London: Penguin, 2003.
Bolaño, Roberto. *2666*. Trans. Natasha Wimmer. London: Picador, 2016.
Borges, Jorge Luis. 'Partial Magic in the *Quixote*.' *Labyrinths: Selected Stories and Other Writings*. Ed. Donald A. Yates and James E. Irby. New York: New Directions, 1964. 193–96.
Brennan, Teresa. *The Transmission of Affect*. Ithaca, NY: Cornell University Press, 2004.
Brooks, Peter. *The Melodramatic Imagination: Balzac, Henry James, Melodrama, and the Mode of Excess*. New York: Columbia University Press, 1985.
———. *Reading for the Plot: Design and Intention in Narrative*. Cambridge, MA: Harvard University Press, 1984.
Brown, Judith M. *Nehru: A Political Life*. New Haven, CT: Yale University Press, 2003.
Burke, Edmund. *A Philosophical Enquiry into the Origin of Our Ideas of the Sublime and Beautiful*. Ed. Adam Phillips. Oxford: Oxford University Press, 1990.
Caldwell, Helen. *The Brazilian Othello of Machado de Assis: A Study of Dom Casmurro*. Berkeley: University of California Press, 1960.
Camus, Albert. *The Plague*. Trans. Stuart Gilbert. London: Penguin, 1960.
Capote, Truman. *Truman Capote: Conversations*. Ed. M. Thomas Inge. Jackson: University Press of Mississippi, 1987.
Chambers, Ross. *Loiterature*. Lincoln: University of Nebraska Press, 1999.
Chandra, Vikram. Foreword. *Dongri to Dubai: Six Decades of the Mumbai Mafia*. By S. Hussain Zaidi. Delhi: Roli Books, 2012. ix–x.
———. *Sacred Games*. London: Faber and Faber, 2007.
Chatterjee, Upamanyu. *English, August: An Indian Story*. New York: New York Review Books, 2006.
Clough, Arthur Hugh. *Amours de Voyage*. London: Macmillan, 1903. *Project Gutenberg*. Web. 27 February 2015.
Coetzee, J.M. 'The Mind of Apartheid: Geoffrey Cronjé.' *Social Dynamics* 17.1 (1991): 1–35.
Cooper, Artemis. *Cairo in the War, 1939–1945*. London: Penguin, 1995.
Craps, Stef. *Postcolonial Witnessing: Trauma Culture Out of Bounds*. Basingstoke: Palgrave Macmillan, 2013.
Culler, Jonathan. *Flaubert: The Uses of Uncertainty*. Ithaca, NY: Cornell University Press, 1974.
———. *The Literary in Theory*. Stanford, CA: Stanford University Press, 2007.
———. *The Pursuit of Signs: Semiotics, Literature, Deconstruction*. London: Routledge, 2001.

Damasio, Antonio. *Descartes' Error: Emotion, Reason, and the Human Brain*. New York: Avon Books, 1994.

———. *The Feeling of What Happens: Body and Emotion in the Making of Consciousness*. New York: Mariner, 2000.

———. *Looking for Spinoza: Joy, Sorrow, and the Feeling Brain*. New York: William Heinemann, 2003.

Daniel, E. Valentine. *Charred Lullabies: Chapters in an Anthropography of Violence*. Princeton, NJ: Princeton University Press, 1996.

Daniel, G. Reginald. *Machado de Assis: Multiracial Identity and the Brazilian Novelist*. University Park: Pennsylvania State University Press, 2012.

Darwin, Charles. *The Expression of the Emotions in Man and Animals*. London: John Murray, 1872.

Deeb, Marius. 'Najib Mahfuz's *Midaq Alley*: A Socio-Cultural Analysis.' *Critical Perspectives on Naguib Mahfouz*. Ed. Trevor Le Gassick. Washington DC: Three Continents Press, 1991. 27–36.

Desai, Anita. 'Sitting Pretty.' *New York Review of Books*. 27 May 1993: 22–26.

Dharwadker, Vinay. 'Emotion in Motion: The *Nāṭyashāstra*, Darwin, and Affect Theory.' *PMLA* 130.5 (2015): 1381–1404.

Dickens, Charles. *Bleak House*. Oxford: Oxford University Press, 2008.

Dufrenne, Mikel. *The Phenomenology of Aesthetic Experience*. Trans. Edward S. Casey. Evanston, IL: Northwestern University Press, 1979.

Durrant, Sam. *Postcolonial Narrative and the Work of Mourning: J.M. Coetzee, Wilson Harris, and Toni Morrison*. Albany: State University of New York Press, 2004.

Dwivedi, O.P., and R.B. Jain. 'Bureaucratic Morality in India.' *International Political Science Review* 9.3 (1988): 205–14.

El-Enany, Rasheed. *Naguib Mahfouz: The Pursuit of Meaning*. London: Routledge, 1994.

Eliasoph, Nina, and Paul Lichterman. 'Culture in Interaction.' *American Journal of Sociology* 108.4 (2003): 735–94.

Fanon, Frantz. *Black Skin, White Masks*. Trans. Richard Philcox. New York: Grove, 2008.

———. *The Wretched of the Earth*. Trans. Constance Farrington. New York: Grove, 1963.

Farrier, David. 'Gesturing Towards the Local: Intimate Histories in *Anil's Ghost*.' *Journal of Postcolonial Writing* 41.1 (2005): 83–93.

Fausto, Boris. *A Concise History of Brazil*. Trans. Arthur Brakel. Cambridge: Cambridge University Press, 2006.

Fenichel, Otto. 'On the Psychology of Boredom.' *The Collected Papers of Otto Fenichel: First Series*. New York: Norton, 1953. 292–302.

Flatley, Jonathan. *Affective Mapping: Melancholia and the Politics of Modernism*. Cambridge, MA: Harvard University Press, 2008.

Flaubert, Gustave. *The Letters of Gustave Flaubert, 1830–1857*. Ed. and trans. Francis Steegmuller. London: Faber and Faber, 1982.

———. *Sentimental Education*. Trans. Robert Baldick. London: Penguin, 1982.

Foucault, Michel. 'Tales of Murder.' *I, Pierre Rivière, Having Slaughtered My Mother, My Sister, and My Brother: A Case of Parricide in the Nineteenth Century*. Ed. Michel Foucault. Trans. Frank Jellinek. Lincoln: University of Nebraska Press, 1982. 199–212.

Freud, Sigmund. 'The Claims of Psychoanalysis to Scientific Interest.' *The Standard Edition of the Complete Psychological Works of Sigmund Freud*. Vol. XIII. Ed. and trans. James Strachey. London: Hogarth Press, 1955. 165–92.

———. 'Further Remarks on the Neuro-Psychoses of Defence.' *The Standard Edition of the Complete Psychological Works of Sigmund Freud*. Vol. III. Ed. and trans. James Strachey. London: Hogarth Press, 1962. 162–85.

———. *The Interpretation of Dreams. The Standard Edition of the Complete Psychological Works of Sigmund Freud*. Vol. IV. Ed and trans. James Strachey. London: Hogarth Press, 1953. 1–338.

———. *Introductory Lectures on Psychoanalysis*. Ed. James Strachey and Angela Richards. Trans. James Strachey. Harmondsworth: Penguin, 1984.

———. 'Some Neurotic Mechanisms in Jealousy, Paranoia and Homosexuality.' *The Standard Edition of the Complete Psychological Works of Sigmund Freud*. Vol. XVIII. Ed. and trans. James Strachey. London: Hogarth Press, 1955. 223–32.

———. *Totem and Taboo. The Standard Edition of the Complete Psychological Works of Sigmund Freud*. Vol. XIII. Ed. and trans. James Strachey. London: Hogarth Press, 1955. 1–162.

———. 'The Unconscious.' *The Standard Edition of the Complete Psychological Works of Sigmund Freud*. Vol. XIV. Ed. and trans. James Strachey. London: Hogarth Press, 1957. 159–215.

Freyre, Gilberto. *The Mansions and the Shanties: The Making of Modern Brazil*. Trans. Harriet de Onís. New York: Alfred A. Knopf, 1963.

Frye, Northrop. *The Secular Scripture: A Study of the Structure of Romance*. Cambridge, MA: Harvard University Press, 1976.

Gabriel, Teshome H. 'Third Cinema as Guardian of Popular Memory: Towards a Third Aesthetics.' *Questions of Third Cinema*. Ed. Jim Pines and Paul Willeman. London: BFI, 1989. 53–64.

Gaylard, Gerald. 'Transculturating the Sympathetic Imagination: Unfamiliar Feelings in Ivan Vladislavić.' *Current Writing: Text and Reception in Southern Africa* 24.1 (2012): 98–108.

Genette, Gérard. *Narrative Discourse: An Essay in Method*. Trans. Jane E. Lewin. Ithaca, NY: Cornell University Press, 1980.

Gilroy, Paul. *Postcolonial Melancholia*. New York: Columbia University Press, 2005.

Goldie, Peter. *The Emotions: A Philosophical Exploration*. Oxford: Oxford University Press, 2002.

Good, Mary-Jo Delvecchio, and Byron J. Good. 'Ritual, the State, and the Transformation of Emotional Discourse in Iranian Society.' *Culture, Medicine, and Psychiatry* 12 (1988): 43–63.

Goodstein, Elizabeth S. *Experience without Qualities: Boredom and Modernity.* Stanford, CA: Stanford University Press, 2005.
Government of India. 'Report of the Sixth Central Pay Commission.' Indian Government Website. 2008. Web. 27 January 2011.
Graham, Richard. *Patronage and Politics in Nineteenth-Century Brazil.* Stanford, CA: Stanford University Press, 1990.
Graham, Sandra Lauderdale. *House and Street: The Domestic World of Servants and Masters in Nineteenth-Century Rio de Janeiro.* Cambridge: University of Cambridge Press, 1988.
Greco, Monica, and Paul Stenner. 'Introduction: Emotion and Social Science.' *Emotions: A Social Science Reader.* Ed. Monica Greco and Paul Stenner. London: Routledge, 2008. 1–21.
Grice, Paul. 'Logic and Conversation.' *Studies in the Way of Words.* Cambridge, MA: Harvard University Press, 1989. 22–40.
Grossberg, Lawrence. 'Postmodernity and Affect: All Dressed Up with No Place to Go.' *Emotions: A Cultural Studies Reader.* Ed. Jennifer Harding and E. Deidre Pribram. London: Routledge, 2009. 69–83.
———. *We Gotta Get Out of This Place: Popular Conservatism and Postmodern Culture.* New York: Routledge, 2013.
Guha, Ranajit. 'Chandra's Death.' *Subaltern Studies V: Writings on South Asian History and Society.* Ed. Ranajit Guha. Delhi: Oxford University Press, 1987. 135–65.
Gupta, Akhil. *Red Tape: Bureaucracy, Structural Violence, and Poverty in India.* Durham, NC: Duke University Press, 2012.
Hansen, Thomas Blom. *Wages of Violence: Naming and Identity in Postcolonial Bombay.* Princeton, NJ: Princeton University Press, 2001.
Heidegger, Martin. *Being and Time.* Trans. John Macquarrie and Edward Robinson. Oxford: Blackwell, 2001.
———. *The Fundamental Concepts of Metaphysics: World, Finitude, Solitude.* Trans. William McNeill and Nicholas Walker. Bloomington: Indiana University Press, 1995.
———. *Introduction to Metaphysics.* Trans. Gregory Fried and Richard Polt. New Haven, CT: Yale University Press, 2000.
Hempelmann, Christian F. 'The Laughter of the 1962 Tanganyika "Laughter Epidemic."' *Humor: International Journal of Humor Research* 20.1 (2007): 49–71.
Henderson, James. *A History of the Brazil: Comprising Its Geography, Commerce, Colonization, Aboriginal Inhabitants, &c.* London: Longman, Hurst, Rees, Orme, and Brown, 1821.
Hobbes, Thomas. *Man and Citizen [Philosophical Rudiments Concerning Government and Society].* Trans. Charles T. Wood, T.S.K. Scott-Craig, and Bernard Gert. Indianapolis, IN: Hackett Publishing, 1991.
Hochschild, Arlie Russell. *The Managed Heart: Commercialization of Human Feelings.* Berkeley: University of California Press, 2003.

Hogan, Patrick Colm. *Affective Narratology: The Emotional Structure of Stories.* Lincoln: University of Nebraska Press, 2011.

———. *The Mind and Its Stories: Narrative Universals and Human Emotion.* Cambridge: Cambridge University Press, 2003.

Holloway, Thomas H. *Policing Rio de Janeiro.* Stanford, CA: Stanford University Press, 1993.

Hull, Matthew S. *Government of Paper: The Materiality of Bureaucracy in Urban Pakistan.* Berkeley: University of California Press, 2012.

Ifowodo, Ogaga. *History, Trauma and Healing in Postcolonial Narratives: Reconstructing Identities.* Basingstoke: Palgrave Macmillan, 2013.

Iliffe, John. *A Modern History of Tanganyika.* Cambridge: Cambridge University Press, 1994.

James, Henry. 'The Art of Fiction.' *Literary Criticism, Volume One: Essays on Literature, American Writers, English Writers.* New York: Library of America, 1984. 44–65.

James, William. *The Principles of Psychology.* 2 vols. New York: Henry Holt, 1890.

Jameson, Fredric. *The Antinomies of Realism.* London: Verso, 2013.

———. *The Political Unconscious: Narrative as a Socially Symbolic Act.* London: Routledge, 2002.

Jeffrey, Craig. *Timepass: Youth, Class, and the Politics of Waiting in India.* Stanford, CA: Stanford University Press, 2010.

Kant, Immanuel. *Critique of Judgment.* Trans. Werner S. Pluhar. Indianapolis, IN: Hackett Publishing, 1987.

Khanna, Ranjana. *Dark Continents: Psychoanalysis and Colonialism.* Durham, NC: Duke University Press, 2003.

Kierkegaard, Søren. *The Concept of Anxiety.* Ed. and trans. Reidar Thomte. Princeton, NJ: Princeton University Press, 1980.

Kim, Sue J. *On Anger: Race, Cognition, Narrative.* Austin: University of Texas Press, 2013.

Kingsbury, Damien. *Sri Lanka and the Responsibility to Protect: Politics, Ethnicity and Genocide.* London: Routledge, 2012.

Klein, Melanie. 'Envy and Gratitude.' *Envy and Gratitude and Other Works, 1946–1963. The Writings of Melanie Klein.* Vol. III. New York: Free Press, 1975. 176–235.

Kleinman, Arthur. *Patients and Healers in the Context of Culture: An Exploration of the Borderland between Anthropology, Medicine, and Psychiatry.* Berkeley: University of California Press, 1981.

Kuhn, Reinhard. *The Demon of Noontide: Ennui in Western Literature.* Princeton, NJ: Princeton University Press, 1976.

Laclau, Ernesto. *Emancipation(s).* London: Verso, 1996.

Lacouture, Jean, and Simonne Lacouture. *Egypt in Transition.* Trans. Francis Scarfe. New York: Criterion Books, 1958.

LeDoux, Joseph. *The Emotional Brain: The Mysterious Underpinnings of Emotional Life*. New York: Simon and Schuster, 1996.

Lefebvre, Georges. *The French Revolution: From Its Origins to 1793*. Trans. Elizabeth Moss Evanson. London: Routledge, 2001.

———. *The Great Fear of 1789: Rural Panic in Revolutionary France*. Trans. Joan White. Princeton, NJ: Princeton University Press, 1982.

Lepenies, Wolf. *Melancholy and Society*. Trans. Jeremy Gaines and Doris Jones. Cambridge, MA: Harvard University Press, 1992.

Leys, Ruth. *The Ascent of Affect: Genealogy and Critique*. Chicago, IL: University of Chicago Press, 2017.

Machado de Assis, Joaquim Maria. *Dom Casmurro*. Trans. John Gledson. New York: Oxford University Press, 1997.

———. *Resurrection*. Trans. Karen Sherwood Sotelino. Pittsburgh, PA: Latin American Literary Review Press, 2013.

Maheshwari, Shriram. 'The All-India Services.' *Public Administration* 49.3 (1971): 291–308.

Mahfouz, Naguib. *Midaq Alley*. Trans. Trevor Le Gassick. New York: Anchor, 1992.

Majumdar, Saikat. *Prose of the World: Modernism and the Banality of Empire*. New York: Columbia University Press, 2013.

Malinowski, Bronislaw. 'The Problem of Meaning in Primitive Languages.' In C.K. Ogden and I.A. Richards. *The Meaning of Meaning: A Study of the Influence of Language upon Thought and of the Science of Symbolism*. New York: Harcourt, Brace and World, 1946. 296–336.

Martin, Theodore. 'The Long Wait: Timely Secrets of the Contemporary Detective Novel.' *Novel: A Forum on Fiction* 45.2 (2012): 165–83.

Marx, Karl. *Selected Writings*. Ed. David McLellan. Oxford: Oxford University Press, 2000.

Massumi, Brian. *Parables for the Virtual: Movement, Affect, Sensation*. Durham, NC: Duke University Press, 2002.

McClennen, Sophia A., and Joseph R. Slaughter. 'Introducing Human Rights and Literary Forms; or, The Vehicles and Vocabularies of Human Rights.' *Comparative Literature Studies* 46.1 (2009): 1–19.

Mehta, Suketu. *Maximum City: Bombay Lost and Found*. New York: Vintage, 2005.

Menon, Ritu, and Kamla Bhasin. *Borders and Boundaries: Women in India's Partition*. Delhi: Kali for Women, 1998.

Miller, D.A. *Narrative and Its Discontents: Problems of Closure in the Traditional Novel*. Princeton, NJ: Princeton University Press, 1981.

———. *The Novel and the Police*. Berkeley: University of California Press, 1988.

Moosa, Matti. *The Early Novels of Naguib Mahfouz: Images of Modern Egypt*. Gainesville: University Press of Florida, 1994.

Moretti, Franco. *Atlas of the European Novel, 1800–1900*. London: Verso, 1999.

———. *The Bourgeois: Between History and Literature*. London: Verso, 2013.

———. *Signs Taken for Wonders: On the Sociology of Literary Forms*. Trans. Susan Fischer, David Forgacs, and David Miller. London: Verso, 2005.

———. *The Way of the World: The Bildungsroman in European Culture*. London: Verso, 1987.

Moussa-Mahmoud, Fatma. 'Depth of Vision: The Fiction of Naguib Mahfouz.' *Third World Quarterly* 11.2 (1989): 154–66.

Myers, David. 'Vikram Seth's Epic Renunciation of the Passions: Deconstructing Moral Codes in *A Suitable Boy*.' *Indian Literature Today, Vol. I: Drama and Fiction*. Ed. R.K. Dhawan. Delhi: Prestige, 1994. 79–102.

Naaman, Mara. *Urban Space in Contemporary Egyptian Literature: Portraits of Cairo*. New York: Palgrave Macmillan, 2011.

Nancy, Jean-Luc. *The Birth to Presence*. Trans. Brian Holmes et al. Stanford, CA: Stanford University Press, 1993.

Nandy, Ashis. 'The Culture of Indian Politics: A Stock Taking.' *Journal of Asian Studies* 30.1 (1970): 57–79.

———. 'Nuclearism, Genocidal Mentality and Psychic Numbing.' *Himāl: The South Asian Magazine* 11.7 (1998): 14–17.

Ndebele, Njabulo. *South African Literature and Culture: Rediscovery of the Ordinary*. Manchester: Manchester University Press, 1994.

Nehru, Jawaharlal. *Jawaharlal Nehru: An Anthology*. Ed. Sarvepalli Gopal. Delhi: Oxford University Press, 1980.

———. *Jawaharlal Nehru's Speeches: Volume Two*. Delhi: Publications Division, Ministry of Information and Broadcasting, Government of India, 1954.

———. 'Let the People Decide.' *Jawaharlal Nehru's Speeches* 100–9.

Ngai, Sianne. 'Merely Interesting.' *Critical Inquiry* 34.4 (2008): 777–817.

———. *Ugly Feelings*. Cambridge, MA: Harvard University Press, 2005.

Obeyesekere, Gananath. *The Work of Culture: Symbolic Transformation in Psychoanalysis and Anthropology*. Chicago, IL: University of Chicago Press, 1990.

Ondaatje, Michael. *Anil's Ghost*. New York: Vintage, 2001.

Pandey, Gyanendra. *Remembering Partition: Violence, Nationalism and History in India*. Cambridge: Cambridge University Press, 2002.

Perera, Sasanka. 'Spirit Possessions and Avenging Ghosts: Stories of Supernatural Activity as Narratives of Terror and Mechanisms of Coping and Remembering.' *Remaking a World: Violence, Social Suffering, and Recovery*. Ed. Veena Das et al. Berkeley: University of California Press, 2001. 157–200.

Plamper, Jan. *The History of Emotions: An Introduction*. Trans. Keith Tribe. Oxford: Oxford University Press, 2015.

Pollock, Sheldon. 'Introduction: An Intellectual History of Rasa.' *A Rasa Reader: Classical Indian Aesthetics*. Ed. and trans. Sheldon Pollock. New York: Columbia University Press, 2016. 1–45.

Prasad, J. 'The Psychology of Rumour: A Study Relating to the Great Indian Earthquake of 1934.' *British Journal of Psychology* 26.1 (1935): 1–15.

Pratt, Mary Louise. *Toward a Speech Act Theory of Literary Discourse*. Bloomington: Indiana University Press, 1977.

Proust, Marcel. *In Search of Lost Time, Vol. I: Swann's Way*. Trans. C.K. Scott Moncrieff and Terence Kilmartin. New York: Modern Library, 2003.

Provine, Robert R. *Laughter: A Scientific Investigation*. New York: Penguin, 2001.

Quayson, Ato. *Aesthetic Nervousness: Disability and the Crisis of Representation*. New York: Columbia University Press, 2007.

———. *Calibrations: Reading for the Social*. Minneapolis: University of Minnesota Press, 2003.

———. *Strategic Transformations in Nigerian Writing: Orality and History in the Work of Rev. Samuel Johnson, Amos Tutuola, Wole Soyinka and Ben Okri*. Oxford: James Currey, 1997.

———. 'Symbolization Compulsion: Testing a Psychoanalytical Category on Postcolonial African Literature.' *University of Toronto Quarterly* 73.2 (2004): 754–72.

Quayson, Ato, Debjani Ganguly, and Neil ten Kortenaar. 'Editorial: New Topographies.' *Cambridge Journal of Postcolonial Literary Inquiry* 1.1 (2014): 1–10.

Rajasingham-Senanayake, Darini. 'The Dangers of Devolution: The Hidden Economies of Armed Conflict.' *Creating Peace in Sri Lanka: Civil War and Reconciliation*. Ed. Robert I. Rotberg. Washington, DC: Brookings Institution Press, 1999. 57–69.

Rankin, A.M., and P.J. Philip. 'An Epidemic of Laughing in the Bukoba District of Tanganyika.' *Central African Journal of Medicine* 9.5 (1963): 167–70.

Rao, Vyjayanthi. 'A New Urban Type: Gangsters, Terrorists, Global Cities.' *Critique of Anthropology* 31.1 (2011): 3–20.

Raymond, André. *Cairo*. Trans. Willard Wood. Cambridge, MA: Harvard University Press, 2000.

Reddy, William M. *The Navigation of Feeling: A Framework for the History of Emotions*. Cambridge: Cambridge University Press, 2001.

Reynolds, Nancy Y. *A City Consumed: Urban Commerce, the Cairo Fire, and the Politics of Decolonization in Egypt*. Stanford, CA: Stanford University Press, 2012.

Robb, Graham. *Balzac: A Biography*. New York: Norton, 1995.

Rodenbeck, Max. *Cairo: The City Victorious*. New York: Vintage, 2000.

Rodrigues, Sarina M., Joseph E. LeDoux, and Robert M. Sapolsky. 'The Influence of Stress Hormones on Fear Circuitry.' *Annual Review of Neuroscience* 32 (2009): 289–313.

Romberg, Bertil. *Studies in the Narrative Technique of the First-Person Novel*. Trans. Michael Taylor and Harold H. Borland. Stockholm: Almqvist and Wiksell, 1962.

Rosenwein, Barbara H. *Emotional Communities in the Early Middle Ages*. Ithaca, NY: Cornell University Press, 2006.

Rowell, Lewis. *Music and Musical Thought in Early India*. Chicago, IL: University of Chicago Press, 1992.

Ryan, Marie-Laure. 'Tellability.' *Routledge Encyclopedia of Narrative Theory*. Ed. David Herman, Manfred Jahn, and Marie-Laure Ryan. London: Routledge, 2005. 589–91.

Said, Edward W. 'After Mahfouz.' *Reflections on Exile and Other Essays*. Cambridge, MA: Harvard University Press, 2000. 317–26.

———. *Culture and Imperialism*. New York: Vintage, 1994.

———. *Freud and the Non-European*. London: Verso, 2003.

Salgado, Minoli. *Writing Sri Lanka: Literature, Resistance and the Politics of Place*. London: Routledge, 2007.

Sartre, Jean-Paul. *Being and Nothingness: An Essay on Phenomenological Ontology*. Trans. Hazel E. Barnes. London: Routledge, 2003.

———. 'Camus' "The Outsider."' *Literary and Philosophical Essays*. Trans. Annette Michelson. New York: Criterion Books, 1955. 24–41.

———. *The Family Idiot: Gustave Flaubert, 1821–1857.* Vol. V. Trans. Carol Cosman. Chicago, IL: University of Chicago Press, 1993.

Saussure, Ferdinand de. *Course in General Linguistics*. Ed. Charles Bally, Albert Sechehaye, and Albert Reidlinger. Trans. Wade Baskin. New York: Philosophical Library, 1959.

Schopenhauer, Arthur. *The World as Will and Representation*. Vol. I. Trans. E.F.J. Payne. New York: Dover, 1969.

Schwarcz, Lília Moritz. 'Machado de Assis: Creator and Character in a Troubled Scene.' *Emerging Dialogues on Machado de Assis*. Ed. Lamonte Aidoo and Daniel F. Silva. New York: Palgrave Macmillan, 2016. 13–25.

Schwartz, Susan L. *Rasa: Performing the Divine in India*. New York: Columbia University Press, 2004.

Schwarz, Roberto. 'The Importing of the Novel to Brazil and Its Contradictions in the Work of Alencar.' *Misplaced Ideas: Essays on Brazilian Culture*. Ed. and trans. John Gledson. London: Verso, 1992. 41–77.

———. *A Master on the Periphery of Capitalism: Machado de Assis*. Trans. John Gledson. Durham, NC: Duke University Press, 2001.

———. 'Misplaced Ideas: Literature and Society in Late Nineteenth-Century Brazil.' *Misplaced Ideas* 19–32.

Scott, Bede. 'Colonial Modernity and Urban Space: Naguib Mahfouz's Cairo.' *Journal of Urban Cultural Studies* 1.2 (2014): 255–72.

———. *On Lightness in World Literature*. New York: Palgrave Macmillan, 2013.

———. 'Roberto Bolaño's *2666*: Serial Murder and Narrative Necrosis.' *Critique: Studies in Contemporary Fiction* 59.3 (2018): 307–18.

Senaratne, Jagath P. *Political Violence in Sri Lanka, 1977–1990: Riots, Insurrections, Counterinsurgencies, Foreign Intervention*. Amsterdam: VU University Press, 1997.

Seoighe, Rachel. *War, Denial and Nation-Building in Sri Lanka: After the End*. London: Palgrave Macmillan, 2017.

Seth, Vikram. *The Golden Gate*. New York: Vintage, 1991.

———. *A Suitable Boy*. New York: Harper Collins, 1993.

Shklovsky, Viktor. 'The Structure of Fiction.' *Theory of Prose*. Trans. Benjamin Sher. Normal, IL: Dalkey Archive Press, 1998. 52–71.
Sirois, François. 'Epidemic Hysteria.' *Hysteria*. Ed. Alec Roy. Chichester: John Wiley, 1982. 101–15.
Somekh, Sasson. *The Changing Rhythm: A Study of Najib Mahfuz's Novels*. Leiden: E.J. Brill, 1973.
Sontag, Susan. 'The Imagination of Disaster.' *Against Interpretation*. London: Vintage, 2001. 209–25.
Spacks, Patricia Meyer. *Boredom: The Literary History of a State of Mind*. Chicago, IL: University of Chicago Press, 1995.
Srivastava, Neelam. *Secularism in the Postcolonial Indian Novel*. London: Routledge, 2008.
Stearns, Peter N., and Carol Z. Stearns. 'Emotionology: Clarifying the History of Emotions and Emotional Standards.' *American Historical Review* 90.4 (1985): 813–36.
Stendhal. *The Red and the Black*. Trans. Roger Gard. London: Penguin, 2002.
Svendsen, Lars. *A Philosophy of Boredom*. Trans. John Irons. London: Reaktion, 2005.
Talib, Gurbachan Singh (ed.). *Muslim League Attack on Sikhs and Hindus in Punjab, 1947*. Amritsar: Shiromani Gurdwara Parbandhak Committee, 1950.
Taussig, Michael. 'Culture of Terror – Space of Death: Roger Casement's Putumayo Report and the Explanation of Torture.' *Comparative Studies in Society and History* 26.3 (1984): 467–97.
Terada, Rei. *Feeling in Theory: Emotion After the 'Death of the Subject.'* Cambridge, MA: Harvard University Press, 2001.
Todorov, Tzvetan. 'The Typology of Detective Fiction.' *The Poetics of Prose*. Trans. Richard Howard. Ithaca, NY: Cornell University Press, 1977. 42–52.
Tomkins, Silvan S. *Affect Imagery Consciousness*. 4 vols. New York: Springer, 1962–92.
Tummala, Krishna K. *Public Administration in India*. Mumbai: Allied Publishers, 1996.
Turner, Victor. 'The Anthropology of Performance.' *The Anthropology of Performance*. New York: PAJ Publications, 1988. 72–98.
Uyangoda, Jayadeva. 'Social Conflicts, Radical Resistance and Projects of State Power in Southern Sri Lanka: The Case of the JVP.' *Building Local Capacities for Peace: Rethinking Conflict and Development in Sri Lanka*. Ed. Markus Mayer, Darini Rajasingham-Senanayake, and Yuvi Thangarajah. Delhi: Macmillan, 2003. 37–64.
Van der Kolk, Bessel. *The Body Keeps the Score: Mind, Brain and Body in the Transformation of Trauma*. London: Penguin, 2014.
Vanaik, Achin. *The Furies of Indian Communalism: Religion, Modernity and Secularization*. London: Verso, 1997.
Vatikiotis, P.J. *The History of Egypt*. London: Weidenfeld and Nicolson, 1980.
Virilio, Paul. 'On Georges Perec.' *AA Files* 45/46 (2001): 15–18.

Voltaire. *Le Mondain*. Ed. Haydn T. Mason. *Œuvres Complètes de Voltaire*. Vol. XVI. Geneva, Banbury, Oxford: Voltaire Foundation, 1968. 295–313.

Ward, Abigail (ed.). *Postcolonial Traumas: Memory, Narrative, Resistance*. Basingstoke: Palgrave Macmillan, 2015.

Whalen, Paul J., and Elizabeth A. Phelps (ed.). *The Human Amygdala*. New York: Guildford Press, 2009.

Wickramasinghe, Nira. *Sri Lanka in the Modern Age: A History*. New York: Oxford University Press, 2014.

Williams, Raymond. *The Long Revolution*. London: Chatto and Windus, 1961.

——. *Marxism and Literature*. Oxford: Oxford University Press, 1977.

——. *Politics and Letters: Interviews with New Left Review*. London: Verso, 2015.

Young, Robert J.C. *Postcolonialism: An Historical Introduction*. Oxford: Blackwell, 2001.

Zaidi, S. Hussain. *Black Friday: The True Story of the Bombay Bomb Blasts*. Delhi: Penguin, 2002.

——. *Dongri to Dubai: Six Decades of the Mumbai Mafia*. Delhi: Roli Books, 2015.

Index

Abu-Lughod, Janet 32
Adorno, Theodor 125, 126
affect studies 16–17, 21, 26
Ahmed, Sara 10n8, 26, 133–34, 161n13
   The Promise of Happiness 8n6
Alencar, José de 85
Algerian War (1954–62) 13–14
Allahabad (India) 70–71n17
Altieri, Charles
   The Particulars of Rapture 43n14
Amnesty International 25, 127, 139, 140n12
amygdala 131–32, 134–35, 145
Anderson, Perry 37n8
anger 12, 16, 17, 19, 20, 24, 26–27, 31, 57–58n1, 59, 60n4, 66, 67, 70, 75, 86
   in Aristotle 36–37n7
   atmosphere of 34, 43
   and colonial order 40–41
   as displaced 36, 40, 41, 50
   as historically constituted 33, 35–36
   as intersubjective 33, 42–43
   and literary discourse 19
   as overdetermined 35–36
   as pathological 50
   as socially determined 33, 35–36
   ubiquity of 33, 34–35
   see also Midaq Alley

Anil's Ghost (Ondaatje) 18, 21, 25, 127–145 *passim*
   and crime fiction 21, 131, 137–43
   fear in 21, 25, 57–58n1, 129–31, 132–45
   generic disturbances in 21, 130, 131, 137–43, 145
   phobic qualities of 21, 131, 135–38, 142, 143–45
   and the Sri Lankan Civil War (1983–2009) 16, 18, 21, 25, 129–31, 132–35, 139–40, 142
   and symbolization compulsion (Quayson) 136, 137n10, 144, 145n16
   see also fear
Antigua 84, 85
Anwer, Megha 155n7
anxiety 2, 5, 8, 15, 24n21, 30, 40–41n9, 46, 49, 60n3, 133, 145n16
apartheid 29, 149–50n1
apatheia 60n4, 163
The Arabian Nights 115–16
Aristotle 20, 60n4, 63n8
   Nicomachean Ethics 36–37n7, 55
   Poetics 124, 130–31n5
   Rhetoric 130–31n5
Auerbach, Erich 11, 125
Aurelius, Marcus 106, 108, 111, 113, 120

Austen, Jane
  Mansfield Park 83–85
autonomic nervous system 26, 66–67, 131–32, 134–35

Babri Masjid (Ayodhya) 18, 151, 158, 167
Bakhtin, Mikhail 112n7
Balzac, Honoré de 2n1, 50, 79–80, 101, 102, 160, 164
  Old Goriot 11, 80n2
  'Sarrasine' 67–68n13
  The Wild Ass' Skin 156–57
Banaras (India) 70–71n17
Baraka, Magda 31
Barros, João de 85
Barthes, Roland 42, 46, 55–56, 57, 65, 66, 67–69, 73, 78n21, 99, 110n4, 112, 114, 124, 160, 166, 167
  'Introduction to the Structural Analysis of Narratives' 152
  The Pleasure of the Text 160
  S/Z 56, 75, 111
Beckett, Samuel 161
Bengal (India) 59, 70–71n17, 148
Benjamin, Walter
  'On the Concept of History' 127
Ben-Ze'ev, Aaron 90
Bersani, Leo 44, 106
The Bhagavad Gita 111, 115
Bharata
  Nāṭyashāstra 12–13, 28
Bharatiya Janata Party (BJP) 61n6, 158
Bihar (India) 44, 47, 62n7
Bihar earthquake (1934) 44–45, 47
Bildungsroman 79–80, 93, 101–3, 123
Bolaño, Roberto
  2666 79, 141n13
boredom 16, 17, 19, 20, 25, 26–27, 57–58n1, 105, 108–9, 124–25, 149–50n1, 151, 160–61, 163n14
  and the absence of desire/energy 106, 109–11, 124
  and the absence of meaning 109
  and bureaucracy 20, 25, 106–7, 118, 124–25
  in Heidegger 108–9
  as historically constituted 7n5
  and interminability 114n9, 118
  and literary discourse 19, 20–21, 25, 26–27, 106–7, 110–11, 119n14, 125–26
  as socially determined 7n5
  and waiting 108–9, 118
  see also English, August: An Indian Story
Borges, Jorge Luis 115–16
Bourbon Restoration (1814–30) 101–2n21
Brazil 17, 24–25, 41–42n11, 81–82, 95–96, 101–2n21
  agregado (retainer) 89
  independence (1825) 17, 81
  Lei Áurea (1888) 83
  patronage 17, 20, 25, 81, 82, 87–88, 89, 92
  Segundo Reinado 81, 82, 87–88, 89–90, 92, 93, 95, 100
  slavery 17, 18–19, 20, 41–42n11, 81, 82, 83, 87, 92, 93, 96
  see also Rio de Janeiro
Brennan, Teresa
  The Transmission of Affect 7–8
Brooks, Peter 47, 48–51, 65, 105, 119, 122, 155, 157
  Reading for the Plot 110
Burke, Edmund 130–31n5

Cage, John 161
  4'33" 108
Cairo (Egypt) 16, 24, 27
  duality of 32–33
  during the Second World War 17, 18, 23, 31–32, 40–41
  and modernity 32, 41–42n11
  see also Egypt
Calcutta (India) 59, 61, 70, 77, 122
Caldwell, Helen
  The Brazilian Othello of Machado de Assis 81
Cambridge Journal of Postcolonial Literary Inquiry 17
Camões, Luís Vaz de
  The Lusiads 85
Camus, Albert
  The Plague 48n16
  The Stranger 111n6
Capote, Truman 47n15

Carson, Anne 132
Chambers, Ross 153–54n5, 164n15
Chandra, Vikram 21, 25, 147–68 *passim*
  see also *Sacred Games*
Chatterjee, Upamanyu 17–18, 20, 105–26 *passim*
  see also *English, August: An Indian Story*
Clough, Arthur Hugh
  Amours de Voyage 64–65
Coetzee, J.M. 29
Colombo (Sri Lanka) 132, 135, 143
Cronjé, Geoffrey 29
Culler, Jonathan 68, 94, 120, 123–24

Damasio, Antonio 131–33, 134, 138–39
Dangarembga, Tsitsi
  The Book of Not 33n4
  Nervous Conditions 33n4
Daniel, E. Valentine 130n3
Dante Alighieri
  Purgatorio 85
Darwin, Charles
  The Expression of the Emotions in Man and Animals 13n13
Delhi (India) 111, 115, 116
depression 60n3
Desai, Anita 63n8
Dharwadker, Vinay 13n13
Dickens, Charles
  Bleak House 118, 125–26
Dom Casmurro (Machado de Assis) 17, 18, 19, 20, 24, 41–42n11, 79–103 *passim*
  agregado (retainer) 89, 92
  anachronies in 97–98, 100, 102
  anisochronies in 98–101, 102
  and the Bildungsroman 79–80, 93, 101–3
  and the cooperative principle (Grice) 94–95
  and European modernity 20, 41–42n11, 83, 87, 92
  jealousy in 16, 19, 20, 24–25, 41–42n11, 57–58n1, 81, 82, 86–87, 90–101, 102, 103
  and liberalism 19, 20, 24, 82, 83, 86, 87, 88, 92, 93, 96, 100, 102
  and patronage 20, 21, 25, 82, 88–92

  and slavery 18, 19, 20, 21, 24, 41–42n11, 82, 84–86, 87, 88, 92, 93, 96, 102
  see also jealousy
Dom Pedro II (emperor) 17, 23, 80, 81
Dufrenne, Mikel 6, 10–13, 43
  The Phenomenology of Aesthetic Experience 1, 28
  world atmosphere 10–11, 12, 15, 20
Dwivedi, O.P. 117n11

Egypt 14, 17, 31
  Anglo-Egyptian Treaty (1936) 17
  see also Cairo
Eliasoph, Nina 10n8
emotion
  affect/emotion distinction 26–27
  affective economies (Ahmed) 10n8
  affective transmission (Brennan) 7–8
  and atmosphere 6–11, 43n14
  background feeling (Damasio) 138–39
  definition of 27
  emotional communities (Rosenwein) 10n8
  emotional labour (Hochschild) 92
  emotional regimes (Reddy) 10n8, 60
  emotionology (Stearns and Stearns) 10n8, 57–58n1
  etymology of 6n4
  feeling rules (Hochschild) 10n8, 57–58n1
  group style (Eliasoph and Lichterman) 10n8
  as historically constituted 6–11, 13–16, 21–23, 27
  as intersubjective 6–10, 12–13, 19, 22, 33, 43n14
  and literary discourse 6–7, 9–11, 13–16, 19, 21–23, 24, 25, 26–27
  and literary tone 10–11
  mobility of 6, 10, 19, 25, 27, 43n14
  and mood 43n14
  as pathological 5, 13–14, 25
  and the postcolonial 13–14, 16–19, 21
  primary and secondary emotions (Damasio) 131–33, 134
  as socially determined 6–11, 13–16, 19, 21–23, 27

185

Affective Disorders

structure of feeling (Williams) 6, 7, 8–10, 13, 15, 19, 23–24, 27, 30
   as transcultural 27–28, 30
   as transhistorical 30
   and trauma 15, 16
   ubiquity of 6, 11
   and the uncanny 15
   see also entries for specific emotions
English, August: An Indian Story (Chatterjee) 17–18, 19, 20, 22, 25, 105–126 *passim*
   and the absence of desire/energy 106, 109–11, 112, 114, 118, 119, 120
   and the absence of meaning 119–20, 124–26
   boredom in 16, 17, 19, 20, 25, 26–27, 57–58n1, 106–7, 109, 110–11, 118, 123–26
   and bureaucracy 18, 19, 20, 21, 22, 25, 106–7, 108, 114, 116–18, 120, 124–25
   and interminability 106–7, 114–18, 119–20
   and the iterative 106–7, 112–14, 123
   and the proairetic code (Barthes) 106, 111–12, 114, 121–23
   and procrastination 116–17, 123
   and realism 20–21, 106, 119, 125–26
   and waiting 108–9, 118
   see also boredom
envy 24n21, 35n5, 81n3

Fanon, Frantz 41
   Black Skin, White Masks 29
   The Wretched of the Earth 13–14, 31
fear 9, 12, 18, 21, 25, 26, 30, 57–58n1, 60n4, 66, 81n3, 90, 91, 130–31n5, 159, 165
   and the amygdala 131–32, 134–35, 145
   in Aristotle 124, 130–31n5
   atmosphere of 134, 142
   as background feeling (Damasio) 138–39
   culture of terror (Taussig) 130
   fear/anxiety distinction 133
   fear psychosis 129
   fear syndrome 129
   Great Fear (1789) 1–3, 6, 30
   in Hobbes 130–31n5
   and literary discourse 25, 130–31, 134–35, 136–45
   mobility of 25, 133, 140, 142
   as non-cathartic 131, 138–39, 142
   as socially determined 142
   and the sublime (Burke) 130–31n5
   as systemic 134
   ubiquity of 130, 133–34, 140, 142
   see also Anil's Ghost
Fenichel, Otto 110n4
Flaubert, Gustave 1, 7n5, 105
   Madame Bovary 43n12, 112n7
   Sentimental Education 105, 110, 122, 125, 126
Foucault, Michel
   'Tales of Murder' 150–51
France 1–3, 7n5, 101–2n21, 150
French Revolution (1789) 1–3
Freud, Sigmund 29, 36, 40–41n9, 92–93, 133, 145n16
   Moses and Monotheism 29
   Totem and Taboo 28n27
Frye, Northrop 143

Gabriel, Teshome 43
Ganges (river) 44, 70
Gaylard, Gerald 16
Genette, Gérard 43n12, 97–99, 113–14, 122n16
   Narrative Discourse 98n19
Goethe, Johann Wolfgang von
   Faust 85
   Wilhelm Meister 80
Goodstein, Elizabeth S. 109n3
Graham, Sandra Lauderdale 91–92n14
Great Fear (1789) 1–3, 6, 30
Grice, Paul 94–95
Guha, Ranajit
   'Chandra's Death' 148–50

Heidegger, Martin 25, 124, 133
   'The Fundamental Concepts of Metaphysics' 108–9
Hobbes, Thomas 130–31n5
   Philosophical Rudiments Concerning Government and Society 127
Hochschild, Arlie Russell 10n8, 57–58n1

Homer
  The Iliad 85
Hugo, Victor
  'Tristesse d'Olympio' 85
Hull, Matthew S. 117n12

Ibrahim, Dawood 158
India 12, 17–18, 44, 57–58n1, 70–71n17, 128, 159n12
  bureaucracy 18–19, 107–8, 116–17
  communal violence 24, 58–62
  corruption 18, 107
  independence (1947) 17, 58, 107
  Partition (1947) 20, 24, 58, 60, 61
  secularism 17n18, 58, 61n6, 76, 77
  Zamindari Abolition Act 62
  see also Mumbai
Indian Administrative Service (IAS) 18, 19, 20, 22, 25, 106, 107, 116, 117n11, 123, 125
Indian Civil Service (ICS) 25, 107
Itaguaí (Brazil) 85

Jain, R.B. 117n11
James, Henry
  'The Art of Fiction' 105
James, William
  The Principles of Psychology 13n13
Jayewardene, J.R. (president) 128n1
jealousy 16, 19, 20, 57–58n1, 79, 90n13
  and competition 25, 90–92
  definition of 81n3, 91
  as displaced 87
  as disproportionate 82, 86–87, 92–93
  and envy 81n3
  in Freud 92–93
  as historically constituted 20, 24–25, 41–42n11, 82, 87, 89–90, 92, 102
  and literary discourse 19, 81, 82, 92–101, 102
  as pathological 19, 24, 81, 82–83n5, 86, 87, 88, 92, 93, 97, 99–100, 102, 103
  as socially determined 20, 24–25, 41–42n11, 81, 82, 87, 89–90, 92, 102
  ubiquity of 92
  see also Dom Casmurro
Jeyifo, Biodun 52–53

Kanafani, Ghassan
  Men in the Sun 14
Kanpur (India) 70
Kant, Immanuel 163
  Critique of Judgement 118n13
Khan, Sir Khizar Hayat (premier) 107n1
Khoury, Elias
  Little Mountain 14
Kierkegaard, Søren 133
Kim, Sue J. 33n4
Klein, Melanie 81n3
Kleinman, Arthur 60n3
Kuhn, Reinhard 109

Laclau, Ernesto
  Emancipation(s) 28n26
laughter epidemic (Tanganyika) 4–5, 6, 30
Lebanon 14
Lefebvre, Georges 2
Lepenies, Wolf 9n7, 114n9
  Melancholy and Society 7n5
Lichterman, Paul 10n8
Lucian
  The True History 85

Machado de Assis, Joaquim Maria 17, 20, 41–42n11, 79–103 *passim*
  The Posthumous Memoirs of Brás Cubas 81–82n4, 95n17
  Resurrection 82–83n5
  see also Dom Casmurro
Maharashtra (India) 151n2
Mahfouz, Naguib 14, 17, 20, 31–53 *passim*
  see also Midaq Alley
Majumdar, Saikat 149–50n1
  Prose of the World 16n17
Malinowski, Bronislaw
  'The Problem of Meaning in Primitive Languages' 71
Martin, Theodore 153n4
Massumi, Brian 26
McClennen, Sophia A. 140n12
metriopatheia 20, 60n4
Midaq Alley (Mahfouz) 17, 18, 20, 24, 31–53 *passim*
  anger in 16, 17, 19, 20, 24, 26–27, 33–36, 38, 39–41, 42–44, 50, 52, 53, 57–58n1, 86

187

and colonial modernity 20, 21, 24, 33–34, 35–36, 37–42, 45–53
envy in 35n5
and melodrama 20, 34, 48–53
and rumour 20, 33–34, 44–48
and the systemic uncanny (Quayson) 36, 42
and tragedy 20, 52
see also anger
Miller, D.A. 118, 164–65
  The Novel and the Police 141
Minas Gerais (Brazil) 83
Monghyr (India) 44
Montaigne, Michel de
  Essays 85
Moretti, Franco 72–73, 79–80, 101, 140–41
  Atlas of the European Novel, 1800–1900 84n7
  The Bourgeois 22
Mumbai (Bombay) 18, 23, 148, 151n2, 152, 156, 162
  communal violence 18, 21, 26, 151, 158, 167
  crime 18, 21, 26, 147–48, 151, 158, 167
  terrorism 18, 21, 26, 151, 158–59, 167
  see also India
Muzaffarpur (India) 44
Myers, David
  'Vikram Seth's Epic Renunciation of the Passions' 63n8

Nancy, Jean-Luc
  The Birth to Presence 31
Nandy, Ashis 159n12
narratology 16, 17, 21
Ndebele, Njabulo 149–50n1
Nehru, Jawaharlal (prime minister) 17–18, 20, 22, 24, 25, 57, 58–62, 63n8, 67, 70–71n17, 76, 77
  'Let the People Decide' 55
Nehruvian Consensus 17n18
nētra mangala (ceremony) 143
Ngai, Sianne 19, 21, 25, 34, 135, 160–62, 163, 167
  stuplimity 21, 25–26, 57–58n1, 148, 151–52, 155n7, 160–63, 167–68
  Ugly Feelings 24n21, 151, 163n14

Obeyesekere, Gananath 29
Okri, Ben 52–53
Ondaatje, Michael 18, 21, 127–45 *passim*
  see also *Anil's Ghost*

Pakistan 59, 117n12, 159n12, 167n17
Palestine 14, 86
Pandey, Gyanendra 48
parasympathetic nervous system (PNS) 66–67, 77
Paris (France) 1, 2n1, 157
Patel, Vallabhbhai (deputy prime minister) 107
Patna (India) 44
Perec, Georges 147, 161
Perera, Sasanka 130, 142
Philip, P.J. 5
Plato
  Phaedo 85
Pollock, Sheldon 13
Prasad, J. 44–45, 47, 48
Pratt, Mary Louise 94–95
Proust, Marcel 114, 160
  In Search of Lost Time 113n8, 166
Provine, Robert R. 5–6n2
psychoanalysis 6n3, 28–29, 122, 133
Putumayo River (Colombia) 130n4

Quayson, Ato 36n6
  Aesthetic Nervousness 42
  symbolization compulsion 15–16, 136, 137n10, 144, 145n16
  systemic uncanny 15–16, 36, 42, 134n8

Rajasingham-Senanayake, Darini 129
Rankin, A.M. 5
Rao, Vyjyanthi 167
rasa (aesthetic theory) 12–13
Reddy, William M. 10n8
  The Navigation of Feeling 60
reticence 24, 25, 56, 63–64
  as affective style 57–58n1
  as emotional regime (Reddy) 24, 25, 60–62, 76, 77
  as emotionology (Stearns and Stearns) 57–58n1
  as feeling rule (Hochschild) 57–58n1

as historically constituted 57–58n1, 61–62, 77
as intersubjective 57–58n1
and literary discourse 55–56, 65–78
and *metriopatheia* (Aristotle) 20, 60n4
as Nehruvian virtue 57, 58–62, 63n8, 67
as socially determined 57–58n1, 61–62, 77
see also A Suitable Boy
Revolution of 1848 (France) 7n5
Richter, Gerhard 161
 Atlas 161
Rio de Janeiro (Brazil) 16, 17, 18, 23, 24, 80, 85, 86, 89n12, 90n13
 casa e rua distinction 91–92n14
 slavery 83, 84
 see also Brazil
Rivière, Pierre 150
Rosenwein, Barbara H. 10n8

Sacred Games (Chandra) 18, 21, 25, 147–68 *passim*
and banality 147–48, 151, 152–55, 159, 162, 165–68
and communal violence 18, 21, 26, 151, 162
and crime 18, 21, 26, 147–48, 151, 154–55
and the false ending (Shklovsky) 165–68
and narratological deviance 155–57, 162, 164–65
nuclei/catalyzers in 152–53, 164–68
and the spectacular 148, 151–52, 155n7, 157, 158, 159, 162–63, 165, 167–68
stuplimity in 21, 25–26, 57–58n1, 148, 151–52, 155n7, 160–63, 167–68
and terrorism 18, 21, 26, 151, 158–59
see also stuplimity
Said, Edward 14, 29, 83–84, 85
 contrapuntal reading 83
 Culture and Imperialism 83
Salgado, Minoli 144n15
Sartre, Jean-Paul 7n5, 111n6
 Being and Nothingness 79
Saussure, Ferdinand de 28

Schopenhauer, Arthur 110–11
Schwarcz, Lília Moritz 89n12
Schwarz, Roberto 15, 22, 81–82, 83, 88, 96, 100
 A Master on the Periphery of Capitalism 81–82n4
 'Misplaced Ideas' 81–82n4
Second French Empire (1852–70) 7n5
Seine (river) 2, 105
Senaratne, Jagath P. 129
Seth, Vikram 17, 20, 55–78 *passim*
 The Golden Gate 63–64n9
 see also A Suitable Boy
Shakespeare, William
 Othello 85
Shiv Sena (political party) 151n2, 158n10
Shklovsky, Viktor 166
Sirois, François 5
Slaughter, Joseph R. 140n12
Sontag, Susan
 'The Imagination of Disaster' 147
Spacks, Patricia Meyer 110, 119n14
Sri Lanka 29
Sri Lankan Civil War (1983–2009) 16, 18, 21, 25, 127–31, 133, 139–40, 142
 casualties 128n2
 Indian peacekeeping force 128
 Janatha Vimukhti Peramuna (JVP) 128, 133
 Liberation Tigers of Tamil Eelam (LTTE) 128, 133, 142
Srikrishna, B.N. (judge) 158n10
Srivastava, Neelam 61n6
Stearns, Carol Z. 10n8, 57–58n1
Stearns, Peter N. 10n8, 57–58n1
Stein, Gertrude
 The Making of Americans 161
Stendhal 11, 79, 101–2n21, 102
 The Red and the Black 164–65
Sterne, Laurence
 Tristram Shandy 156
stuplimity 21, 25–26, 57–58n1, 148, 151–52, 155n7, 160–63, 167–68
 definition of 151, 160–62
 see also Sacred Games
Sue, Eugène
 The Mysteries of Paris 157

189

A Suitable Boy (Seth) 17, 18, 20, 22, 24, 25, 55–78 *passim*, 110
  and affective moderation 25, 56–57, 60n4, 61–62, 68, 74, 77
  and the autonomic nervous system 66–67, 77
  and communal violence 21, 24, 58–62, 73–75
  and the emotional regime (Reddy) 24, 25, 60–62, 76, 77
  and the hermeneutic code (Barthes) 55–57, 66, 67, 68, 77
  and *metriopatheia* (Aristotle) 20, 60n4
  nuclei/catalyzers in 22, 68–73, 78
  and phatic communion 71–72
  reticence of 20, 24, 25, 56–58, 61–62, 63–78
  see also reticence
Svendsen, Lars 109n3
sympathetic nervous system (SNS) 66–67

Tacitus 85
Tagore, Rabindranath 115
Tanganyika 4–5, 30
Taussig, Michael 130n4
tellability 154–55
Todorov, Tzvetan 137, 142, 156n8

Tolstoy, Leo
  War and Peace 160, 166
Tomkins, Silvan
  Affect Imagery Consciousness 13n13
Turner, Victor 119

Uttar Pradesh (India) 70–71n17, 109n2, 158
Uyangoda, Jayadeva 128n1

Van der Kolk, Bessel 66
Virilio, Paul
  'On Georges Perec' 147
Vishva Hindu Parishad (VHP) 158
Voltaire
  Le Mondain 70n16

Wagner, Richard 85
Williams, Raymond
  The Long Revolution 8
  Politics and Letters 9
  structure of feeling 6, 7, 8–10, 13, 15, 19, 23–24, 27, 30

Young, Robert J.C. 23
  Postcolonialism 23n20

Zaidi, S. Hussain 158n11